WEEKEND Adventures

FOR CITY-WEARY PEOPLE

Also by Carole Terwilliger Meyers:

How to Organize a Babysitting Cooperative and Get Some *Free* Time Away From the Kids

Eating Out With the Kids in San Francisco and the Bay Area

Getting in the Spirit: Annual Bay Area Christmas Events

WEEKEND Adventures

FOR CITY-WEARY PEOPLE

CAROUSEL PRESS

OVERNIGHT TRIPS IN NORTHERN CALIFORNIA
CAROLE TERWILLIGER MEYERS

CAROUSEL PRESS
P.O. Box 6061
Albany, CA 94706
415/527-5849

Library of Congress Cataloging-in-Publication Data

Meyers, Carole Terwilliger.
   Weekend adventures for city-weary people, overnight trips in northern California/Carole Terwilliger Meyers.
      p. cm. — (Weekend adventures for city-weary people, overnight trips in the U.S.A.)
   Includes index.
   ISBN 0-917120-09-4
   1. California, Northern—Description and travel—Guide-books.
   2. Family recreation—California, Northern—Guide-books. I. Title.
II. Series: Meyers, Carole Terwilliger. Weekend adventures for city-weary people, overnight trips in the U.S.A.
F867.5.M48 1988
917.94'0453—dc19   88-10869
                                                                CIP

Printed in the United States of America

10 9 8 7 6 5 4 3

for Gene

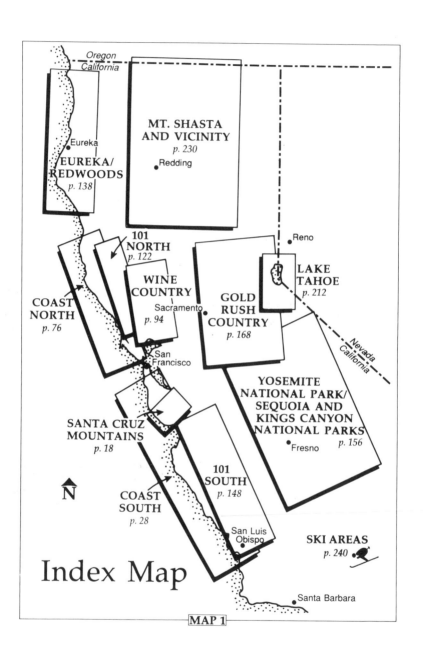

Oregon
California

Eureka

EUREKA/
REDWOODS
p. 138

MT. SHASTA
AND VICINITY
p. 230

Redding

**101
NORTH**
p. 122

Reno

**WINE
COUNTRY**
Sacramento
p. 94

**LAKE
TAHOE**
p. 212

**COAST
NORTH**
p. 76

**GOLD
RUSH
COUNTRY**
p. 168

Nevada
California

San
Francisco

**YOSEMITE
NATIONAL PARK/
SEQUOIA AND
KINGS CANYON
NATIONAL PARKS**
p. 156

**SANTA CRUZ
MOUNTAINS**
p. 18

Fresno

N

**101
SOUTH**
p. 148

**COAST
SOUTH**
p. 28

San Luis
Obispo

SKI AREAS
p. 240

Index Map

Santa Barbara

MAP 1

CONTENTS

Map 1 (index map)
INTRODUCTION 1
TRAVELING WITH CHILDREN 3
    Planning Trips 3
        Lodging Reservations 4
        Packing 5
    Helpful Hints in the Car 6
        Safety and Comfort 6
        Food 7
        Entertainment 9
        Stops 10
        When Things Degenerate 10
    Hints for When You're There 11
        Souvenirs 11
        At the Beach 11
    The Goodie Bag 12
    Traveling With Teens 14
    Condominiums 15
GUIDELINES FOR INTERPRETING THIS BOOK 17
SANTA CRUZ MOUNTAINS 19
Map 2 18
    San Lorenzo Valley 19
    Los Gatos/Saratoga 22
COAST SOUTH 29
Map 3 28
    Highway 1 Lodgings and Attractions 29
    Santa Cruz 31
    Capitola 39
    Monterey Peninsula 42
    Monterey 42
    Pacific Grove 50
    Carmel 54
    Big Sur 64
    San Simeon/Cambria 67
    Morro Bay 72
COAST NORTH 77
Map 4 76
    Highway 1 Lodgings and Attractions 77
    Mendocino 83
    Fort Bragg 91

WINE COUNTRY 95
Map 5 94
  Sonoma 96
  Yountville 102
  St. Helena 107
  Calistoga 112
  Clear Lake 118
101 NORTH 123
Map 6 122
  Santa Rosa 123
  Guerneville/Russian River 126
  Healdsburg 131
  Geyserville 134
  Hopland 136
  Ukiah 136
  Willits 137
  Eureka/Redwoods 137
  Map 7 138
101 SOUTH 149
Map 8 148
  San Juan Bautista 149
  Salinas 151
  Gonzales 152
  Pinnacles National Monument 153
  San Miguel 153
  Paso Robles 154
  San Luis Obispo 154
YOSEMITE NATIONAL PARK 157
Map 9 156
SEQUOIA AND KINGS CANYON NATIONAL PARKS 165
GOLD RUSH COUNTRY 169
Map 10 168
  Jamestown 170
  Sonora 172
  Columbia State Historic Park 173
  Murphys 175
  Angels Camp 178
  San Andreas 179
  Mokelumne Hill 180
  Jackson 181
  Sutter Creek 183
  Volcano 184
  Amador City 187

Drytown   188
Shingle Springs   188
El Dorado   188
Placerville   189
Coloma   190
Auburn   192
Grass Valley   192
Nevada City   196

SACRAMENTO   203

LAKE TAHOE   213
Map 11   212
South Lake Tahoe   213
North Lake Tahoe   222

MT. SHASTA AND VICINITY   231
Map 12   230
Lake Shasta   232
Lassen Volcanic National Park   233
Lava Beds National Monument   235
Trinity Alps   237
Yreka   239

WINTER SNOW FUN   241
Map 13   240
Downhill Skiing   241
Cross-country Skiing   242
Snow Play   242
Dressing Kids for the Snow   243
Way Up North   244
South Lake Tahoe   245
North Lake Tahoe   246
Donner Summit   249
East   252
South   253

FAMILY CAMPS   259

HOUSEBOATS   265

RIVER TRIPS   267

PACK TRIPS   269

CAMPING   271

MISCELLANEOUS ADVENTURES   273

INDEX   278

CREDITS   286

ABOUT THE AUTHOR   287

ORDER FORM   291

FEEDBACK   293

INTRODUCTION

It is frustrating to discover after you're home that an area where you've just vacationed had an interesting attraction you didn't know about. It also isn't much fun to find out too late that there was a better or cheaper (depending on what you're after) lodging you could have booked into... or a restaurant you would have enjoyed trying.

This book is designed so that you can quickly determine what is of special interest in the area being visited. Listings are selected based on the fact that they are in some way special—bargain rates, welcoming of families, aesthetically pleasing, historically interesting, etc. Phone numbers—many of which are toll-free 800 numbers—necessary for obtaining further information are included. (I have found that writing for information is too slow and unreliable, so I recommend that you instead always call for a brochure or to make a reservation.)

The destinations in this book radiate out from the immediate San Francisco Bay Area. Most make good two- or three-day weekend trips; all can easily be adapted to longer stays. For information on San Francisco and destinations which are closer in, refer to my book *Eating Out with the Kids in San Francisco and the Bay Area.*

With the aid of this book, you will find trip-planning easier and you'll get the most out of a weekend away.

TRAVELING WITH CHILDREN

PLANNING TRIPS

Those of you without children may still be able to glean a few ideas from this section. However, feel free to skip on. Those of you with children had better read carefully. You (and I) need all the help we can get.

- Write or call the Chamber of Commerce or Visitors Bureau in the area you plan to visit. Ask them for specific recommendations for families, and have them send all pertinent literature.

- Have your children help pick a destination and plan the trip. Look at maps together. (You may want to consider joining the California State Automobile Association, which offers excellent maps and services to members.) Create a flexible travel schedule. Plan to allow sufficient travel time between destinations so that you can make spontaneous exploration stops along the way.

- Pre-planning is crucial for a successful trip. Plan a daily agenda. But don't pack it too tightly. Leave time for simple pleasures such as napping and slurping ice cream cones. Allow for some "separation" time: adults going their separate ways with one child; adults taking turns staying with the kids while one gets free time; etc. Establish guidelines on spending money, snacks, bedtime, TV use, etc.

- Plan to start the trip early in the morning and to arrive at your destination early in the day so you will have time to relax.

- When you arrive, reread the appropriate sections in this book to familiarize yourself with local facilities. Also, check the Yellow Pages in the telephone book for further information on things to do:

babysitting services	bicycle rentals
horseback riding/ stables	public swimming pools/ plunges
restaurants	skating rinks

  Also, check the local newspapers and tourist guides for current special events and activities.

- Hang a detailed map of California on a wall in your home. Use colored pushpins or flags to mark places you have visited. Children especially enjoy doing this.

- Consider doing what the military daddy did in the movie *The Great Santini*. He moved his family out for a car trip in the middle of the night. It might work. Traffic is lighter then, and the kids just might sleep.

Lodging Reservations

- Make advance reservations at motels and campgrounds to avoid disappointment and a frantic, last-minute search for anything— and the possiblity of finding nothing. Inquire about any special rates or packages which are available. Reservations sometimes save you money as well. Inexpensive rooms often are reserved first, leaving the expensive (albeit usually more luxurious) rooms for last-minute arrivals. Always ask for a written confirmation. Take it along as proof of your reservation. If you must cancel, do so as soon as possible. A complete refund is usually available with at least 48 hours notice.

  C.T.M.'s Rule of the Road: *The tendency to get sick increases in direct proportion to the approach of a trip. This is even more likely if you've paid a non-refundable deposit on accommodations.*

- If you require a crib, reserve one at the time you make your room reservation. Otherwise, you may find none available when you arrive. Or purchase a portable crib to use when traveling. A pattern for making a particularly nice fabric and wood crib appears in *Sunset* magazine (May 1983; p.182).

- If your child still wets, take along a plastic sheet to protect the bed.

- Children are sometimes allowed to sleep on the floor of their parents' room at no charge. If you want to do this, you'll need to take along sleeping bags for them. Inquire ahead of time about the lodging's policy.

- On longer trips an occasional splurge on two rooms, or a suite, can be a treat for everyone—especially if you have two or more older children. For this reason, I am especially fond of all-suite hotels and condominiums.

Packing

- Make a checklist of all the items you need to gather or buy for your trip. For instance, if you are going to a beach or river area in the summer, you will want to consider taking along the following items:

swimsuits	sand toys
towels	inner tubes
suntan lotion	sandals/tennis shoes
beach blanket	air mattress
back rest	balls
sun umbrella	

And remember that if you do forget something, most of the destinations mentioned in this book are near a store where you can buy emergency replacements.

- Remember to take along travelers' checks or adequate cash. Surprisingly, some lodging and dining facilities in vacation areas do not accept out-of-town checks or credit cards.

HELPFUL HINTS IN THE CAR

Traveling anywhere in a car with children can be a trying experience for everyone concerned. Even short trips can be exhausting and leave everyone in real *need* of a vacation. (Does anyone know where I can purchase the kind of taxi that has bulletproof, soundproof glass separating the parents from the kids—I mean the driver from the passengers?) Here are some suggestions on how to make a family car trip a more pleasurable experience.

Safety and Comfort

- California residents are required by law to use a car seat for children who are under age four or who weigh less than 40 pounds and are advised to restrain children up to age 15 with seat belts. For detailed information on the importance of car seats and brand recommendations, refer to *Consumer Reports* at your library. A fabric liner makes a car seat easier to clean and protects a child from the danger of hot plastic.

- Use a luggage rack to handle trunk overflow. For comfort, leave as much space as possible in the passenger section.

- Take along blankets and pillows for napping. Buy some new towels for your bathroom, and put the old ones in the trunk of your car. They make good covers for hot car seats and can be used in countless other ways: rolled up as a pillow, for mopping up spills, etc.

- Keep a first-aid kit in your trunk. Stock it with:

bandages	children's aspirin and
antiseptic	aspirin substitute

safety pins   thermometer
tweezers   scissors
a roller bandage   adhesive tape
cotton swabs   gauze pads
washcloth   soap
sunblock   flashlight
a compact sewing kit
a few dimes for emergency phone calls

These items will fit inside a large, empty coffee can or in an old lunchbox.

- If you have a toddler, pack electrical outlet covers and a safety gate.

- Keep a package of medium-sized self-locking plastic bags in your car's trunk. These are handy for holding many things: messy items such as bibs, diapers, and wet bathing suits; items children collect; etc.

Food

- Pack a supply of non-messy snacks for the road. Some ideas:

fruit rolls   dried apple rings
raisins   granola bars
cheese   apples
animal crackers   bananas
fig newtons   small boxes of dry cereal
small cans or boxes of juice, straws

- You might want to pack these snacks in a separate lunch box or shoe box for each child. Let them eat as they are hungry. Don't forget to put in a few packaged moist towelettes for clean-up.

- Provide the kids with a bag of *Cheerios* or *Froot Loops* and some dental floss for stringing edible necklaces. They will love you, and their dentist will too.

- For clean-ups, pack damp paper towels or a damp wash-cloth in a plastic bag or covered container.

- Consider packing only water for drinks. When spilled, it isn't sticky. A fun idea for older children is to recycle commercial plastic containers which resemble lemons and limes. Empty the citrus juice, remove the insert (an ice pick helps), rinse, and fill with water. Children can then squirt drinks into their mouths with a minimum of mess and bother. Another idea is to give each child their own small thermos of water. Or give each child a collapsible cup to use for drinks from the family thermos. Many years ago I bought a stainless steel thermos for our family car trips. It has turned out to be a wise investment.

- For long trips, stock an ice chest with milk and fruit and other nutritious but perishable foods.

- Picnic when possible. After the cramped experience of a car ride, a restaurant can sometimes feel too confining. Gas station attendants can be helpful in providing directions to a local park with a playground.

- Avoid eating in the car. Though it saves time, it offers no chance to stretch.

- Make disposable bibs by using an old "sweater guard" to hold a table napkin around baby's neck.

- Use a molded plastic bib when dining. This is especially wonderful for catching ice cream drips. To clean it, all you have to do is wipe or rinse.

- A bottle warmer which plugs into the car's cigarette lighter can be useful when traveling with a baby. Also, removable screens for the car's windows keep the sun off baby and out of eyes.

- For a baby no longer on formula but still on a bottle, try putting 1/3 cup (2 2/3 oz.) of powdered milk in a baby bottle. When milk is needed, add water to make 8 oz. and shake. This eliminates the need for refrigeration and is handy any time you are away from home.

Entertainment

- Turn your children into navigators. Give each their own map and let them determine how far it is to the next town. Give them a wide felt-tip pen to trace the route as you go.

- Provide each child with a notepad to use as a trip diary. Encourage them to make entries each day. Older children can do this alone. For younger children, you can write down what they dictate. Have crayons available for illustrations. If you have an instant print camera, let each child take a few pictures each day to illustrate the diary.

- Children make good use of a portable tape recorder. My family especially enjoys listening to prerecorded story tapes together. It is also fun to record a travel diary as you go. But when one of our children turns on the music in our car, they also put on their earphones.

- *Colorforms* plastic cutouts are fun for younger children. They adhere easily to the passenger's side window and leave no marks.

- Have a few wrapped presents on hand to use for distracting children during restless times. Select items which are good additions to the goodie bag (see p. 12). If they're learning to tell time and have their own watch, consider writing specific instructions such as, "Open at 10:42."

- Hang a shoebag on the back of the front seat or on the car door for storing games and miscellaneous items.

- Keep a good travel game book in the glove compartment. Use it only when really necessary. When everyone is happy, leave well enough alone.

Stops

- A quick, inexpensive breakfast stop at a donut shop can help you get on the road fast.

- Make a rest stop every few hours or as the situation dictates. This is a good time to eat, enjoy a sightseeing side trip, or let children run off some pent-up energy in a park.

- Organize a scavenger hunt during a park stop or after a picnic. Give each child a list of items (pine cone, twig shaped like a letter, something from an animal, two different leaves, etc.) and see who can find the most in a given amount of time. Have a prize for all participants.

- Pack an inflatable beach ball to encourage active movement when you stop.

- Buy gas in small quantities. Never fill the tank unless you are driving in desolate areas. This will require you to stop more frequently, giving passengers time to stretch, get drinks, and visit the restroom.

When Things Degenerate

- Try the "mad bag/glad bag" trick. Give each child a bag filled with nickels or dimes at the beginning of the trip. (It seems pennies are no longer exciting.) Mom and dad begin the trip with an empty bag. When a child has been deemed naughty, he must give up a coin to the parents' bag. If you are a liberated parent, you can let it work the other way too. Any coins left in the child's bag at the end of the trip are his to keep. This works even better with dollars.

- Adults take turns driving. The nondriving adult sits in the back seat with one (two, three...) child while the other child sits in the front seat with the driver. This helps keep squabbles to a minimum and also gives the back-seat parent and child a chance to spend some time together. And, even though many adults will not jump at the chance to sit in the back seat, most children will jump at the chance to sit in the front seat.

- I've heard tell of a parent who keeps a fly swatter with her in the front seat. It allows her to easily reach a troublemaker in the back seat.

- When all else fails, travel in a motorcycle with a side-bucket. Daddy and one kid sit on the cycle, mommy and another sit in the bucket. This may be a very unsafe and inconvenient form of travel, but you won't hear a word.

HINTS FOR WHEN YOU'RE THERE

Souvenirs

- Post cards are an inexpensive souvenir. Let your children select a few at each destination. Have your children use them to illustrate their diaries. Or keep them as a collection, held together with a rubber band or ribbon. Or write diary entries on the back and keep a post card diary. Or keep a post card diary and then actually send each post card to themselves as you travel so they will have mail when they get home. Or let them write a post card to a friend, cut it up, and send it in an envelope for an instant puzzle post card. Or assign each of the kids a number of relatives to send post cards to. When the natives get restless in the condo, notice that it's time for them to write post cards.

At the Beach

- To help get all your gear from the car to the beach, consider using a molded plastic sled (borrowed from your winter gear). Pack everything in the sled and drag it along the sand to your chosen spot. Filled with a little water, it also makes a great place for a baby to splash and play safely.

- Remove the floor from an old playpen and use it to corral a toddler at the beach. Or turn your regular one upside down to provide shade.
- Have the kids fill their buckets with water and carry them back to the car for rinsing sandy feet.

THE GOODIE BAG

A good way to keep children occupied and happy on a car trip is to provide each with his own goodie bag. For the bag itself you might use an old purse, a recycled lunch box, a back pack (especially good for plane trips), a small basket, a shopping bag, a small suitcase, a plastic bucket, or a covered metal cake pan. Whichever container you choose, be sure to have a separate one for each child and try to fill them with the same items (or equivalent items if their interests differ). Labeling the contents with each child's name will avoid some conflict. A flat, hard container makes a good foundation for writing and coloring. Things you might put inside include:

pads of paper	small scraps of
scotch tape	colored paper
colored pencils/	gummed paper shapes
washable felt pens	or stickers
midget cars	magic slate
finger puppets	eraser
little people toys	magnetic games
car games	shoestring sewing cards
workbooks	magnifying glass
pencil box	photo viewer toy
blunt scissors	small chalkboard
card games	and chalk
crayons	felt board and shapes
coloring books	glue stick

pipe cleaners
snap-lock plastic
    beads
paper dolls
origami paper
play dough

etch-a-sketch toy
sponge puzzle
plastic bags to
    hold collectibles
spiral notebook
story books

The items you choose to put in the goodie bag will depend on your child's age. Be sure to keep the bag stocked and ready to go, and keep your eyes open for new items to unveil on future trips. For younger children, don't forget to bring along their lovies— teddy bear, blanket, etc.

Have older children shop with you for new goodie bag items a few days before the trip. The anticipation of playing with the newly selected items will work in your favor.

I think you will find the goodie bag so useful that you will begin using it in other ways—on a rainy day, when your children are sick, when you leave them with a babysitter, and maybe even when you dine out in a restaurant.

Picnic Goodie Bag

I like to stop at a delicatessen for picnic fare. To help make our picnics more comfortable, I always keep in the trunk of our car: a picnic blanket, a day pack (for those picnic spots that require a hike to reach), and a plastic pull-string bag stocked with paper plates, cups, napkins, plastic eating utensils, straws, a can opener, and a corkscrew.

Musical Goodie Bag

For family fun by the campfire or fireplace, pack a musical goodie bag. The following inexpensive items can be purchased in most music shops:

slide whistle   plastic flute

kazoo   whistle
small tambourine   wooden rhythm blocks
jew's-harp   ratchet
gongs   rasps
bells   harmonica
cymbals

Beach Play Goodie Bag

Many of these items can be gathered from your kitchen.
Remember to avoid glass. I like to store them all in one big
plastic bucket and save it especially for trips to the water.

spray bottle   bucket
spatula   funnel
scoop   cookie cutters
pastry brush   strainer
plastic cups   pancake turner
measuring spoons

TRAVELING WITH TEENS

Since my oldest child has become a teenager, I've often
lamented the trials of traveling with one. Of course, I had
trials even *before* he was a teen. Now I just have *different*
ones.

I've found that the very best solution to the problem is to let
him stay home. This really does work best for everyone concerned. I like him to stay with a friend or relative when he
doesn't accompany us, and I only allow this option for weekend trips. For longer family vacations, I still insist he come
with us. I believe it is important that we have these experi-
ences together.

Since I have another younger child who is still fairly enthused
about going places and doing things with her parents, I don't

feel a void when the teen is not with us. I find, instead, that we have a much more enjoyable time. And on those now rarer occasions when he does accompany us, we all consider it a special treat.

Other suggestions include:

• Let them invite a friend along.

• Plan a trip somewhere they desperately want to go.

• Plan a one-parent, one-child trip. Perhaps a river rafting trip or a backpacking expedition.

• Put them in charge of something they would enjoy: taking photographs, planning several outings, etc.

• My teen enjoys staying behind in our room while we adults go out to dinner. He especially enjoys this when he can watch a movie on cable TV and/or order from room service. Sometimes we hire him to babysit for his younger sister; he earns extra trip money, and we adults get a break.

• Be careful about letting them stay with someone else for long periods while you vacation without them. A side effect can be that a letting-up on your rules by the temporary caretaker can make it difficult to reestablish order when you return.

CONDOMINIUMS

Condominiums are a good choice for family lodging, especially when the stay is for longer than a weekend. Prices are usually competitive with motels, and you get additional space in the form of extra bedrooms, a living room, and a kitchen. Vacation money can be stretched by making use of the kitchen to prepare breakfast and to put together a picnic lunch. Barbecues are sometimes available and are fun for cooking the evening meal. Occasional meals out then become more affordable.

Many condo complexes offer shared recreational facilities such as a pool, jacuzzi, and tennis courts. They also usually have amenities such as laundry facilities and fireplaces. In the winter, packages with nearby ski resorts are often available.

Sharing a condo with another family can cut expenses even further or, at the very least, allow a choicer location. Cooking and shopping chores can be shared, and each couple can get a night out by taking turns babysitting. Be sure, though, to get it clear what happens if one family cancels out after the deposit is paid.

The reservation numbers listed in this book are usually for an owners' rental service. Because maid service and office expenses have to be covered, the units cost more than when rented directly from the owner. If you like staying in condos, be alert for advertised units. You'll save money that way.

If you ever find yourself wondering why you brought the kids along, keep in mind that they are very useful in figuring out how to turn strange TVs on and off.

And above all remember, as someone once said,
Happiness is a journey, not a destination.

GUIDELINES FOR INTER-PRETING THIS BOOK

This book is organized by geographical area. Each chapter has the following subsections:

A LITTLE BACKGROUND: historical and general background information about the area; what kinds of activities to expect.

VISITOR INFORMATION: address and phone number of Chamber of Commerce or Visitors Bureau.

ANNUAL EVENTS: where to get further information. Listings are in chronological order. When no address or phone number is listed, contact the Chamber of Commerce or Visitors Bureau for information.

GETTING THERE: the quickest, easiest driving route from San Francisco; scenic driving routes, other transportation options.

STOPS ALONG THE WAY: noteworthy places to stop for meals or sightseeing.

WHERE TO STAY: a select sampling of lodging facilities listed alphabetically and, when available, including the following information: name, street address, toll-free 800 reservations number, area code and phone number, price range per night for two people/four people (see price code below), months closed, policies regarding children (whether there is a *children stay free in parents' room* policy; whether facility is *unsuitable for children under a specified age);* availability of TVs, kitchens, bathtubs, fireplaces, views; whether there is room service, a complimentary breakfast (continental or full), or a restaurant; recreational facilities: pool, jacuzzi, tennis courts. Private baths are generally in all rooms unless otherwise stated.

♥ before a listing indicates facility is inappropriate for children.

$ = under $50; $$ = $50-$75; $$$ = $75-$100; $$$+ = over $100.

WHERE TO EAT: a selective sampling of worthwhile restaurants listed alphabetically and, when available, including the following information: name, address, phone number, meals served (B/L/D/SunBr), days open; availability of highchairs, booster seats, children's portions; price range (see price code below); whether reservations are needed or accepted; credit cards accepted (see code below). Always call to confirm any information, as it frequently changes.

♥ before a listing indicates a romantic atmosphere.

$ = inexpensive. Dinner for one adult might cost up to $10.

$$ = moderate. Dinner for one adult might cost from $10 to $20.

$$$ = expensive. Dinner for one adult might cost over $20.

Projected costs are based on dinner prices and are exclusive of drinks, dessert, tax, and tip.

Credit Cards: American Express (AE), Carte Blanche (CB), Diners Club (DC), MasterCard (MC), BankAmericard/Visa (V)

WHAT TO DO: activities and sights in the area which are of special interest, listed alphabetically. Some of these facilities are closed on major holidays. Always call first to verify hours.

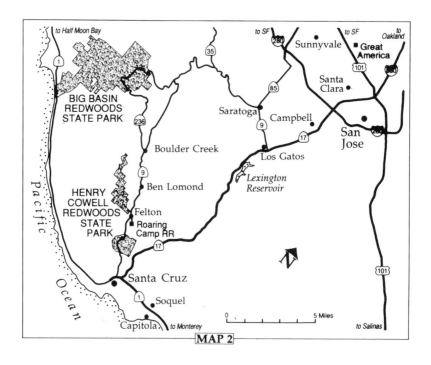

MAP 2

SANTA CRUZ MOUNTAINS

SAN LORENZO VALLEY

■ *A LITTLE BACKGROUND*

Hidden in a dense redwood forest, this once-popular resort area is now a little frayed around the edges. Mostly relics left from a heyday that is long past, the area's motels and cabins are generally far from luxurious. Still, the abundance of trees, trails, and swimming holes, as well as reasonable prices, make it a choice destination for bargain-hunting vacationers.

■ *VISITOR INFORMATION*

San Lorenzo Valley Chamber of Commerce *Boulder Creek 95006, 408/335-2764.*

■ *GETTING THERE*

Located approximately 70 miles south of San Francisco. Take Highway 280 to Highway 84 to Highway 35 to Highway 9.

■ *WHERE TO STAY*

Ben Lomond Hylton Motel *9733 Highway 9, Ben Lomond, 408/336-2292; 2-4/$-$$; cribs; TVs; some tubs; heated pool; continental breakfast.* These motel rooms are shaded by tall redwoods.

19

Griffin's Fern River Resort Motel *5250 Highway 9, Felton, 408/335-4412; 2/$, 4/$$; all TVs; some kitchens, porches, gas fireplaces.* These modern cabins are located on the river across from Henry Cowell Redwoods State Park. The five-acre lot features a redwood-shaded outdoor recreation area with volleyball, tetherball, and Ping Pong, and guests have use of a private beach on the river.

Jaye's Timberland Resort *8705 Highway 9, Ben Lomond, 408/336-5479; 2/$$, 4/$$-$$$; 2-night minimum on weekends, 5-night minimum in summer; cribs; all TVs, kitchens; some fireplaces; pool (heated in summer).* These modern cabins are scattered on spacious grounds shaded by redwoods.

Merrybrook Lodge *13420 Big Basin Way, Boulder Creek, 408/338-6813; 2-4/$-$$; 2-night minimum weekends; cribs; TVs, refrigerators; some kitchens, fireplaces.* Tucked in the redwoods, some of these cabins and motel units overlook a creek.

■ WHERE TO EAT

Scopazzi's Restaurant *Big Basin Way, Boulder Creek, 408/338-4444; L W-Sat, D W-Sun; highchairs, booster seats, children's portions; reservations suggested; $$; AE,MC,V.* This spacious, rustic 1904 mountain lodge is known for its Italian food. You can get cannelloni, veal scaloppine, and chicken cacciatore as well as fried prawns, pepper steak flambe, and quail en cocotte. Children should be pleased to see the menu also offers a hamburger, grilled cheese sandwich, and spaghetti.

♥ **Tyrolean Inn** *9600 Highway 9, Ben Lomond, 408/336-5188; L/D daily; booster seat; reservations suggested on weekends; $$; all cards.* Diners feast here on exquisite Austrian/German cuisine such as sauerbraten and schnitzels. Desserts include fresh apple strudel and Black Forest cake. With 24-hour notice, the kitchen will prepare venison, duck l'orange, or any specialty desired. In good weather lunch is available on the patio. Dinner is enjoyed in a romantic, cozy dining room heated by two fireplaces. Cottages are available should you desire to stay the night.

■ WHAT TO DO

Big Basin Redwoods State Park *21600 Big Basin Way, Boulder Creek, 408/338-6132; day use $3.* California's oldest state park, Big Basin has over 50 miles of hiking trails. Self-guiding **Redwood Trail** leads to interesting redwoods such as the **Animal Tree** and the **Chimney Tree**. Another 3 1/2-mile trail leads to **Berry Creek Falls**—a good spot for a swim. A Nature Lodge features exhibits, and campsites are available.

Covered Bridge *off Graham Hill Rd., Felton.* Built over the San Lorenzo River in 1892, this creaky, decaying redwood bridge can still be walked on and is now a State Historical Landmark. Measuring 34 feet high, it is the tallest bridge of its kind in the U.S.

Henry Cowell Redwoods State Park *Felton, 408/335-4598.* A number of trails lead through this park's redwood groves. Campsites are available.

Highlands County Park *8500 Highway 9, Ben Lomond, 408/336-8551; daily 10-dusk; pool 12-5 summer only, adults $1.50, under 17 $1; parking $1 in summer.* The grounds of this old estate have been transformed into a park with pool, playground, and picnic tables. Nature trails lead to a sandy river beach.

Roaring Camp & Big Trees Narrow-Gauge Railroad *Graham Hill Rd., Felton, 408/335-4484; operates daily, call for schedule; adults $10.50, 3-15 $7.50.* This six-mile, hour-long train ride winds through virgin redwoods and crosses over a spectacular trestle. About the time passengers start feeling a little restless, the train makes a short stretch stop at **Cathedral Grove**—an impressive circle of tall, 800-year-old redwood trees said to have a 3,000-year-old root system! Another stop is made at **Bear Mountain**, where riders may disembark for a picnic or hike and then return on a later train. An outdoor chuckwagon barbecue operates near the depot *(Sat & Sun 12-3, May-Oct),* and the **Red Caboose Saloon** dispenses short order items. Be sure to save some tidbits for the hungry ducks in the lake. And remember to bring sweaters. Though this area enjoys warm to hot weather in the summer, it can get chilly on the train ride. Many special events are scheduled each year, including a **Steelhead Special** for fisherman in the winter and a chocolate **Easter egg hunt** for kids during spring vacation.

Swimming Holes.

Ben Lomond County Park *Mill St., Ben Lomond, 408/336-5639; daily 12-5 in summer; adults $1.50, under 17 $1.* A sandy beach and good river swimming are available at this dammed-up swimming hole. Shaded picnic tables with barbecue facilities are also provided.

Boulder Creek Park *Middleton Ave. east of Highway 9, Boulder Creek.* This swimming hole has both shallow and deep areas and a sandy beach. Picnic tables and barbecue facilities are in a shady area.

LOS GATOS/SARATOGA

■ *A LITTLE BACKGROUND*

Tucked in the lush, green Santa Cruz mountains, Los Gatos is known for its many antique shops. Nearby Saratoga is a small and quiet town.

■ *VISITOR INFORMATION*

Los Gatos Chamber of Commerce *P.O. 1820, (5 Montebello Way), Los Gatos 95030, 408/354-9300.*

Saratoga Chamber of Commerce *P.O. Box 161, Saratoga 95070, 408/867-0753.*

■ *GETTING THERE*

Located approximately 60 miles south of San Francisco. Take Highway 101 to Highway 17 to the Los Gatos exit.

■ *WHERE TO STAY*

The Inn at Saratoga *20645 Fourth St., Saratoga, 800/543-5020, 408/867-5020; 2-4/$$$+; cribs; TVs, refrigerators, bathtubs; continental breakfast.* This brand new five-story hotel has an old-time Victorian feeling combined with modern luxurious amenities and a contemporary decor. Set in a quiet canyon behind busy Highway 9, its rooms all face a forest of old eucalyptus through which winds gurgling Saratoga Creek. Afternoon wine and appetizers are served in the cozy parlour and outdoors on a sylvan patio. Families will appreciate that **Wildwood Park**, and its ample playground, is just across the creek.

La Hacienda Inn *18840 Saratoga-Los Gatos Rd., Los Gatos, 408/354-9230; 2/$$-$$$+, 4/$$$+; children under 6 free; cribs; TVs, refrig-*

erators; some fireplaces, bathtubs; heated pool (unheated Nov-Apr), jacuzzi; continental breakfast, restaurant. Tucked away from the main highway, this pleasant motels features cozy, redwood-trimmed rooms with private patios. A large lawn, suitable for children's play, and an exercise cycle are available to guests.

Los Gatos Garden Inn *46 E. Main St., Los Gatos, 408/354-6446; 2/ $$,4/$$$+; 3-night minimum on kitchen units; all TVs, bathtubs; some kitchens; continental breakfast; pool (summer only).* These rustic Spanish bungalows are in a quiet location just two blocks from Old Town.

Los Gatos Lodge *50 Saratoga Ave., Los Gatos, 800/231-8676, 408/ 354-3300; 2-4/$$-$$$+; children under 12 free; cribs; TVs; some refrigerators, bathtubs, private hot tubs; heated pool (unavail. Nov-Feb), jacuzzi; room service, restaurant.* Located on attractive, spacious grounds, this modern motel makes a putting green, shuffleboard, and lawn games available to guests.

Sanborn Park Hostel *15808 Sanborn Rd., Saratoga, 408/741-9555.* This gorgeous, rustic building is constructed of logs and located in a secluded redwood grove in the foothills of the Santa Cruz mountains. It's a naturally fragrant, quiet area with plenty of hiking trails. Just down the road **Sanborn-Skyline County Park** offers campsites, picnic tables, and the **Youth Science Institute**. See also p.25.

■ WHERE TO EAT

The Chart House *115 N. Santa Cruz Ave., Los Gatos, 408/354-1737; D daily; highchairs, booster seats, children's portions; reservations suggested; all cards.* Enjoy a special dinner inside this stately old Victorian. The menu features prime rib, steaks, and fresh seafood. All dinners include a salad with homemade dressing, plus both hot sourdough and squaw bread.

The Good Earth *206 N. Santa Cruz Ave., Los Gatos, 408/395-6868; B/ L/D daily; highchairs, children's menu; $; AE,DC,MC,V.* A good spot for a quick, light meal or snack, the menu here offers whole grain breads, organic beef, and a large selection of vegetarian items. There are also homemade soups, sandwiches, salads, hot entrees, omelettes, health-food shakes, and good-for-you desserts. An extensive children's menu includes pancakes, noodles, a peanut butter & jelly sandwich, and several burgers.

Mimi's *in Old Town, Los Gatos, 408/354-5511; L/D daily, Sat & SunBr; highchairs, booster seats, children's portions; reservations suggested; $$; MC,V.* Anytime is a good time to dine outside among the hanging geraniums here, but I think the best time is at brunch when apple pancakes and egg dishes served with superb homefries are on the extensive menu. The lunch menu features an eclectic mix of soups, salads, sandwiches, and pastas. Children's items include the house blintzes, grilled peanut butter, grilled cheese, and a hamburger. The wait for a railing-side table is worth it. Besides getting to enjoy looking out into ancient oaks, you'll be able to look down into a well-groomed **topiary garden**. Exotic coffees, ice cream sundaes, and desserts—carrot cake, cheesecake with a pecan-walnut crust—end the menu.

Mountain Charley's *15 N. Santa Cruz Ave., Los Gatos, 408/354-7090; call for hours and current music schedule.* You'll want to know about this lively bar if you get thirsty while you're in town. A live band performs nightly, making a visit to this gigantic, jumping saloon an exciting experience. Age minimum 21.

Pedro's *316 N. Santa Cruz Ave., Los Gatos, 408/354-7570; L/D daily, SunBr; highchairs, booster seats, children's portions; no reservations; $$; MC,V.* This popular spot features an authentic Mexican decor and huge servings of tasty Mexican dishes. Unusual menu items include chimichangas (deep-fried flour tortillas filled with spicy shredded beef and topped with guacamole and sour cream), quesadillas (large flour tortillas filled with Jack cheese and topped with guacamole and sour cream), and—the house specialty—a crab enchilada. There is often a wait to get in. Some people pass the time sipping Margaritas and munching cornchips and salsa outside on the patio or in the cozy bar.

■ WHAT TO DO

Congress Springs Vineyards *23600 Congress Springs Rd./Highway 9, Saratoga, 408/867-1409; tasting daily 11-5.* Established in 1892, this winery is located at the end of a steep, woodsy backroad. Before heading up, you might want to pick up a picnic in town at **Florentine Pasta Factory & Trattoria** *(14510 Big Basin Way)*.

Domaine M. Marion Winery *300 College Ave., Los Gatos, 408/395-7914; tasting daily 11-4:30, tour at 1.* This upstart winery recently took over the historic site, high in the hills above town, formerly occupied by the Novitiate Winery. Low prices, high quality, and artist-designed labels qualify the wines as a bargain. A picnic area with a view of the town is situated just outside the stone cellar tasting room.

Garrod Farms Stables *22600 Mt. Eden Rd., Saratoga, 408/867-9527; daily 8:30-5; $12.50/hr.* Shetland ponies are available for children under nine to ride; an adult must walk them with a lead rope. Anyone over nine can ride the trails which roam over 200 acres.

Hakone Japanese Gardens *21000 Big Basin Way, Saratoga, 408/867-3438 x43; M-F 10-5, Sat & Sun 11-5; free.* Now a city park, this garden was originally constructed by a private individual to typify a mid-17th century Zen garden. It includes a Japanese-style house built without nails or adhesives, a pond stocked with colorful koi, and an authentic Tea Ceremony room. Tea is served in the garden on weekends.

Los Gatos Museum *4 Tait St., Los Gatos, 408/354-2646; Tu-Sun 10-4; free.* Housed in a Spanish-style building, circa 1907, this small museum features exhibits on natural science and contemporary fine arts. The tiny **Forbes Mill Museum** *(75 Church St., 408/395-7375),* located in the remains of a flour mill dating from 1854, focuses on town history.

Old Town *50 University Ave., Los Gatos, 408/354-6596.* Once the town elementary school, this attractive complex is now a series of interesting shops and restaurants. Free entertainment is often scheduled in an outdoor amphitheatre.

Parks. Twelve-acre **Oak Meadow Park** *(off Blossom Hill Rd. in Los Gatos)* has picnic facilities, baseball diamonds, hiking trails, and a well-equipped playground with a real fire engine and airplane to climb on. **Billy Jones Wildcat Railroad,** a miniature steam locomotive, operates Tuesdays through Sundays in summer, weekends in the spring and fall. The 175-acre **Vasona Lake County Park** *(also off Blossom Hill Rd.)* is dominated by a huge reservoir where you can rent canoes and sailboats, feed hungry ducks and seagulls, and fish—not to mention use the barbecue facilities and playground and visit the **Youth Science Institute.**

Villa Montalvo *15400 Montalvo Rd., Saratoga, 408/741-3421. Arboretum: daily 9-5; free. Gallery: Tu-Sun 1-4; adults 50¢, under 19 free.* Once the summer home of U.S. Senator James Phelan, this majestic Mediterranean-style estate now is the county center for fine arts. It also serves as a bird sanctuary. Self-guided nature trails wind through the 175-acre estate gardens. Theatrical events are often staged in the natural outdoor amphitheater and **Carriage House Theater.**

■ *WHAT TO DO NEARBY*

The Gaslighter Theater *400 E. Campbell Ave., Campbell, 408/866-1408; Th 8pm, F 8:30, Sat 6:30 & 9:30; tickets $8.75 & 9.50.* A staff member says that this cozy theater is located "in lovely downtown Campbell—Santa Clara County's fastest growing ghost town." And, indeed, at night this seems to be the only show in town. After being greeted in the street and at the door by the exhuberant cast, the whole family has fun inside hissing the villain and cheering the hero—while munching on complimentary popcorn. The two-part shows are not at all subtle—making them great for school-age children. Shows include both a melodrama (like *Ignorance Isn't Bliss* or *No Mother to Guide Her*) and vaudeville (dancing, singing, comedy) performance.

Great America *on Great America Parkway off Highway 101 or Highway 237, Santa Clara, 408/988-1776; call for schedule; $15.95, 3-6 $7.95, under 3 free.* There's no question about it. The thrill rides here are spectacular, the roller coasters great shocking fun. Then there are the Yankee Clipper and Logger's Run flume rides, the double-decker carousel, and the Sky Whirl—the world's first triple-arm Ferris wheel. Smurf Woods features special rides and activities for children under 12.

Rosicrucian Egyptian Museum *Park Ave./Naglee, San Jose, 408/287-2807; Sat-M 12-4:40, Tu-F 9-4:40; adults $3, 12-17 $1; strollers not permitted.* Collection highlights include mummies, fine jewelery, and a full-size reproduction of a 4,000-year-old rock tomb—the only such tomb in the United States. The surrounding buildings and grounds are stunning; allow time for a stroll. An adjacent Planetarium presents shows daily.

Winchester Mystery House *525 S. Winchester Blvd., San Jose, 408/247-2101; tours daily 9:30-4, longer in summer; adults $8.95, 6-12 $4.95; strollers not permitted.* The story goes that Sarah Winchester, heir to the $20 million Winchester rifle fortune, believed that to make amends for a past wrong-doing she had to build additions to her home continuously, 24-hours-a-day. Her eccentric ideas resulted in some unusual features: asymmetrical rooms, narrow passageways, zigzag staircases, and doors opening into empty shafts. The tour takes in ll0 rooms, climbs more than 200 steps, and covers almost a mile. Picnic tables are available in the courtyard.

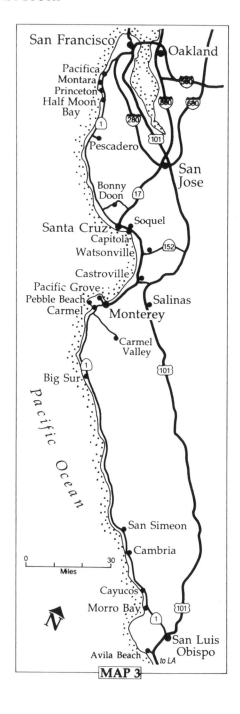

COAST
SOUTH

HIGHWAY 1 LODGINGS
AND ATTRACTIONS

■ *VISITOR INFORMATION*

Half Moon Bay/Coastside Chamber of Commerce *P.O. Box 188, (225 S. Cabrillo Highway), Half Moon Bay 94019, 415/726-5202.*

Harvest Trails *765 Main St., Half Moon Bay 94019.* For a free map to the area's farms, send a self-addressed, stamped legal-size envelope.

■ *ANNUAL EVENTS*

Chamarita *May.* Held here for over 100 years, this Portuguese festival includes a barbecue and carnival.

Art and Pumpkin Festival *October.* Children are invited to wear costumes and participate in the **Great Pumpkin Parade**. Rounding out the fun are pumpkin-carving and pie-eating contests, arts and crafts booths, a variety of pumpkin foods, and assorted on-going entertainment. Nearby pumpkin patches are open for picking.

■ *GETTING THERE*

The trip down Highway 1 from San Francisco features a breath-taking, cliff-hugging ride along the Pacific Ocean. Half Moon Bay, with its restful farmland vistas, is located about 25 miles south.

■ *WHERE TO STAY/WHAT TO DO*

PACIFICA

Sea Breeze Motel *100 Rockaway Beach, 415/359-3903; 2/$-$$, 4/$$; cribs; TVs; restaurant.* This is the destination if you're looking for a quick, inexpensive escape. Rooms are simple motel-style, but the beach is only a few steps away and a merry restaurant, **Nick's**, is just next door.

MONTARA

Montara Lighthouse Hostel *16th St., 415/728-7177; rooms for families and couples available.* This restored 1875 lighthouse is now the cliffside setting for a picturesque retreat. Lodging is in a modern duplex—formerly the lightkeeper's quarters. Facilities include two kitchens, a laundry, a volleyball court, a private beach, an outdoor hot tub (fee), and bicycle rentals. A continental breakfast is available at an additional charge. See also p.273.

Fitzgerald Marine Reserve *in El Granada, 415/728-3584.* Excellent tidepooling can be enjoyed here. Walks are led by naturalists on weekends when low tides permit. Call for schedule.

HALF MOON BAY

♥ **San Benito House** *365 Main St., 415/726-3425; 2/$$-$$$+; unsuitable for children; some shared baths; sauna; continental breakfast, restaurant.* Upstairs, the guest rooms feature solid walls, high ceilings, and bathrooms with old-fashioned tubs. Downstairs, the charmingly decorated dining room invites romantic dining. Owner/chef Carol Mickelsen makes use of fresh local produce and seafood in her accomplished preparation of California cuisine with a French country influence, and the kitchen is famous for its delicious French pastries. Make reservations when you book your room, as this cozy restaurant is also very popular with locals. A deli dispenses quick, inexpensive meals *(M-Sat 11-3)*, and a lively Western-style saloon *(daily from 4pm)* is the perfect spot for a nightcap. Guests can also take a stroll in the formal English garden and, perhaps, indulge in some competition on the croquet lawn.

Horseback riding. Sea Horse Ranch *(415/726-2362)* and **Friendly Acres** *(415/726-9871)* are the places to go. Hayrides are also available.

A picnic can be put together by visiting the old-fashioned **Cunha**

Country Store *(Main St./Kelly Ave., 415/726-4071)*, which has been in the same building for over fifty years, and the **Half Moon Bay Bakery** *(514 Main, 415/726-4841)*, which is still using its original brick ovens and is known for its great French bread and Portuguese sweet bread. The spectacular beaches are popular destinations in summer; **Dunes Beach** is my favorite.

Whale-watching expeditions leave from nearby Princeton-By-The-Sea. They are sponsored by the **Oceanic Society** *(415/474-3385)* and the **Whale Center** *(415/654-6621)*. Reservations are necessary.

PESCADERO

Pigeon Point Lighthouse Hostel *Pigeon Point Rd., 415/879-0633; rooms for families and couples available.* Built in 1871, this scenic lighthouse is the second tallest on the West Coast. Visitors are housed in adjacent bungalows, and an outdoor hot tub is available (fee). Public tours of the lighthouse are given on Sundays from 10 to 3. Excellent tidepools are located just to the north. See also p.273.

Ano Nuevo State Reserve *New Year's Creek Rd., 415/879-0227, 879-0228; tours Nov-Apr; reservations necessary (Ticketron 415/974-6391); $3.* Huge elephant seals return to this beach each year to mate and bear their young. Docent-guided tours, lasting 2 1/2 hours and covering three miles, take visitors close enough to observe the seals basking in the sun or sleeping. Usually that is the extent of the activity seen, but occasionally one of the weighty bulls roars into battle with a challenging male.

Depending on the season, you can **pick-your-own** boysenberries, kiwi fruit, artichokes, or Christmas trees across the street at **Coastways Ranch** *(415/879-0414)*.

SANTA CRUZ

■ *A LITTLE BACKGROUND*

Santa Cruz has long been a popular summer beach resort and is close enough to San Francisco to visit just for the day. The weather is reliably clear and sunny, and the beach features fine sand and a gentle surf. In fact, it is a Very Southern California-style beach town. The beach people add to the simile with zinc on their noses, surfboards hanging out of their cars, and The Beach Boys blaring from their tapedecks.

■ *VISITOR INFORMATION*

Santa Cruz Area Chamber of Commerce *P.O. Box 921, (105 Cooper St., suite 243), Santa Cruz 95061, 408/423-1111.*

■ *ANNUAL EVENTS*

Watsonville Fly-In *May; Watsonville, 408/724-3849.* An assortment of antique planes provide an interesting air show.

Cabrillo Music Festival *July; U.C.Santa Cruz campus, 408/476-9064.* Held inside a tent, this is said to be one of the country's best small music festivals. It includes a variety of classic and contemporary works as well as world premieres.

Brussels Sprout Festival *October; at the Boardwalk, 408/423-5590.* Is your tummy ready to sample chocolate-covered sprouts, sprout water taffy, sprout chip cookies, and guacasprout dip? What about sprout pizza and sprouts-on-a-stick? Those who remain unconvinced may taste the more conventional recipes demonstrated by local restaurants.

■ *GETTING THERE*

Located approximately 80 miles south of San Francisco. Take Highway
101 or Highway 280 to Highway 17, or Highway 1 all the way.

■ *WHERE TO STAY*

♥ **Babbling Brook Bed & Breakfast Inn** *1025 Laurel St., 408/427-
2437; 2/$$$-$$$+; 2-night minimum on weekends; unsuitable for
children under 13; all bathtubs; some fireplaces, private decks; full
breakfast.* Shaded by tall redwoods, this secluded hillside inn was
built as a log cabin in 1909. Rooms were added through the years,
and the inn was renovated in 1981. It is on the National Register of
Historic Places and is the oldest and largest (12 rooms) B&B in the
area. An acre of beautfully landscaped grounds, with paths and covered footbridges, surrounds the inn, and complimentary wine and
cheese are served each afternoon by the fireplace in the parlor.

Casa Blanca Motel *101 Main St., 408/423-1570; 2/$$-$$$+, 4/$$$+;
2-night minimum on summer weekends; cribs; all TVs, ocean views;
some kitchens, fireplaces, bathtubs; restaurant.* Located across the
street from the beach, this converted 1918 mansion features spa-
cious, nicely decorated rooms. More modern rooms are available in
a 1950s annex. Elegant steak and seafood dinners and a Sunday
brunch are served in an adjoining restaurant, where children's por-
tions and highchairs are available.

Dream Inn *175 W. Cliff Dr., 800/662-3838, 408/426-4330; 2-4/$$$-
$$$+; 2-night minimum on summer weekends; children under 12
free; cribs; all TVs, bathtubs; some refrigerators; heated pool,
jacuzzi; room service, 2 restaurants.* This 10-story hotel is located
right on the beach. Each room has a private balcony or patio over-
looking the beach and ocean. The pool and jacuzzi are one story up
from the sand and enjoy the same view.

Ocean Echo Motel & Cottages *401 Johans Beach Dr., 408/462-4192;
2/$$-$$$, 4/$$$; 2-night minimum in summer; cribs; all TVs, refrig-
erators; some kitchens, bathtubs, ocean views.* Located a few miles
south of the Boardwalk, these attractive units are on a private beach.

Santa Cruz Hostel *425 King St., 408/423-8304; summer only.* A permanent year-round hostel is in the works, but meanwhile guests
sleep on mattresses on the floor of a school gym. See also p.273.

Motel Row. Many more motels are located in the area surrounding the
Boardwalk, including some inexpensive ones dating from the 1930s.
They are often available at the last minute.

■ *WHERE TO STAY NEARBY*

Pajaro Dunes *2661 Beach Rd., Watsonville, 800/7-PAJARO, 408/722-9201; 2-4/$$$+; 2-night minimum; cribs; all TVs, kitchens, fireplaces, bathtubs; some ocean views, private saunas; 19 tennis courts.* Located in the shoreline dunes, this complex of condominiums and homes has bicycle rentals and a small parcourse among its facilities.

■ *WHERE TO EAT*

Cocoanut Grove *400 Beach St., 408/423-2053; SunBr; highchairs, booster seats, children's portions; reservations suggested; $$; MC,V.* In the '30s and '40s this marvelous room was popular as a ballroom for big band dances. The second-floor dining room overlooks the beach and, on warm days, the domed glass ceiling is opened to the fresh sea air. Among the opulent array of brunch foods are create-your-own omelettes, prepared before your very eyes until 11 a.m. A buffet of fresh fruits, salads, relishes, cheeses, muffins, breakfast meats, and egg items is carefully maintained and available throughout. Then, to top it all off, there is a calorie-laden pastry table. Choice of drink is also included. Children are nicely accommodated, and dress varies from beach-casual to dressy.

The Crow's Nest *2218 E. Cliff Dr., 408/476-4560; L/D daily; highchairs, booster seats, children's portions; reservations suggested on weekends; $$; AE,MC,V.* Dine outdoors, protected by a glass windbreaker, while watching the yachts come and go from the **Santa Cruz Yacht Harbor.** Seals also are often observed frolicking close to shore. Steak, seafood, and both an oyster and salad bar are available. So is a hamburger.

El Palomar *1344 Pacific Ave., 408/425-7575; L M-Sat, D M-Sun; highchairs, booster seats; $; no reservations; MC,V.* Located in what was once the lobby of the old Palomar Hotel, this restaurant serves well-prepared, authentic Michoacan-style Mexican food. Tortillas are made by hand each day, and there is a large selection of Mexican beers. Unusual menu items include crisp flautas, pozole (pork and hominy stew), carne asada (barbecued beef), and occasionally menudo (tripe soup). The fresh seafood specials are also usually quite interesting. Children might especially enjoy the sopes (little tortillas shaped like boats and filled with chicken, guacamole, or tasty ground beef).

India Joze *1001 Center St., 408/427-3554; L/D daily; highchairs, booster seats, children's portions; reservations suggested for din-*

ner; $$; MC,V. The day of the week determines the type of Asian cuisine you'll find on this exciting, exotic menu. Monday through Wednesday it is Mid-East Asian, Thursday and Friday it's East Indian, and Saturday and Sunday it's Indonesian. Each August the menu reflects the fact that the restaurant is the home of the **International Calamari Festival.** The pleasant dining area is light and airy, and live entertainment is scheduled some evenings. The kitchen is well-known for its splendid desserts, which may be enjoyed sans meal in an informal dining area outside the restaurant. Before or after a meal here, you may want to browse in the adjoining **Santa Cruz Art Center** shops.

Old Theatre Cafe *106 Walnut Ave., 408/426-0544; B/L daily, D Tu-Sat; highchairs, booster seats; $; no cards.* This European-style coffee shop serves particularly good breakfasts. But it is best known for its German-Austrian bakery, which puts out such delights as Black Forest cake and Napoleons.

Santa Cruz Brewing Company *516 Front St., 408/429-8838; L/D daily; booster seats; $; MC,V.* This cheerful spot claims to be "the first brewery on California's central coast since prohibition." It dispenses made-on-the-premises brews: an European-style Lighthouse Lager, a Lighthouse Amber, and a dark Pacific Porter. Children might like the root beer made from an old-time recipe. Like the brews, the pub food is made fresh on the premises and includes "spiedies" (grilled skewers of pork), oyster shots (spicy oysters in a shot glass), beer bread (made from the spent grains of beer-making), and shark bites (battered deep-fried thresher shark). All this, plus an assortment of sandwiches and "munchies."

Tampico Kitchen *822 Pacific Ave., 408/423-2241; B/L/D daily; highchairs, booster seats, children's portions; $; reservations suggested; MC,V.* Tasty Mexican food is served here in an American cafe-style atmosphere. Especially noteworty are the nachos (tortilla chips smothered with cheddar cheese, chiles, and onions), the taquitos (crisp corn tortillas rolled around shredded beef and topped with sour cream and guacamole), and the anesthetizing margaritas. Children tend to favor the quesadillas (a tortilla folded around melted cheese), and for dessert everyone seems to enjoy the flan topped with whipped cream.

■ WHAT TO DO

Beach & Boardwalk *400 Beach St., 408/423-5590; from 11am, daily June-Sept, weekends Oct-May, call for hours; admission to Boardwalk free; individual fee for rides, all-day ride ticket $11.95; minia-*

ture golf $2.75/person. Fortunately, this is one boardwalk which has not degenerated over the years. Built in 1907, it was spiffed up a few years ago with a cheerful painting. Now the only boardwalk left on the West Coast, it offers a variety of arcade games, fast-food stands, and souvenir shops, plus nineteen major rides and five kiddie rides. The half-mile-long concrete walkway parallels a clean, gorgeous beach. Thrill rides include the **Giant Dipper**—a rickety wooden roller coaster built in 1924 and rated by *The New York Times* as one of the ten best in the country—and Logger's Revenge—a refreshing water flume ride. An old-fashioned merry-go-round—built in New Jersey by Looff in 1911 and one of only four remaining classic carousels in California—features 70 hand-carved horses and 2 chariots as well as its rare, original 342-pipe Ruth band organ and a brass ring toss. Both the roller coaster and the carousel are now national historic landmarks. All this and indoor miniature golf, too!

Bonny Doon Vineyard *2 Pine Flat Rd., Bonny Doon, 8 miles north of town, 408/425-3625; tasting Sat & Sun 12-5:30, in summer Tu-Sun.* This pleasant side trip takes you along a meandering country road to the tiny town of Bonny Doon. Picnic facilities are available in a redwood grove complete with creek. Winery specialties include Pinot Noirs, Chardonnays, and exotic Rhone-like Cuvees.

Joseph M. Long Marine Laboratory *N.W. End Delaware, 408/429-4308; Tu-Sun 1-4; free.* This marine research station for U.C. Santa Cruz features an aquarium of local sea life and an 81-foot blue whale skeleton. Guided tours are sometimes available to observe the sea lions and dolphins.

Lighthouse Point *on West Cliff Dr.* **Seal Rock**, home to a herd of sea lions, is visible off shore from the small, brick **Mark Abbott Memorial Lighthouse** which now houses the **Santa Cruz Surfing Museum** *(408/429-3429; daily, Apr-Sept 12-5, Oct-Mar 11-4; free).* Surfers can be viewed in action from nearby **Steamer's Lane**.

Mission Santa Cruz *126 High St., 408/426-5686; daily 2:30-5, call ahead to check schedule; by donation.* The original mission, built in 1794, had a history of destruction. This half-size replica is built near the original mission site and houses a small museum.

Municipal Wharf *near the Boardwalk.* You can walk or drive to the end of this half-mile-long pier. Fishermen angle from the side, and seafood restaurants, snack stands, and picnic tables are scattered along its length. Deep-sea fishing trips originate at concessions located here.

Mystery Spot *1953 Branciforte Dr., 3 miles north of town, 408/423-8897; daily 9:30-4:30; adults $3, 5-11 $1.50.* Gravitational forces appear to be defied in this small, quiet, and cool spot in the redwoods. Finding it can be a bit of a mystery, too.

Natural Bridges State Beach *on West Cliff Dr., 408/423-4609; daily 8am-sunset; $3/car.* Enjoy a picnic in the sun on the sandy beach, or in the shade at sturdy tables. The sandstone arches after which the beach is named have collapsed, but there are still tidepools to explore. Swimming in the ocean is not safe, but sometimes a lagoon forms where small children may safely wade. From October to March large numbers of Monarch butterflies make their homes here. A 3/4-mile nature trail leads to good viewing points where they can be observed hanging in clusters on mature eucalyptus trees. Guided walks are also often scheduled.

Octagon County Historical Museum *118 Cooper St., 408/425-2540; M-Sat 12-5; free.* Exhibits inside this circa 1882 building, formerly the County Hall of Records, change regularly.

Pacific Garden Mall *Pacific Ave. between Water & Cathcart Sts.* These five landscaped blocks comprise downtown Santa Cruz. The park-like setting features many conventional stores as well as boutiques, art galleries, and restaurants—many of which are located inside restored historic buildings. The **Bookshop Santa Cruz** *(at 1547)* is great for browsing and has a pleasant courtyard in the back where you can relax and enjoy a snack.

Santa Cruz City Museum *1305 E. Cliff Dr., 408/429-3773; Tu-Sat 10-5, Sun 12-5; adults $1.* Located across the street from wonderful

Once upon a time at Natural Bridges State Beach

Seabright Beach, this museum displays the county's natural treasures. Exhibits include Indian relics and costumes as well as an unusual collection of sea shells.

The Last Supper *526 Broadway, 408/426-5787; Tu-Sun 10-4; by donation.* Located in the **Santa Cruz Art League galleries**, this life-size sculpted interpretation of Leonardo da Vinci's painting took ten years to complete.

University of California, Santa Cruz Campus *1156 High St., 408/429-0111; free parking Sat & Sun, M-F $2.* Acquaint yourself with this scenic campus by taking a self-guided walking tour. Maps are available at the Public Information Office. Guided walking and van tours are given free each weekday at 10:30 and 1:30. Call 408/429-4008 for reservations. The Arboretum *(408/427-2998; W, Sat, Sun 2-4)* has an extensive collection of plants from Australia and New Zealand and of South African protea. A free shuttle bus loops the grounds during the school year but does not run in the summer. Hungry? Try the **Whole Earth Restaurant** which serves organic vegetarian food and is open to the public.

CAPITOLA

■ *A LITTLE BACKGROUND*

Dating to 1861, this historic seaside resort was the state's first. Now it is an artsy-craftsy beach town. The lovely mile-long beach is sheltered between two bluffs and offers swimming in calm ocean waters or wading in the fresh water of Soquel Creek. Be cautious, however, as sometimes that creek water isn't so fresh.

Fronting the beach, The Esplanade is lined with coffee houses and restaurants serving everything from hamburgers to lobster. Many have outdoor patios overlooking the beach.

Because it is such a popular spot, in the summer free shuttle buses are in service to take visitors from parking lots on Bay Avenue to the beach. Some shuttle bikes are also available for loan.

■ *VISITOR INFORMATION*

Capitola Chamber of Commerce *P.O. Box 234, (410 Capitola Ave.), Capitola 95010, 408/475-6522.*

■ *ANNUAL EVENTS*

Begonia Festival *September.* This popular festival includes a sand sculpture contest, arts and crafts fair, and floating parade of flower-covered boats down Soquel Creek. It is interesting to note that the only other begonia festival in the world is held in Ballarat, Australia.

■ *GETTING THERE*

Located approximately 5 miles south of Santa Cruz.

■ *WHERE TO STAY*

Capitola Inn *822 Bay Ave., 408/462-3004; 2-4/$$-$$$+; children under 14 free; cribs; all TVs, bathtubs; some kitchens, fireplaces; 3 restaurants on property; heated pool.* This tasteful, modern lodging facility operates a free shuttle bus to the beach daily in summer.

Capitola Venetian Hotel *1500 Wharf Rd., 408/476-6471; 2/$$-$$$+, 4/$$$-$$$+; 2-night minimum on weekends; cribs; all TVs, kitchens; some fireplaces, bathtubs, ocean views.* This mini-village of charming pastel stucco apartments is located right on the beach. Built in 1929, it is said to have been the first condominium complex in the U.S.

Harbor Lights Motel *5000 Cliff Dr., 408/476-0505; 2/$-$$$, 4/$$-$$$; cribs; all TVs, refrigerators; some kitchens, fireplaces, ocean views.* This ordinary motel boasts an extraordinary location just across from the beach.

■ *WHERE TO EAT*

Greenhouse at the Farm *5555 Soquel Dr., Soquel, 408/476-5613; L/D daily, SunBr; highchairs, booster seats, children's portions at dinner; $$; AE,DC,MC,V.* This century-old, five-acre farm is still producing goods for the kitchen. Diners are seated in the converted garden greenhouse next to a cozy fireplace or in the Victorian front room of the former farmhouse. Entree choices include quiches, hamburgers, fresh fish, steaks, and hickory-smoked ribs—all served with delicious freshly baked breads and including access to a well-supplied salad bar. Several homemade soups and hot chocolate made with steamed milk from the espresso machine are also available. Delectable desserts are prepared by the kitchen's own pastry chef. The farm also houses gift and wine shops, a nursery, and a bakery.

Mimi's Ice Cream Cart. In summer be on the lookout for pretty Mimi pedaling her ice cream bike. She also peddles cold ice cream to hot and hungry tourists. It's been awhile since I've seen Mimi. I do hope she's still around and hasn't become just another wispy legend.

♥ **Shadowbrook** *1750 Wharf Rd., 408/475-1511; D daily, Sat & SunBr; highchairs, booster seats, children's portions; reservations suggested; $$$; AE,MC,V.* Located on the banks of Soquel Creek, this popular restaurant is said to be haunted by the man who built it as a summer home in 1917. Diners descend to the romantic restaurant either by riding a bright red, self-operated cable car down a flower-laden hill from the street above or by strolling down a winding path. The menu features prime rib, salmon, and abalone as well as continental cuisine. Dinners include a salad or clam chowder and fresh sourdough and brown breads. Don't like to eat vegies? Trying drinking them here in a "mocktail"—an award-winning non-alcoholic drink devised by the restaurant's owner. Entertainment and dancing are scheduled nightly in summer, weekends the rest of the year.

■ *WHAT TO DO*

Antonelli Brothers Begonia Gardens *2545 Capitola Rd., Santa Cruz, 408/475-5222; daily 9-6; free.* Acres of indoor plants, ferns, and beautiful begonia baskets may be viewed and purchased here. Peak of bloom is August and September, but a good show may be enjoyed June through November. Picnic tables are available in the Hanging Begonia Room.

Bargetto Winery *3535 N. Main St., Soquel, 408/475-2258; tasting M-Sat 9-5:30, Sun from 11.* This small family winery is known for fruit wines, including olallieberry and apricot (my personal favorite), and excellent homemade wine vinegars. Pack a picnic to enjoy on the rustic outdoor patio overlooking gurgling Soquel Creek.

MONTEREY PENINSULA

■ A LITTLE BACKGROUND

Popular for years because of its proximity to San Francisco, this area (Monterey, Pacific Grove, and Carmel) is well-established as a vacation destination. All types of overnight accommodations and restaurants are available. Once the off-season was the entire winter. Now, due to the area's immense popularity, there is no off-season. It is essential that you have reservations for lodging as well as for most of the more popular restaurants.

■ GETTING THERE

Located approximately 40 miles south of Santa Cruz.

■ STOPS ALONG THE WAY

Giant Artichoke Restaurant *11261 Merritt St. (off Highway 1), Castroville, 408/633-3204; daily 7am-7:30pm; booster seats; no cards.* Located in "the artichoke capital of the world," this novelty restaurant makes a good rest stop. You can snack on artichoke specialties such as french-fried artichokes with mayonnaise dip, artichoke soup, artichoke nut cake, and steamed artichokes. Other more standard short-order items are also on the menu.

MONTEREY

■ VISITOR INFORMATION

Monterey Peninsula Chamber of Commerce Visitors & Convention

Bureau *P.O. Box 1770, (380 Alvarado St.), Monterey 93942, 408/ 649-1770.*

■ *ANNUAL EVENTS*

Bing Crosby Golf Tournament *January; Pebble Beach, 408/372-4711.*

Adobe House Tour *April; 408/372-2608.* This is a very popular self-guided walking tour.

Scottish Highland Games *July; 408/899-3864.* See athletic competitions as well as Highland dancing, bagpipe bands, and a sheepdog show at this benefit for cerebral palsy.

Laguna Seca Races. Historic Automobile Races *August;* **Grand Prix** *October; 408/373-1811.*

Concours d'Elegance *August; 408/649-8500.* View classic vintage and antique automobiles at this classy Pebble Beach event.

Jazz Festival *September; 408/373-3366.*

■ *WHERE TO STAY*

Casa Munras Garden Hotel *700 Munras Ave, 800/222-2446, 408/375-2411; 2/$$-$$$+, 4/$$$; children under 12 free; cribs; all TVs; some fireplaces, bathtubs; restaurant; heated pool.* The grounds are spacious, attractive, and peaceful at this large motel-like facility, and all rooms are furnished with brass beds.

Hyatt Regency Monterey *One Old Golf Course Rd., 800/228-9000, 408/372-7171; 2-4 $$$-$$$+; children under 12 free; restaurant; 2 pools, 2 hot tubs, parcourse, 6 tennis courts.* Located on the outskirts of town, this quiet resort offers 579 luxurious rooms. Many face the scenic **Old Del Monte Golf Course**, which is adjacent to the property. A lounge provides live entertainment in the evenings.

Monterey Beach Hotel *2600 Sand Dunes Dr., 800/242-8627, 408/394-3321; 2-4/$$$-$$$+; children under 12 free; cribs; all TVs, bathtubs; some refrigerators, ocean views; room service, restaurant; heated pool, jacuzzi, fitness room.* Located right on the beach, this hotel offers spectacular views of Monterey Bay from its higher-priced rooms. A recreational trail is available to guests.

Monterey Peninsula Hostel *408/373-4167; summer only.* Accommodations consist of mattresses on the floor in a school gymnasium. See also p.273.

Monterey Sheraton *350 Calle Principal, 800/325-3535, 408/649-4234; 2-4/$$$-$$$+; children under 18 free; cribs; restaurant;*

heated pool, jacuzzi, sauna. Located near the Wharf, this attractively designed hotel is built on the former site of the grand old Hotel San Carlos. Rooms are quiet and tastefully appointed, and two people are employed full-time just to take care of the flowers and plants! A health club is available to guests, and an attractive bar features live jazz in the evening.

Motel Row. Modern motel accommodations abound on Munras Avenue.

■ WHERE TO EAT

Abalonetti *57 Fisherman's Wharf, 408/373-1851; L/D Th-M, daily in summer; highchairs, booster seats, children's portions; $; AE,MC.* This tiny, unpretentious restaurant is named for a famous dish in which the squid is pounded tender, breaded, and sauteed in butter. So, not surprisingly, over half the menu is devoted to versions of the house specialty—calamari (squid). Other seafood and Italian dishes are also available, and there is a good view of Monterey Bay.

Clock Garden *565 Abrego, 408/375-6100; L M-F, D daily, SunBr; booster seats; $$; reservations suggested for dinner, AE,DC,MC,V.* Diners have a choice of sitting inside this historic adobe, among the collection of antique clocks, or outside in a lovely courtyard garden. Weekend brunch features delicious hot muffins, orange marmalade served in a scooped-out orange shell, and frothy Ramos Fizzes. Reservations are not taken then or for lunch, so be there when they open or expect a wait. The dinner menu features roasts, ribs, steak, and lots of fresh fish, and the kitchen is well-known for its Greek lemon soup.

Consuelo's *361 Lighthouse Ave., 408/372-8111; L/D daily, SunBr; highchairs, booster seats, children's portions; reservations suggested; $$; all cards.* Situated in an elegant two-story Victorian mansion dating from the 1880s, this Mexican restaurant might be more appropriately located in one of the area's historic adobes. Rooms in the house have been turned into semi-private dining areas, and the menu offers typical Mexican fare as well as a few more unusual items. A personal favorite is the flauta—a chewy flour tortilla filled with shredded beef, rolled, and then deep-fried and topped with a very good guacamole. Among the children's items are a soft quesadilla (sort of a Mexican grilled cheese sandwich) and a hamburger. Meals begin with complimentary appetizers of both spicy carrots and peppers and a giant crisp flour tortilla topped with melted cheese and served elegantly on a pedestal tray. Desserts include unusual pina colada and Kahlua cheesecakes as well as more traditional flan. Ole!

Mark Thomas' Outrigger *700 Cannery Row, 408/372-8543; L/D daily; highchairs, booster seats, children's portions; reservations suggested; $$; all cards.* Seafood and steak dominate the menu, but a hamburger is also available. Diners are seated in a dimly-lit, noisy dining room featuring spectacular views of Monterey Bay. The comfortable bar juts out over the water and makes a good spot to enjoy a potent tropical drink concoction and perhaps some—careful with this one parents—puu puus (appetizers). Live entertainment is scheduled on Friday and Saturday evenings.

Mike's Seafood *25 Fisherman's Wharf, 408/372-6153; B/L/D daily; highchairs, booster seats, children's portions; no reservations; $; all cards.* Arrive before sundown to take advantage of the excellent bay views afforded from the tables of this busy and popular seafood restaurant. Steaks, hamburgers, and chicken are also on the menu.

Sancho Panza *590 Calle Principal, 408/375-0095; L/D daily; highchairs, booster seats; $; AE,MC,V.* Once inside you will see why this claims to be the funkiest Mexican restaurant in town. It reminds me of a Mexican roadhouse. I especially like the touch of old Mexican newspapers recycled as placemats. The patio is decorated with weathered hatch covers and timbers salvaged from Cannery Row's old sardine boats. The history of the building, known as **Casa Guttierez**, is described as "a Mexican country inn...located in a historic adobe built in 1841...by a young Mexican for his bride." Fifteen children were raised here by that bride! The adobe was built when Monterey was still part of Mexico and is now protected by the State of California. My favorite menu items are the chispa (cheese and salsa on a flour tortilla), tostada (huge), chile verde burrito, guacamole, and Mexican hot chocolate flavored with cinnamon and crushed almonds. Freshly fried tortilla chips and salsa accompany each meal.

♥ **The Sardine Factory** *701 Wave St., 408/373-3775; D daily; children's portions; reservations suggested; $$$; all cards.* This building once housed a canteen patronized by cannery workers. Now it is home to this elegant, dimly-lit award-winning restaurant. The kitchen offers fresh seafood and continental-style fare and is known for its white veal and well-aged beef. All dinners are accompanied by a plate of antipasto, hot cheese bread, soup, and a salad presented with *chilled* forks. Children are welcome, but I wouldn't want to be caught here with any whose behavior is unpredictable.

The Warehouse Restaurant *Cannery Row/Prescott, 408/375-1921; L M- Sat, D daily, SunBr; highchairs, booster seats, children's portions; $; no reservations; all cards.* The menu here features Italian items such as ravioli, lasagna, fettucini, and various kinds of spaghetti and individual-size pizzas. Seafood is also available. All dinners include an award-winning clam chowder and visits to a salad bar.

Wharfside Restaurant *60 Fisherman's Wharf, 408/375-3956; L/D daily; highchairs, booster seats, children's portions; $$; reservations accepted; all cards.* In the window downstairs you can watch the various varieties of ravioli (meat and spinach, cheese, squid, salmon, shrimp, crab, lobster) being laboriously prepared. Dining takes place upstairs, where great views of the bay are to be enjoyed. The menu is rounded out with other pastas and seafood, and there are plenty of reasonably-priced side orders which should please children. Sandwiches and pizza are available only at lunch.

■ WHAT TO DO

Allen Knight Maritime Museum *550 Calle Principal, 408/375-2553; Tu-F 1-4 (in summer from 10), Sat & Sun 2-4; free.* See ship models, bells, compasses, and related items and learn about the area's naval history. At press time this museum was scheduled to move to Custom House Plaza.

California Heritage Guides *10 Custom House Plaza, 408/373-6454.* Guided walking tours through Monterey's historic area are arranged to fit your interests, schedule, and budget. Call for details and reservations.

California's First Theater *Pacific/Scott, 408/375-4916; call for schedule and reservations; adults $5, under 13 $3.* Children over age 5

may enjoy visiting this ex-saloon and former boarding house for sailors. The first play was presented here in 1847, and the Troupers of the Gold Coast are still going strong. Nowadays the melodramatic shows and olios change periodically, but they are still presented in the tiny theater just like they were in the old days. Best seating for kids is on benches in the back. **Jack Swan's Tavern** serves a pub menu in the lobby; reservations are suggested for a pre-show dinner.

Cannery Row. Once booming with sardine canneries, Cannery Row became a ghost town in 1945 when the sardines mysteriously disappeared from the area's ocean. Now this mile-long road houses restaurants, art galleries, shops, a **Bargetto Winery** tasting room, the **Spirit of Monterey Wax Museum**, and the new **Monterey Bay Aquarium** (see p.48). To get in the mood, you might want to read John Steinbeck's *Cannery Row*. Lee Chong's Heavenly Flower Grocery in Steinbeck's novel is now **The Old General Store** (#835), La Ida's Cafe is now **Kalisa's** (#851), and Doc's lab is now a private club (#800).

Edgewater Packing Company *640 Wave St., 408/649-1899; open daily, restaurant from 7:30am, merry-go-round and shops from 11.* This family entertainment center has a game room with both antique pinball machines and modern video games, a toy store which children and limber adults can enter by crawling through a kitten's mouth, and a candy shop stocked with cotton candy, candy apples, and popcorn. It also has what may be the world's fastest merry-go-round, and you can rent regular bikes—as well as unusual multi-passenger surrey bikes—to ride on the scenic new bike trail which hugs the bay.

El Estero Park *Del Monte Ave./Camino El Estero/Fremont Blvd.* Enjoy hiking and bike trails and a lake filled with hungry ducks. Paddle boats and canoes may be rented, and children may fish from boats. By the lake on Pearl Street, **Dennis the Menace Playground** features equipment designed by Hank Ketchum, creator of *Dennis the Menace* and a former resident of the area. Notable are a hedge maze and suspension bridge. Picnic tables and a snack concession are available.

Fisherman's Wharf. Lined with restaurants and shops, the Wharf also offers some inexpensive entertainment. Sometimes an organ grinder greets visitors at the entrance with a friendly monkey anxious to take coins from children's hands. Freeloading sea lions live around the wharf pilings. If you toss them a fish (available at the bait shops), they will put on a show. A **diving bell** provides a 30-foot plunge into the water for a fish's-eye view of Monterey Bay. Several businesses offer bay cruises and deep-sea fishing expeditions.

Kitty Hawk Kites *1 Reservation Rd., Marina, 408/384-2622.* If you've ever longed to take up hang-gliding, this is the place to do it. Located on the dunes east of town, this school offers a three-hour beginning course with five flights for $47. Reservations are necessary.

Monterey Bay Aquarium *886 Cannery Row, 408/375-3333; daily 10-6; adults $7, 3-12 $3.* There's something new on old Cannery Row. Built on the site of what was once the row's largest sardine factory, this spectacular $40 million facility is the world's largest seawater aquarium. Well-arranged and architecturally interesting, it provides a close-up view of the underwater world of Monterey Bay—an area known for its spectacular and varied marine life. Among the 83 habitat tanks are one which displays a kelp forest in what is the tallest exhibit tank in the country. Another displays the area's playful sea otters. More than 5,000 fish, mammal, bird, invertebrate, and plant specimens are on display, and most are native to Monterey Bay. Don't miss the special walk-through aviary of shorebirds and the bat ray petting pool. Children might especially enjoy the Touching Pool, where they can handle a variety of starfish and other tidepool life. A fast-food cafeteria and pricier restaurant are available inside; picnic tables are provided outside.

Monterey Bay Kayaks *693 Del Monte Ave., 408/373-KELP; Tu-F 10-*

6, Sat & Sun 8:30-6; $48/4-hr tour. Observe the sea lions and otters up close near Fisherman's Wharf and along Cannery Row. The tour includes a half-hour of safety instruction. Kayaks hold two people. Children must be at least 13 and accompanied by an adult. More extensive and demanding trips are also available.

Monterey Peninsula Museum of Art *559 Pacific St., 408/372-7591; Tu-Sat 10-4, Sun 1-4; free.* Located downtown, this museum exhibits regional art and photography.

Monterey State Historic Park *1 Custom Plaza, 408/649-7118; daily 10-5; adults $3.50, 6-17 $2.* Part of the California State Park System, this park consists of ten historical sites and preserved adobes. The fee admits you to all of the buildings and gardens and includes guided tours of the very special **Stevenson House** (said to be haunted by a forelorn woman dressed in black), the **Larkin House**, and the **Casa Soberanes**. Begin your tour at the **Custom House**.

Presidio of Monterey Museum *Pacific St. north of Decatur St., 408/242-8414; M-F 9-12, 1-3; free.* The history of "Old Fort" Hill is told through dioramas, artifacts, and photographs. Among ten historic sites located next to the museum are a 2,000-year-old Indian village site and ceremonial "rain rock," the ruins of Fort Mervine, and the site of Father Serra's 1770 landing.

Fisherman's Wharf

PACIFIC GROVE

■ *VISITOR INFORMATION*

Pacific Grove Chamber of Commerce *P.O. Box 167, (Forest/Central Aves.), Pacific Grove 93950, 408/373-3304.*

■ *ANNUAL EVENTS*

Each year in late October hundreds of thousands of **Monarch butterflies** return to Pacific Grove to winter on the needles of favored local pine trees. There they dangle in

huge clusters and are often overlooked as dull pieces of bark. They migrate all the way from western Canada and Alaska and stay until March, when they again fly north. Somewhat of a mystery is how they find their way here each year since, with a lifespan of less than a year, no butterfly makes the trip twice. The stunning orange and black Monarchs somehow program this information into their progeny, which then return to these same trees the following fall and repeat the cycle.

Monarchs like to flutter about on sunny days between the hours of 10 a.m. and 4 p.m. and this is the best time to view them. In fact, when temperatures drop below 55 degrees, the monarchs can't fly. So on cold and foggy days, which are quite common in this area, they huddle together. Clinging to the trees with closed wings—they react to the weather somewhat like a golden poppy.

Leave your nets at home. To discourage people from bothering these fragile, lovely creatures, in Pacific Grove molesting a butterfly is a crime carrying a $500 fine.

To celebrate the annual return of the butterflies, the town of Pacific Grove, also known as Butterfly Town USA, hosts a special parade each year. School children dress up as butterflies and march along with the more traditional bands and majorette corps. Afterwards the local PTA sponsors a bazaar and carnival where celebrants enjoy old-fashioned fun and homemade foods.

Each April there is a **Victorian Home Tour**. Children under 12 are not permitted. Take your teenagers.

■ *WHERE TO STAY*

Andril Fireplace Cottages *569 Asilomar Blvd., 408/375-0994; 2- 4/$$-$$$; cribs; all TVs, kitchens, fireplaces.* These woodsy cottages make for very comfortable lodging, especially for longer stays. The sixteen units surround a shady courtyard stocked with picnic tables.

Asilomar Conference Center *800 Asilomar Blvd., 408/372-8016; 2/$-$$, 4/$$-$$$; children under 2 free; cribs; all bathtubs; some kitchens, fireplaces, ocean views; full breakfast, dining room; heated pool.* Though this facility is used mainly as a conference grounds, it is part of the California State Park System. When underbooked, rentals are made available to the general public. Reservations may not be made more than a month in advance; last-minute accommodations are often available. In Spanish the word asilomar means "refuge by the sea" and, indeed, the grounds are located in a quiet, scenic area just a short walk from the ocean. Guests and non-guests are welcome to participate in inexpensive, family-style conference meals at 7:30, noon, and 6; reservations are not necessary.

Beachcomber Inn *1996 Sunset Dr., 800/237-5885, 408/373-4769; 2-4/ $$-$$$; 2-night minimum on weekends; cribs; all TVs, bathtubs; some kitchens, ocean views; continental breakfast; restaurant; heated pool, sauna.* Factors rendering this otherwise ordinary motel special include its oceanfront location, the availability of some rooms with waterbeds, and free bikes for the use of guests.

Butterfly Grove Inn *1073 Lighthouse Ave., 408/373-4921; 2$$-4/$$-$$$; all TVs; some kitchens, fireplaces; pool, jacuzzi.* This facility offers a choice of suites in a vintage house or motel rooms. It is located on a quiet side street next to a two-acre field of easily accessible trees particularly favored by the Monarchs.

Butterfly Trees Lodge *1150 Lighthouse Ave., 800/332-6966, 408/372-0503; 2-4/$$-$$$+; 2-night minimum on weekends; cribs; all TVs; some kitchens, fireplaces, ocean views; continental breakfast; pool, sauna, jacuzzi.* Located adjacent to a favorite butterfly nesting spot, this attractive and quiet motel schedules complimentary wine and cheese tastings each afternoon.

Centrella Hotel *612 Central Ave., 408/372-3372; 2-4/$$$-$$$+; 2-night minimum on weekends; children under 12 free; cribs; some TVs, refrigerators, fireplaces, bathtubs, ocean views; some shared baths; full breakfast.* This restored turn-of-the-century Victorian has won awards for its interior decor. Rooms are furnished with antiques, and some bathrooms have clawfoot tubs. Families with children under 12 are accommodated only in the more expensive cottage suites.

♥ **Seven Gables Inn** *555 Ocean View Blvd., 408/372-4341; 2/$$$-$$$+; 2-night minimum on weekends; unsuitable for children under 12; all ocean views; some refrigerators, bathtubs; continental breakfast.* Located across the street from the ocean, this cheerful yellow Victorian mansion, built in 1886, lets both rooms and cottages. High Tea is served each afternoon.

Motel Row. Numerous motels are located at the west end of Lighthouse Avenue and on Asilomar Boulevard.

■ *WHERE TO EAT*

♥ **Old Bath House** *620 Ocean View Blvd., 408/375-5195; D daily; booster seat; reservations suggested; $$$; all cards.* French and northern Italian cuisine are served here amid elegant Victorian decor. Every table has a good view of Monterey Bay. Entrees include roast rack of lamb, Australian lobster in pastry, and seafood cannelloni. Divine desserts are made in the restaurant's own pastry kitchen. Past selections have included mocha almond cheesecake and a cream puff filled with French vanilla ice cream and topped with hot fudge sauce.

Tinnery *631 Ocean View Blvd., 408/646-1040; B/L/D daily; highchairs, booster seats, children's portions; $$; all cards.* Located at **Lover's Point**—the southern tip of Monterey Bay—this comfortable, casual restaurant offers outstanding views of the bay. Breakfast is particularly pleasant—with omelettes, egg dishes, and blueberry pancakes on the menu. The eclectic international dinner menu includes appetizers such as nachos and deep-fried zucchini and entrees such as tempura prawns, chicken picatta, and barbecued spareribs.

■ *WHAT TO DO*

Butterfly Viewing. The densest clusters of Monarchs occur behind the Butterfly Grove Inn. Other good viewing spots are by the Butterfly Trees Lodge and on the west side of **George Washington Park** along Melrose Street south of Pine Avenue. A statue honoring the butterfly is located at Lover's Point; a few butterflies can also occasionally be seen fluttering there.

Lover's Point Marina *626 Ocean View Blvd.* There is a pleasant beach here for sunbathing and wading. A grassy picnic area with barbecue pits is also available, and a public pool is open in summer.

Pacific Grove Museum of Natural History *165 Forest Ave., 408/372-4212; Tu-Sun 10-5; free.* Learn about the natural history of Monterey County through exhibits of butterflies, marine and bird life, native plants, shells, and Indian artifacts. Each year during the third weekend in April, this tiny museum sponsors a **Wildflower Show** with displays of as many as 500 varieties.

Point Pinos Lighthouse *on Asilomar Blvd., about 2 blocks north of the end of Lighthouse Ave., 408/372-4212; Sat & Sun 1-4; free.* The Coast Guard gives guided tours of this oldest continuously operating Pacific Coast lighthouse—built in 1855 out of granite quarried in the area. Doc's Great Tide Pool, from Steinbeck's *Cannery Row,* is located here. The area surrounding the lighthouse is a good spot to walk, picnic, and observe sea otters.

Poor Man's 17-Mile Drive. There is no charge for this scenic 4.2-mile drive which passes rugged seascapes and some impressive Victorian homes. Begin at Ocean View Boulevard and 3rd Street. At Point Pinos turn left on Sunset Drive. Tidepooling is good in several spots. From April to August beautiful lavender ice plant cascades in full bloom over the rocky beach front.

CARMEL

■ A LITTLE BACKGROUND

A well-established weekend destination, Carmel is best known for its abundant shops, cozy lodging, and picturesque white sand beach. It is also known for the things which it doesn't have. No street signs, streetlights, electric or neon signs, jukeboxes, parking meters, or buildings over two stories high are allowed in town. No sidewalks, curbs, or house numbers are found in the residential sections. These absent items help Carmel keep its small-town feeling.

But do be careful. Eccentric laws in the town make it illegal to wear high-heeled shoes on the sidewalks, throw a ball in the park, play a musical instrument in a bar, or dig in the sand at the beach other than when making a sand castle.

Because Carmel is such a popular destination, it is important to make reservations for your accommodations far in advance, especially if you want to stay in one of its quaint inns. It seems that almost every weekend some special tournament, race, or house tour is scheduled in the area, making available lodging perpetually scarce.

■ VISITOR INFORMATION

Carmel Business Association *P.O. Box 4444, (Vandervort Court on San Carlos/Ocean), Carmel 93921, 408/624-2522.*

Tourist Information Center *P.O. Box 7430, (Mission/5th St.), Carmel 93921, 408/624-1711.* This private agency is very helpful with information and will make lodging reservations.

■ ANNUAL EVENTS

Bach Festival *July; P.O. Box 575, Carmel 93921, 408/624-1521.* Some of the performances are held at the Carmel Mission.

■ *WHERE TO STAY*

Carmel River Inn *Highway 1 at the bridge, 408/624-1575; 2-4/$-$$; 2-night minimum; cribs; all TVs; some kitchens, fireplaces, bathtubs, river views; heated pool.* Located on the outskirts of town on the banks of the Carmel River, this lodging facility has ten acres of space for children to romp and explore. Guests have a choice of motel rooms or individual cottages.

Colonial Terrace Inn *San Antonio/13th, 408/624-2741; 2/$$-$$$+, 4/ $$$-$$$+; cribs; all TVs; some kitchens, fireplaces, ocean views; continental breakfast.* In business since 1925, this crisp, attractive lodging is located in a quiet residential area just one block from the beach.

♥ **The Green Lantern** *7th/Casanova, 408/624-4392; 2/$$-$$$+, 4/ $$$+; unsuitable for children under 12; all TVs; some fireplaces, bathtubs; continental breakfast.* An inn since 1926, this pleasant group of rustic multi-unit cottages is located on a quiet sidestreet just a few blocks from the village and two blocks from the beach.

Highlands Inn *on Highway 1, 4 miles south of town, 800/682-4811, 408/624-3801; 2-4/$$$-$$$+; children under 18 free; cribs; all TVs, VCRs, refrigerators, bathtubs; some kitchens, fireplaces, ocean views; room service, 2 restaurants; heated pool.* Located on the scenic outskirts of town, this inn was built in 1916 and extensively remodeled in 1984. The accommodations are luxurious, the cliffside setting spectacular, and guests may choose between lanai rooms and cottages. It is the perfect choice for a self-indulgent splurge. Hamburgers are on the menu at the **California Market** and may be enjoyed outside on a balcony overlooking the rugged coastline.

The Homestead *Lincoln/8th, 408/624-4119; 2/$$-$$$; 2-night minimum on weekends; all TVs; some kitchens, fireplaces.* Painted a cheery rust red, this remodeled home provides a variety of interesting rooms. It is conveniently located on a quiet corner garden lot just a few blocks from the village.

Lamp Lighters Inn *Ocean/Camino Real, 408/624-7372; 2/$$$-$$$+, 4/$$$+; cribs; all TVs; some kitchens, fireplaces, bathtubs, ocean views.* This gingerbread village has charming rooms and cottages and a convenient location between the village and the ocean. It very well may fulfill your fairytale fantasies. Several cottages accommodate families; one called the "Hansel and Gretel" has a sleeping loft for the kids. Accommodations in an annex, located one block closer to the beach, are a little less expensive.

La Playa Hotel *Camino Real/8th Ave., 800/582-8900, 408/624-6476;*

2-4/$$$+; cribs; children under 12 free; all TVs, refrigerators; some fireplaces, bathtubs, ocean views; room service, restaurant; heated pool. This luxury three-story, Spanish-style hotel is conveniently located just two blocks from the beach and four blocks from town. Taking up an entire block, it is the largest hotel in town and features beautifully maintained grounds which are always abloom with colorful flowers. The beds in the 75 thick-walled rooms all have rustic carved headboards sporting the hotel's mermaid motif.

Lincoln Green Inn *Carmelo/15th, 408/624-1880; 2-4/$$$+; 2-night minimum on weekends; cribs; all TVs, kitchens, fireplaces, bathtubs.* Located on the outskirts of town just a few blocks from where the Carmel River flows into the ocean, this cluster of four comfortable English housekeeping cottages features living rooms with cathedral-beamed ceilings and stone fireplaces.

The Lodge at Pebble Beach *on 17-Mile Drive, Pebble Beach, 408/624-3811; 2-4/$$$+; 2-night minimum on weekends; cribs; all TVs, refrigerators, fireplaces, bathtubs; some ocean views; room service, 3 restaurants; heated pool, children's wading pool, sauna, 14 tennis courts.* Complete luxury and the best of sporting facilities await guests. Golfers will enjoy playing some of the best courses in the country. Horse rentals and equestrian trails are nearby—as are jogging and hiking trails, a parcourse, and several pools. Even if you don't stay in one of the bungalows or houses, you might want to stop in and enjoy the spectacular ocean view over a drink or meal.

Normandy Inn *Ocean Ave./Monte Verde, 408/624-3825; 2/$$$-$$$+, 4/$$$+; cribs; all TVs; some kitchens, fireplaces, bathtubs; continental breakfast; heated pool.* This inn is conveniently located on the town's main shopping street. Rooms are comfortably appointed and tastefully decorated, and the pool area is invitingly secluded. For breakfast, coffee and croissants are served in a French Provincial kitchen located off the lobby.

Pine Inn *Ocean Ave./Monte Verde, 408/624-3851; 2-4/$$$-$$$+; cribs; all TVs, bathtubs; some refrigerators, ocean views; 1 fireplace; room service, restaurant.* Elegantly decorated in Victorian style, this inn claims to be the oldest in town. It is conveniently located on the main shopping street.

♥ **San Antonio House** *San Antonio/7th, 408/624-4334; 2/$$$-$$$+; 2-night minimum on weekends; unsuitable for children under 13; all fireplaces; some kitchens, bathtubs; continental breakfast.* This attractive guesthouse offers large rooms, a lovely garden, and a location in a quiet residential area just one block from the beach.

♥ **Sea View Inn** *Camino Real/12th, 408/624-8778; 2/$$-$$$; 2-night* *minimum on weekends; unsuitable for children under 12; some shared baths; continental breakfast.* Located three blocks from the beach, this converted three-story Victorian home offers pleasantly appointed rooms. Sherry is served to guests each afternoon.

♥ **Stonehouse Inn** *8th/Monte Verde, 408/624-4569; 2/$$$-$$$+; unsuitable for children under 14; all shared baths; some ocean views; full breakfast.* Built by local Indians in 1906, this rustic stone country house is close to the village. The original owner often entertained well-known artists and writers. The antique-furnished rooms are now named after some of those guests.

♥ **Vagabond's House Inn** *4th/Dolores, 408/624-7738, 624-7403; 2/ $$- $$$+; 2-night minimum on weekends; unsuitable for children under 13; all TVs; some kitchens, fireplaces, bathtubs; continental breakfast.* This English Tudor-style building features cozily furnished rooms opening off a quiet, rustic, flower-bedecked courtyard.

■ OTHER

♥ **John Gardiner's Tennis Ranch** *Carmel Valley, 408/659-2207; Apr-Nov; $1,550-$1,650/person includes lodging, meals, and tennis instruction; some kitchens, fireplaces; 2 pools, jacuzzi.* Begun by John Gardiner in 1957, this legendary tennis retreat has been visited by three presidents (Nixon, Ford, Reagan). Tennis clinics run Sunday through Friday and include 25 hours of instruction. Most are set up for mixed doubles; several are just for women. With fourteen courts and only fourteen guest rooms, there is never any waiting. And, indeed, there shouldn't be at these prices. Lodging is in luxurious cottages on beautifully landscaped grounds, and meals are sumptuous.

■ WHERE TO EAT

Clam Box Restaurant *Mission/5th, 408/624-8597; D Tu-Sun; closed most of Dec; highchairs, booster seats, children's portions; no reservations; $$; no cards.* Customers wait as happily as clams in the constant line to get into this tiny, cozy restaurant. That's because they know they're going to enjoy themselves once they get a table. The menu is predominantly seafood. Some children may be happy to know there is also a hamburger on the menu.

Cottage of Sweets *Ocean/Lincoln, 408/624-5170; daily 10-6.* Among the sweet surprises in this charming candy cottage are imported chocolates, diet candy, gourmet jelly beans, and taffy.

Em Le's *Dolores/5th, 408/625-6780; B/L daily; highchairs, booster seats; $; no cards.* Cozy and always crowded, this casual spot offers a large variety of breakfast items. Wild blueberry pancakes and buttermilk waffles (in choice of light or dark) are my personal favorites. Pleasant views of the sidewalk traffic and counter seating add to its special Carmel charm.

Hector De Smet Bakery *Ocean/Lincoln, 408/624-6265; daily 6:30am-8pm.* Caramel apples, Cookie Monster cupcakes, and alligators and turtles made of marzipan bread are just a few of the delicacies available at this popular bakery. The large selection of pastries and drinks may be enjoyed on the premises or as you walk the boutique-laden Carmel streets.

Hog's Breath Inn *San Carlos/5th, 408/625-l044; L M-Sat, SunBr, D daily; booster seats; no reservations; $$; AE,DC,MC,V.* Owned by actor, director, and former mayor of Carmel Clint Eastwood, this rustic, secluded spot exudes a casual, cozy atmosphere. Redwood burl tables and comfortable, colorful, and appropriate director's chairs are scattered outdoors under a rambling old oak tree. Guests are warmed by fireplaces and heaters when the temperature chills. Seating is also available inside. The brunch menu offers eggs Benedict, omelettes, and eggs served with homemade blueberry muffins and homefried potatoes. Lunch features wonderful homemade soups, salads, sandwiches, and hamburgers. It is perfectly acceptable to stop in just for a drink. Hot drinks and simple drinks tend to be best.

Jack London's Bar & Bistro *San Carlos/5th, 408/624-2336; L/D daily, SunBr; booster seats; $-$$; V.* Even locals come here to enjoy the excellent bar drinks and cozy bistro atmosphere. Kids can have fancy "virgin" drinks. Specialties include individual-size pizzas, a variety of hamburgers, and deep-fried calamari. Fresh fish selections change daily. Rich, velvety pasta carbonara Milano and a New York steak round out the eclectic menu. Dinner entrees come with a generous house salad topped with Roquefort dressing. Sunday brunch includes a complimentary glass of champagne with menu items such as strawberry crepes and French toast made with a Grand Marnier batter.

♥ **La Boheme Restaurant** *Dolores/7th, 408/624-7500; D daily; closed most of Dec; booster seat, children's portions; no reservations; $$; MC,V.* Cozy and colorfully decorated, this petite cafe serves one prix-fixe menu each evening. Soup, salad, entree, and vegetable are included. The French and Italian country-style dishes are served informal family-style.

Mediterranean Market *Ocean/Mission, 408/624-2022; daily 9-6.* This well-stocked delicatessen offers freshly marinated artichoke hearts, sandwich meats, cheeses, skinny French baguettes, exotic beers, wines, bottled waters, and soft drinks. Caviar is also available—as are picnic baskets to carry it all away in. Located practically next door is **Wishart's Bakery** *(408/624-3870; daily 8-6:30),* which dispenses freshly baked breads and desserts. After selecting luncheon supplies, head out to the beach for a pleasant picnic.

Mrs. M's Fudge *Mission/6th, 408/624-5331; daily 10:30-9; AE,MC,V.* Seventeen kinds of homemade fudge and unusual "snow fruit" (apricots, peaches, pears, cherries, and walnut-stuffed prunes partially dipped in white chocolate) are just a few of the diet-deserting goodies available here. Real sugarplums are available around Christmas.

♥ **Patisserie Boissiere** *Mission/Ocean, 408/624-5008; B/L/D daily; highchairs; reservations suggested; $$; MC,V.* The menu at this very elegant little French spot offers snacks of homemade soups and quiches as well as more substantial entrees. Though it would be hard to do so, don't overlook the Parisian pastries: lemonpot cheesecake, chocolate eclairs, a wide variety of meringues, babas au rhum, and plenty more.

Rocky Point *12 miles south of town on Highway 1, 408/624-2933; L/D daily; highchairs, booster seats, children's portions; reservations suggested; $$$; MC,V.* Take a scenic drive down the coast toward Big Sur, and stop here for a charcoal-broiled steak or fresh seafood dinner. The spectacular view is included in the steep menu prices. Lunch—when sandwiches and hamburgers are on the menu—is a relative bargain.

Scandia *Ocean/Lincoln, 408/624-5659; B/L/D daily; highchairs, booster seats, children's portions; reservations suggested; $$; AE, MC, V.* Pretty and pink is the dining room at this old standby. The bargain Early Bird dinner, served from 4 to 6:30, comes with kavli flatbread and a French baguette, homemade soup or salad, and fresh vegetables. Entree choices include fresh fish, prepared in exemplary manner, and traditional Danish meatballs (frikadeller). Children's portions are a choice of hamburger steak or linguine marinara. Though children are welcome, they don't fit in well in the evening when the atmosphere is quite romantic.

Swedish Restaurant *Dolores/7th, 408/624-3723; B/L daily; highchairs, booster seats; no reservations; $; no cards.* This charming spot is my favorite for breakfast. A large window allows diners to view the busy sidewalk traffic, and a fireplace warms the tiny dining room. Portions are generous, and most items are served with toasted homemade breads. Swedish pancakes with lingonberries, a specialty, are memorably delicious. Breakfast items are also available at lunch.

The Thunderbird *3618 The Barnyard, 408/624-9414; L daily, D Tu-Sun; highchairs, booster seats, children's portions; reservations suggested; $$; MC,V.* Dine among world-famous authors in this combination bookstore/restaurant. Sandwiches and hamburgers are available at lunch, full meals at dinner, coffee-and during the off hours.

Tuck Box English Tea Room *Dolores/Ocean, 408/624-6365; B/L/ afternoon tea W-Sun; booster seats; no reservations; $; no cards.* Featuring fairytale architecture and verily reeking of quaintness, this tiny dining room can be quite difficult to get into. If you ever notice it without a long line in front, go! Seating is also available on an outdoor patio. The limited breakfast menu offers simply prepared eggs served with delightful fresh scones and either homemade olallieberry preserves or orange marmalade. At lunch there are sandwiches, salads, and omelettes (the house specialty) as well as Welsh rarebit and a daily entree special. Afternoon tea features scones and cakes and, of course, plenty of English tea.

■ WHAT TO DO

Beaches.

Carmel Beach *at the foot of Ocean Ave., 408/626-1255.* Known for its white powdery sand and spectacular sunsets, this world-famous beach is a choice spot for a refreshing walk, a picnic, or flying a kite, but swimming is unsafe. A **sand castle contest** is held here each October.

Carmel River State Beach *at the end of Scenic Rd., 408/649-2836; daily 9-dusk; free.* Very popular with families, this fresh-water lagoon is also a bird sanctuary. Picnic facilities are available, and open fires are allowed.

San Jose Creek. Scuba divers come from all over to enjoy the undersea beauty of Carmel Bay. This is one of their favorite diving spots and is a good place to observe them while you picnic.

Brass Rubbing Centre *Mission/8th, 408/624-2990; M-Sat 10:30-5, Sun from 12.* Once upon a time people would travel all the way to England to make wax-on-paper impressions of the brass plaques embedded in the floors of old churches. But the brasses there have become so worn that this practice is now forbidden. This inexpensive hobby can still be enjoyed in shops like this one, where you can make rubbings of brass reproductions.

Come Fly a Kite *Ocean/Mission in Carmel Plaza, 408/624-3422; daily 10-5.* Pick up a kite here and then head for the beach—the perfect spot to launch it.

Dansk II *Ocean/San Carlos, 408/625-1600; daily 10-6.* Get bargain prices on discontinued items and seconds from this expensive line of kitchen merchandise.

Mission San Carlos Borromeo del Rio Carmelo *3080 Rio Rd., 1 mile south of town off Highway 1, 408/624-3600; M-Sat 9:30-4:30, Sun 10:30-4:30, services on Sun; by donation.* Father Junipero Serra established this mission in 1770; he is buried here at the foot of the altar. A museum displays Indian artifacts, mission tools, and re-creations of the original mission kitchen and California's first library. A beautifully landscaped courtyard garden accents the cemetery where over 3,000 mission Indians are buried. A **fiesta** is held each year on the last Sunday in September.

Pebble Beach Equestrian Center *Portola Rd., Pebble Beach, 408/624-2756; group rides daily at 10 & 2, $25/person; reservations required.* It's strictly English saddles here. Rides follow the extensive bridle trails which wind through lovely Del Monte Forest. Lessons are available.

Point Lobos State Reserve *3 miles south of town off Highway 1, 408/ 624-4909; daily 9-dusk; $3/car*. Described as "the greatest meeting of land and water in the world," Point Lobos allows the opportunity to see the rustic, undeveloped beauty of the Monterey Peninsula. Self-guiding trails are available, and guided ranger walks are scheduled daily in summer. Sea otters may often be seen in the 1,250-acre reserve's protected waters. An interesting story has this area as the model for Spyglass Hill in Robert Louis Stevenson's *Treasure Island*. Dress warmly and bring along your binoculars and camera and maybe a picnic, too.

17-Mile Drive *located at Pebble Beach exit off Highway 1 between Carmel and Monterey, 408/649-8500; daily; $5/car*. The scenery on this world-famous drive is a combination of showplace homes, prestigious golf courses, and raw seascapes. Sights include the **Restless Sea**, where several ocean crosscurrents meet; **Seal and Bird Rock**, where herds of sea lions and flocks of shoreline birds congregate; the **Pebble Beach Golf Course**, one of three used during the annual **Bing Crosby Pro-Am Tournament**; and the landmark **Lone Cypress** clinging to its jagged, barren rock base. Picnic facilities and short trails are found in several spots. Consider splurging on lunch or dinner at one of the three ocean-view restaurants (one is a reasona-

bly-priced coffee shop) at the elegant Lodge at Pebble Beach (see p.56). If you call ahead for reservations, the gate fee will be waived.

Thinker Toys *Ocean/Mission in Carmel Plaza, 408/624-0441; M-Sat 9:30am-9pm, Sun 10-6.* This super toy store offers an exciting selection of puppets, dolls, workbooks, and puzzles. In another part of the Plaza, an annex houses a large inventory of model trains. This is the place to bring your kids to choose a souvenir.

Tor House *26304 Ocean View Ave., 408/624-1813; tours F & Sat on the hour 10-3, reservations required; adults $5, teenagers $1.50, no children under 12.* Poet Robinson Jeffers built this medieval-style house and tower retreat out of huge granite rocks hauled up by horse from the beach below. He did much of the work himself and was of the opinion that the manual labor cleared his mind and, as he put it, "my fingers had the art to make stone love stone." All of his major works and most of his poetry were written while he lived with his wife and twin sons on this craggy knoll overlooking Carmel Bay.

BIG SUR

■ *A LITTLE BACKGROUND*

Big Sur is such a special place that many people who have been here don't feel generous about sharing it. However, facilities are so limited that I can't imagine it getting overrun with tourists. Except, perhaps, in the thick of summer, when the weather is best.

The town of Big Sur seems to have no center. It stretches along Highway 1 for six miles offering a string of amenities. Then, as one continues driving south, the highway begins a 90-mile stretch of some of the most spectacular scenery in the U.S.

Note that the river's bottom here is rocky. Bring along waterproof shoes for the kids.

■ *VISITOR INFORMATION*

Big Sur Chamber of Commerce *P.O. Box 87, Big Sur 93920, 408/ 667- 2100.*

■ *GETTING THERE*

Located approximately 25 miles south of the Monterey Peninsula.

■ *WHERE TO STAY*

Big Sur Lodge *408/667-2171; 2-4/$$-$$$; some kitchens, fireplaces,*

bathtubs; restaurant; heated pool, sauna. Located in Pfeiffer-Big Sur State Park, this facility offers modern motel rooms and use of the park's facilities (see p.67). Rooms are scattered throughout the spacious, grassy grounds, where deer are often seen grazing. Those close to the pleasant pool area seem most desirable. Guests have access to a recreation room equipped with Ping Pong and pool tables, some video games, and a large assortment of recycled paperbacks. A casual, reasonably-priced restaurant serves meals all day.

Esalen Institute *408/667-3000; hot tubs.* Located on a breath-taking crest above the ocean, this legendary educational facility offers lodging and dining in conjunction with its workshops. Space is open to the general public when they are underbooked. Then a bed space runs $60 to $115 per person per day and includes three meals. Special family rates are available. Self-exploration workshops include massage, Rolfing, vision improvement, etc. Call for further details and a copy of of the workshop catalogue.

Ripplewood Resort *Highway 1, 408/667-2242; 2-4/$$, 4/$$; closed most of Dec; children under 12 free; some kitchens, fireplaces.* Rustic, pleasantly decorated redwood cabins are located both above and below the highway. The ones below are in a dense, dark grove of redwoods. They are more expensive than the ones above the highway, but they are also more lovely and only a stone's throw from the Big Sur River.

♥ **Ventana Inn** *Highway 1, 800/628-6500, 408/667-2331; 2/$$$+; 2-night minimum on weekends; no children under 21; all TVs (satellite reception), bathtubs; some kitchens, fireplaces, ocean views; continental breakfast, restaurant; 2 heated pools, jacuzzi, sauna.* The striking, clean-lined architecture of this inn has won awards, and the restaurant, which serves lunch and dinner, is known for its California-style cuisine. Its spectacular secluded location in the hills 1,200 feet above the ocean makes it a good choice for a restive, revitalizing, and hedonistic retreat. Clothing is optional around the pool. Campsites are available at an adjacent facility.

■ WHERE TO EAT

Big Sur Inn *408/667-2377; B/D Th-M; highchairs, booster seats; reservations suggested for dinner; B$, D$$$; no cards.* My favorite meal here is breakfast, especially when it's raining outside and I've managed to secure a table in front of the fireplace. The mellow, rustic, and informal setting is a complementary background to the fresh, simple, and wholesome foods produced by the kitchen. Dinner is more expensive and sedate, and children don't fit in as well. No alcohol is served; inquire about bringing your own. Rustic, casual lodging is also available, but it is usually booked up far in advance.

Glen Oaks Restaurant *408/667-2623; D daily, SunBr; highchairs, booster seats; reservations suggested; $; MC,V.* Classical music and fresh flowers greet diners inside this log cabin-like building. Cornmeal cakes and whole trout with eggs are on the breakfast menu; dinner is a selection of continental seafood and pastas.

Nepenthe *408/667-2345; L/D daily; highchairs; no reservations; $$; AE,MC,V.* Located at the top of a cliff 808 feet above the ocean and offering a breathtaking view of the coastline, this famous restaurant was designed by a student of Frank Lloyd Wright. When weather is mild, lunchers can dine outside on the casual terrace. The menu features simple food such as steak, fresh seafood, roasted chicken, homemade soup, and a very good hamburger. It is also possible to stop in at the bar for just a drink. The atmosphere has mellowed since the days the restaurant gained notoriety for turning away then-Senator John F. Kennedy— because he wasn't wearing shoes. Now it seems to be living up to the promise of its name, which refers to a mythical Egyptian drug that induced forgetfulness and the surcease of sorrow. **Cafe Amphora** *(408/667-2660)*, located downstairs, serves medium-priced brunch and lunch items on a patio with the same striking view. It is an especially good choice in the afternoon for a refreshing cold drink and, perhaps, one of their excellent pastries. The classy **Phoenix** gift shop makes for pleasant browsing before or after dining.

■ *WHAT TO DO*

Big Sur is so non-commercial that there is little to list in this section. Note that because TV reception in the area is poor, lodgings do not provide TVs. Bring along a good book and relax, swim in the river, picnic on the beach, or take a hike through the woods. And look out for poison oak.

Pfeiffer Beach. Look for unmarked Sycamore Canyon Road on the west side of Highway 1. This narrow road begins about 1.7 miles south of **Fernwood Resort** and winds for two lovely miles to a beach parking lot. The only easily accessible public beach in the area, it features striking rock formations and arches carved out by the very rough surf. Children can wade in a stream which meanders through the sandy beach but should be kept out of the turbulent ocean. If it all looks vaguely familiar, it may be because this is where Elizabeth Taylor and Richard Burton acted out some love scenes in their movie *The Sandpiper.*

Pfeiffer-Big Sur State Park *408/667-2315.* Facilities include hiking trails, river swimming, picnic tables, a campground, and ranger-led nature walks and campfires as well as an open meadow where you can play baseball or throw a frisbee.

Point Sur Light Station *north of town, 408/667-2315; Sun 10-1.* Built in 1889, this lighthouse is now open for strenuous 2 1/2-hour guided tours. Because there is a parking problem, only the first 15 cars to arrive can be accommodated.

SAN SIMEON/CAMBRIA

■ *A LITTLE BACKGROUND*

Located in the small town of San Simeon on the wind-blown coast south of Big Sur, the spectacular **Hearst Castle** is perched atop La Cuesta Encantada (the enchanted hill) and is filled with art treasures and antiques from all over the world. Though considered by William Randolph Hearst to be unfinished, the castle contains 38 bedrooms, 31 bathrooms, 14 sitting rooms, a kitchen, a movie theater, 2 libraries, a billiard room, a dining hall, and an assembly hall! Exotic vines and plants grace the lovely gardens, and wild zebras, goats, and sheep graze the hillsides—remnants of the private zoo which once included lions, monkeys, and a polar bear.

Before 1958 visitors could get no closer than was permitted by the coin-operated telescope located on the road below. Now maintained by the State of California as a Historical Monument, the castle is open to the public. Four tours are available; all include a scenic bus ride up to the castle.

Reservations for the castle tours are essential and may be made by calling 1-800-446-PARK or 619/452-1950. Tickets may also be purchased at the castle after 8 a.m. on the day of the tour, but often none are available. And when they are available, they are usually sold out before noon. The charge for each tour is $10 for adults, $5 for children 6-12.

Tour 1 is suggested for the first visit and includes gardens, pools, a guest house, and the main floor of the castle.

Tour 2 covers the upper floors of the castle, including Mr. Hearst's private suite, the libraries, a guest duplex, the kitchen, and the pools.

Tour 3 covers the 36-room guest wing, and includes the pools and a guest house.

Tour 4 stresses the gardens and is somewhat of a behind-the-scenes tour. It includes the elegant 17-room Casa del Mar guest house and the pools and is given April through October only.

Note: Children under six are free only if they sit on their parent's lap on the bus ride. You will be walking about 1/2 mile and climbing approximately 300 steps on each tour; wear comfortable shoes. Strollers are not permitted. Tours take approximately two hours.

■ *VISITOR INFORMATION*

San Simeon Chamber of Commerce *P.O. Box 1, San Simeon 93452, 805/927-3500.*

Cambria Chamber of Commerce *767 Main St., Cambria 93428, 805/ 927- 3624.*

■ *GETTING THERE*

Located approximately 75 miles south of Big Sur.

For a more leisurely trip try the train package offered by Key Tours *(1510 Parkside Dr. #100, Walnut Creek, 415/945-8687).* Via train is the way guests used to travel to the castle in its heyday. Invitations then always included train tickets. Today travelers can still relax and enjoy the scenery—while Amtrak's Coast Starlight transports them to San Luis Obispo. There, after seeing the local sights, they are transferred to a bus for a tour of the coast, a stop in Cambria, and on to San Simeon for the night. The next day participants are bussed to the famed castle for a guided tour, then down scenic Highway 1 for a stop in the fishing village of Morro Bay, and then back to San Luis Obispo for the trip home. The package does not include meals. Rates vary. Special rates are available for children. Call for details.

■ *WHERE TO STAY*

Cambria Pines Lodge *2905 Burton Dr., Cambria, 805/927-4200, 927-3827; 2-4/$$-$$$; cribs; all TVs; some bathtubs; restaurant in summer; heated indoor pool, jacuzzi, sauna.* Located on a tree-lined hill above town, this spacious lodging facility consists mostly of cabins. A few lodge rooms are also available. Use of the large indoor pool and jacuzzi are available to the general public for a small fee.

Cavalier Inn *9415 Hearst Dr., San Simeon, 800/528-1234, 805/927-4688, 2-4/$$-$$$; cribs; all TVs, VCRs, bathtubs; some refrigerators, fireplaces, ocean views; restaurant; 2 heated pools, jacuzzi.* Located just 200 feet from the ocean, this large motel complex offers modern comforts.

♥ **Pickford House** *2555 MacLeod Way, Cambria, 805/927-8619; 2/$$- $$$, 4/$$$; children under 16 free; all bathtubs; some fireplaces; full breakfast.* This recently built inn boasts rooms bearing the names and personalities of eight silent film stars. For instance, the Valentino Room is furnished with dark-wood antiques and the beds are covered with red satin comforters. Breakfast features the traditional Danish fritters known as aebleskivers. Though families are welcome, there is a stated preference that children be at least 13 years old.

■ *WHERE TO EAT*

Brambles Dinner House *4005 Burton Dr., Cambria, 805/927-4716; D daily; highchairs, booster seats, children's portions; reservations suggested; $$; all cards.* Located inside an English-style cottage with Victorian decor, this homey restaurant offers a menu dominated by steaks, prime rib, and fresh seafood. A hamburger and two sizes of English trifle are also available.

Grey Fox Inn *4095 Burton Dr., Cambria, 805/927-3305; B/L M-F, Sat & SunBr, D daily; highchairs; reservations suggested; $$; all cards.* Enjoy delightful meals and terrace dining in this cozy, converted Spanish-style home. Lunch features a soup and salad bar as well as a sandwich menu; at dinner it's continental-style entrees and fresh fish.

Picnique in the Pines *727 Main St., Cambria, 805/927-8727; B/L Tu-Sat, SunBr; highchairs, booster seats, children's portions; reservations suggested; $; MC,V.* There are Belgian waffles and ricotta cheese crepes for breakfast. Lunch brings on salads, giant croissant sandwiches, and a quiche special.

Sebastian's General Store/Patio Cafe *Highway 1, 805/927-4217; store: daily 8:30-6; cafe: B/L daily, closed Nov-Mar; children's portions; no reservations; no cards.* Built in 1852 and moved to its

present location in 1878, this store is now a State Historical Landmark. Inexpensive short-order items are served in the outdoor cafe.
In winter watch for Monarch butterflies congregating in the adjacent
eucalyptus and cypress trees.

■ *WHAT TO DO*

Pewter Plough Playhouse *824 Main St., Cambria, (805) 927-3877;
shows F & Sat; tickets $7.* Plays and art films are scheduled regularly
in this intimate theatre.

The Soldier Factory *789 Main St., Cambria, 805/927-3804; daily 10-
5.* This store makes an ideal souvenir stop. You can find everything
from an inexpensive unpainted pewter animal to a dearly-priced and
elaborately painted *Alice in Wonderland* chess set. Assorted sizes
and styles of pewter soldiers from various wars are also for sale. The
majority of items are designed, molded, and cast on the premises.
The owner's private collection of toy soldiers is also on display.

William Randolph Hearst State Beach *daily 8am-sunset; $2/car.* This
is a very nice swimming beach with a fishing pier.

MORRO BAY

■ *A LITTLE BACKGROUND*

A huge volcanic rock, visible from just about everywhere in town, is the reason Morro Bay is sometimes called "the Gibraltar of the Pacific." It stands 576 feet high and is now a State Monument. Peregrine falcons, an endangered species, nest at the top.

Commercial fishing is the town's main industry, with albacore and abalone the local specialties. Lodgings often fill up on weekends. Make reservations well in advance.

■ *VISITOR INFORMATION*

Morro Bay Chamber of Commerce *895 Napa St., Morro Bay 93442, 800/231-0592, 805/772-4467.*

■ *GETTING THERE*

Located approximately 30 miles south of San Simeon.

■ *WHERE TO STAY*

Blue Sail Inn *851 Market St., 800/336-0707, 807/772-7132; 2-4 $$-$$$+; cribs; all TVs, refrigerators, bathtubs; some fireplaces, bay views; jacuzzi.* This new lodging is centrally located and overlooks Morro Rock.

Breakers Motel *780 Market Ave., 800/932-8899, 805/772-7317; 2-4/ $$-$$$; cribs; all TVs, refrigerators; some fireplaces, bathtubs, bay views; heated pool, jacuzzi.* This modern motel is located on pleasant, attractive grounds.

Cabrillo Motel *890 Morro Ave., 800/222-9915, 805/772-4435; 2-4/$$; cribs; all TVs, fireplaces; some kitchens, bay views; indoor jacuzzi.* This is an attractive, quiet motel.

The Inn at Morro Bay *800/321-9566, 805/772-5651; 2/$$; children under 12 free; cribs; all TVs; some fireplaces, bay views; restaurant; heated pool, toddler pool.* Located at the southern end of town in Morro Bay State Park, this large motel complex makes a quiet, restful spot to spend the night. A golf course and heron rookery are adjacent.

Point Motel *3450 Toro Lane, 805/772-2053; 2/$, 4/$$; all TVs; some*

kitchens, bay views. Located at the northern end of town, this tiny motel offers bargain rates and beach access. A fully-equipped apartment on the beach is also available.

■ *WHERE TO EAT*

Dorn's Original Breakers Cafe *801 Market Ave. 805/772-4415; B/L/D daily; highchairs, booster seats, children's portions; reservations suggested; $; no cards.* Hearty breakfasts, a dinner menu featuring fresh fish and steaks, and a great bay view are reasons to visit this casual restaurant.

The Great American Fish Company *1185 Embarcadero, 805/772-4407; L/D daily; highchairs, booster seats, children's portions; no reservations; $$; MC,V.* Items grilled over mesquite include fresh fish and shark. Fresh local prawns and Monterey squid, both deep-fried, are also available. Non-fish enthusiasts will appreciate the availability of a steak and hamburger.

Hungry Tiger *861 Market Ave., 805/772-7321; L M-Sat, SunBr, D daily; highchairs, booster seats, children's portions; reservations suggested; $$$; all cards.* This first-class restaurant features great bay views and is known for the fresh lobster it has flown in regularly. Fresh fish items, steak, and chicken are also available.

Rose's Landing *725 Embarcadero, 805/772-4441; L Sat & Sun, D daily; children's portions; reservations essential; $$; all cards.* The best view here is from the downstairs bar. However, the upstairs restaurant has decent views from most of the tables, and that is where the food is. Seafood and steaks dominate the menu. Complete dinners include clam chowder, salad, potato, vegetable, bread, beverage, and dessert.

■ *WHAT TO DO*

Centennial Stairway/Giant Chess Board *Embarcadero/Front, 805/ 772-1214 x226.* At the base of this 44-step stairway is one of the two largest chess boards in the U.S. (the other is in New York City's Central Park). The redwood chess pieces stand two- and three-feet high and weigh from 18 to 30 pounds—making a game here physical as well as mental exercise. From noon to 5 p.m. each Saturday the Morro Bay Chess Club sponsors chess on the giant 16- by 16-foot concrete board; the general public is welcome to challenge. The board is available to the public from 8 to 5 daily, except for the hours mentioned above. Reservations must be made by filling out an application at the Recreation Office. Call for details.

Clam Digging. Go to it! World-famous Pismo clams may be dug up on the beach just about anywhere.

Fishing. Fish from the pier, or go out on a chartered fishing boat.

Morro Bay Aquarium *595 Embarcadero, 805/772-7647; daily from 9, closing time varies; adults $1, 5-11 50¢.* This teeny, tiny aquarium is a draw for the gift shop located in front. However, the price is right, and over 300 live marine specimens may be observed. Some preserved specimens are also displayed, and very noisy seals beg to be fed.

Morro Bay State Park *at the southern end of town, 805/772-2560.*

> **Bird Sanctuary.** Following a trail through the marsh and hills allows for the possiblity of catching glimpses of over 250 species of birds. This is said to be the third largest bird sanctuary in the world.

> **Heron Rookery.** No one is allowed inside the rookery—one of the last where the Great Blue Heron may be found—but the herons may be viewed from an observation area.

> **Museum of Natural History** *805/772-2694; daily 10-5; adults $1, 6- 17 50¢.* Located on a scenic perch over the bay, this museum presents lectures, slide shows, and movies about the wildlife and Indian history of the area. Guided tours are sometimes available. In the winter, inquire about walks to see the Monarch butterflies which congregate in nearby eucalyptus groves.

Morro Rock Playground *east of Morro Rock.* Children are sure to enjoy this idyllic playground in the sand.

Tiger's Folly II *214 Beach St., 805/772-2257; daily June-Sept, Sat & Sun Oct-May, call for schedule; adults $6, 5-12 $3.* Take a one-hour harbor cruise aboard this sternwheeler. A Sunday champagne brunch cruise is also available; reservations are necessary.

■ *WHAT TO DO NEARBY*

Avila Beach *20 miles south of town off Highway 101.* This tiny, old-fashioned beach community is a great place to watch surfers and to swim in a generally mild surf.

Cayucos *6 miles north of town on Highway 1.* This pleasant little beach town has a fine beach with a gentle surf and a string of inexpensive motels. There is a 400-foot pier to fish from, and equipment rentals are readily available. Consider a meal at **The Way Station** *(78 N. Ocean, 805/995-1227)*, a 19th century traveler's rest stop once again functioning as such.

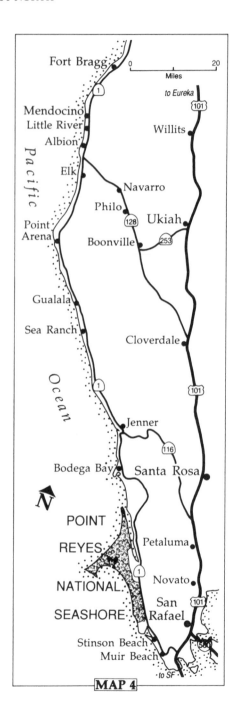

MAP 4

COAST
NORTH

HIGHWAY 1 LODGINGS AND ATTRACTIONS

■ *VISITOR INFORMATION*

Redwood Empire Association *One Market Plaza, Spear Street Tower, suite 1001, San Francisco 94105, 415/543-8334.* Information on the counties north of San Francisco may be obtained Monday through Friday from 9 to 4:30. A Visitor's Guide is available by mail for $1; for a Wine Guide send a legal-size stamped, addressed envelope. Both are available free if picked up in person.

■ *GETTING THERE*

From San Francisco, take Highway 101 to Highway 1 north.

■ *A WORD OF CAUTION*

The rocky cliffs and beaches along the coast are scenic and beautiful. In our awe we sometimes forget that they are also dangerous. Standing at the edge of a cliff with the surf pounding at our feet is tempting, but people have been washed out to sea doing just that. Don't be one of them. Be careful. Stay on trails. Obey posted signs. And take special care not to let children run loose.

■ *WHERE TO STAY/WHAT TO DO*

MUIR BEACH

The Pelican Inn *415/383-6000; 2/$$$+; closed M; cribs; 1 bathtub; full English breakfast; restaurant.* Built in 1979 to resemble a 16th century English country inn, the Pelican offers snug rooms furnished with English antiques, canopied beds, and oriental carpets. Children are welcome but must be accommodated in the small rooms on a rollaway. Elegant pub fare and afternoon tea are available in the dining room.

Slide Ranch *(see p.277.)*

STINSON BEACH

Steep Ravine Cabins *1 mile south of town, 800/444-7275, 916/ 323-2988; 2-4/$; wood stoves.* Perched on a rocky bluff overlooking the ocean, each of these primitive cabins sleeps up to five people. There is no electricity or running water, and guests must provide their own bedding, cooking equipment, and light. Paths lead down to the beach. This facility is in **Mount Tamalpais State Park.**

POINT REYES

Inns of Point Reyes *415/663-1420.* Call for information on the area's B&Bs.

Point Reyes Hostel *415/663-8811.* Formerly a ranch house, this hostel offers a kitchen and outdoor barbecue as well as two cozy common rooms with wood-burning stoves. See also p.273.

Point Reyes National Seashore *west of Olema, 415/663-1093; daily; free.* Known for its beaches and hiking trails, this area has plenty of interesting things for visitors to do. Many activities are clustered around the Park Headquarters. A **Visitors Center** houses a working seismograph and a variety of nature displays. A short walk away **Kule Loklo**, a replica Miwok Indian village, has been re-created using the same tools and materials as the Indians themselves originally used. The **Morgan Horse Ranch**, where pack and trail animals for the national parks are raised and trained, schedules feeding times at 8 a.m. and 4 p.m. Trails beginning near the headquarters include the self-guided **Woodpecker Nature Trail**, the mile-long self-guided **Earthquake Trail** which follows the San Andreas fault, and the popular 4.4-mile **Bear Valley Trail** which winds through meadows, fern grottos, and forests before ending at the ocean. The area has over 70 miles of equestrian trails, and horses may be rented at two nearby stables. Or bring your bikes. Further away from the headquarters is the **Point Reyes Lighthouse**, where it is claimed winds have been recorded blowing at 133 miles per hour—the highest rate in the continental U.S. The bottom line is that it gets mighty windy, cold, and wet at this scenic spot. The lighthouse, reached by maneuvering 300 steps down the side of a steep, rocky cliff, is a popular spot in winter for viewing migrating grey whales. Campsites are available.

BODEGA BAY

Bodega Bay Lodge *Highway 1, 800/368-2468, 707/875-3525; 2-4/$$$-$$$+; 2-night minimum on Sat; children under 12 free; cribs; all TVs, refrigerators, bathtubs; some fireplaces, ocean views; continental breakfast; solar-heated pool, jacuzzi, sauna, exercise room.* This is an attractive modern motel.

JENNER

Murphy's Jenner Inn *Highway 1, 707/865-2377; 2/$-$$$, 4/$$$; 2-night minimum on weekends; some kitchens, woodstoves, bathtubs, ocean views; 2 hot tubs.* Tucked into a curve in the highway at the point where the Russian River runs into the Pacific Ocean, this inn offers a choice of cabins, lodge rooms, or private homes. The communal lounge has a cozy stone fireplace and library filled with books and games. Classical music, jazz, and plays are sometimes presented live on weekends.

Salt Point Lodge *23255 Highway 1, 20 miles north of town, 707/847-3234; 2/$-$$$, 4/$$$; 2-night minimum on weekends; cribs; all TVs; some fireplaces, ocean views; restaurant; jacuzzi, sauna.* Located across the street from the Pacific Ocean, this modern motel provides a large expanse of lawn dotted with a swingset and tether ball equipment. A small restaurant features ocean views and an ambitious, expensive dinner menu. Dishes made with local oysters are featured along with fresh fish, chicken, lamb, and beef items and a variety of tempting homemade desserts. Breakfast is less expensive.

♥ **Timber Cove Inn** *21780 N. Highway 1, 14 miles north of town, 707/847-3231; 2/$$$-$$$+; 2-night minimum on weekends Mar-Dec; unsuitable for children; some fireplaces, ocean views; restaurant.* Perched on a rocky seaside cliff, this inn offers many rooms with magnificent ocean views and some with sunken tubs and private jacuzzis. The lobby bar and dining room feature a dramatic Japanese-modern style of architecture and ocean views. You know you're here when you see the tall Bufano sculpture jutting above the lodge.

Fort Ross State Historic Park *19005 Highway 1, 11 miles north of town, 707/865-2391; daily 10-4:30; $2/car.* Built by Russian and Alaskan hunters in 1812 as a trading outpost, this historic fort has been authentically restored by the state. The compound consists of two blockhouses equipped with cannons, a small Russian Orthodox chapel, two commandant's houses, and a barracks. Self-guided tours are available via audio wands. Guided tours are scheduled on Sunday afternoons; call for reservations. Picnic tables are available. Outside the gates, on a picturesque bluff at the edge of the ocean, visitors can mingle with a flock of grazing sheep; a path there leads down to the beach. An architecturally striking new **Visitors Center** is located adjacent to the parking area. **Living History Days** are held periodically— allowing visitors to step back in time to 1836. Soldiers perform musket drills and fire cannons, candlemakers demonstrate their skills, and a blacksmith pounds at his forge.

Kruse Rhododendron State Reserve *22 miles north of town, 707/847-3221.* Reached via a four-mile long dirt road, this park is known for its spring floral display. Five miles of hiking trails take visitors over picturesque bridges and through fern-filled canyons.

Salt Point State Park *20 miles north of town, 707/847-3221.* This is a popular spot with skin divers and also choice for a walk along the beach. **Stump Cove** has an easy, short trail down to its scenic beach; campsites are available.

SEA RANCH

Homes: Rams Head Realty *707/785-2427;* **Sea Ranch Rentals** *707/785-2579; 2-4/$$$+; 2-night minimum, 1-week July & Aug.; cribs; all kitchens, fireplaces; some bathtubs; heated pool (unavail. Jan-*

Mar), jacuzzi, sauna, 3 tennis courts. Staying in an award-winning vacation home and enjoying the beauty of the wind-swept coastal scenery here are two compelling reasons to visit. A bar and restaurant are located in the nearby lodge, and there are hiking and jogging trails and a children's playground. Horse rentals and a 9-hole golf course are available at extra charge.

Lodge: *60 Sea Walk Dr., 707/785-2371; 2-4/$$$-$$$+; 2-night minimum on weekends; children under 5 free; cribs; all bathtubs; some fireplaces, ocean views; room service, restaurant.* At this rustic modern facility each room has two double beds; two also feature private courtyards with hot tubs. Guests have access to the facilities described for the homes.

GUALALA

Mar Vista Cottages *35101 Highway 1, 707/884-3522; 2-4/$$; crib; all refrigerators; some kitchens, fireplaces, ocean views; hot tub.* These cottages are just a short walk from a sandy beach with a gentle surf. Two ponds and assorted geese and ducks are located on the nine-acre property.

♥ **The Old Milano Hotel** *38300 Highway 1, 707/884-3256; 2/$$$-$$$+; 2-night minimum on Sat; unsuitable for children under 16; some kitchens, fireplaces, bathtubs, ocean views; some shared baths; room service, full breakfast, restaurant; jacuzzi.* Built originally in 1905 as a railroad rest stop and pub, this cliffside Victorian hotel is now recorded in the National Register of Historic Places. A cottage and a converted caboose are available in addition to the hotel rooms—all of which are named after Italian operas.

Serenisea *36100 Highway 1, 707/884-3836; 2-4/$-$$$; 2-night minimum on weekends; all kitchens, fireplaces, ocean views; some TVs, bathtubs; hot tubs, sauna.* These ocean-front cabins and houses are located on a scenic bluff.

♥ **St. Orres** *36601 Highway 1, 707/884-3303; 2/$$-$$$+; 2-night minimum on weekends; unsuitable for children; some kitchens, fireplaces, bathtubs, ocean views; some shared baths; full breakfast, restaurant; hot tub, sauna.* Built of weathered old wood in a Russian style of architecture, this unusual inn offers rooms as well as three detached cabins. Guests may enjoy a memorable meal in the striking three-story-tall dining room.

♥ **Whale Watch Inn** *35100 Highway 1, 707/884-3667; 2/$$$+; 2-night minimum on weekends; unsuitable for children under 18; some fireplaces, ocean views, bathtubs; continental breakfast.* Perched on an oceanside cliff, this contemporary lodging facility offers plenty of peace and quiet.

POINT ARENA

Point Arena Lighthouse *2 miles off Highway 1, 707/882-2777; daily 11-2:30; adults $2, under 16 50¢.* Originally built in 1870, this lighthouse was destroyed in the '06 quake and then rebuilt. It was finally automated in 1976. Visitors may take a self-guided tour of a museum filled with old photos and featuring a whale watching room. Then it's a 145-step climb (equivalent to six stories) up the 115-foot light for a guided tour of the tower. Those who want to stay the night can book one of the bargain three-bedroom, two-bath lightkeeper's homes located adjacent.

ELK

♥ **Harbor House** *5600 Highway 1, 707/877-3203; 2/$$$+; weekends only in Dec; 2-night minimum on Sat; unsuitable for children; some fireplaces, ocean views; full breakfast and dinner included.* Built entirely of redwood in 1917, this lovely inn has five rooms and four cottages. Meals are served in a beautifully appointed dining room with a spectacular ocean view. A path leads to a private beach where guests may sun, explore tidepools, and gather driftwood.

MENDOCINO

■ *A LITTLE BACKGROUND*

For a rejuvenating, quiet escape from the hectic pace of city life, pack up your car and head for Mendocino. Now an Historical Monument, this tiny artists' colony is built in a pastel Cape Cod-style of architecture and exudes the feeling that it belongs to a time past. To really slow down your system, consider parking your car and not using it for the duration of your visit. You can get anywhere in town via a short walk.

Keep in mind that Mendocino has a limited water supply and be careful not to waste. Also, there is a Volunteer Fire Department whose alarm has been known to go off in the middle of the night. Resembling the scream of an air raid siren, it can be quite startling—even if you know what it is.

The night life here is of the early-to-bed-early-to-rise variety. My family's agenda usually consists of dinner out,

a stroll through town, a nightcap at the Mendocino Hotel or Sea Gull Inn, and then off to bed.

Be sure to make your lodging reservations as far in advance as possible; in-town lodging is limited and popular.

■ VISITOR INFORMATION

Fort Bragg-Mendocino Coast Chamber of Commerce *P.O. Box 1141, (332 N. Main St.), Fort Bragg 95437, 707/964-3153.*

■ GETTING THERE

Located approximately 150 miles north of San Francisco. Take Highway 101 to Highway 1, or Highway 101 to Highway 128 to Highway 1.

■ *STOPS ALONG THE WAY*

PICNIC SPOTS.

On the drive to Mendocino, a picnic makes a good lunch stop. Several wineries off Highway 101 have picnic facilities (see Geyserville, p.135). More picnic spots are found along Highway 128 in Boonville: **Indian Creek City Park**, located just east of town, and the **Masonite Corporation Demonstration Forest**, just past Navarro. The **Anderson Valley Historical Museum** *(707/895-3207; F-Sun 1-4, from 11 in summer; free)*, a one-room red schoolhouse located just west of town, is also a worthwhile stop. (Note that in Boonville the townspeople speak an unusual dialect known as "Boontling." For example, public telephones are labeled "Buckey Walter.")

WINERIES.

Edmeades Vineyards *(5500 Highway 128, 707/895-3232; tasting daily 11-5, in summer 10-6; tours by appt.)* is located atop a scenic hill just west of town in Philo. Across the street, **Navarro Vineyards** *(5601 Highway 128, 800/537-9463, 707/895-3686; tasting daily 10-5; tours by appt.)* operates in a striking modern facility and offers tasting of varietal grape juices for children. Both have picnic areas.

LODGING.

Among the interesting lodging in this area is the **Highland Ranch** *(800/544-1211, 707/895-3294; per person charge is based on age; closed Nov-Mar; 2-night minimum; crib; all fireplaces; unheated pool (unavail. Nov-Mar), hot tub, 2 tennis courts)*. There are the rural pleasures of fishing, swimming, and canoeing in three ponds, and most days horseback riding is available at additional charge. Supervised activities for children 6 and older are provided in summer. Lodging is in modern redwood cabins with fireplaces, and three full meals are included. Secluded **Bear Wallow Resort** *(707/895-3335)* features cabins with fireplaces, and the circa 1912 **Toll House Inn** *(707/895-3630)*, situated on a former sheep ranch, offers quiet B&B accommodations and a relaxing jacuzzi. Also, the cozy **Anderson Valley Home Hostel** *(707/895-2138)* has four inexpensive beds (see also p.273).

■ *WHERE TO STAY*

♥ **Joshua Grindle Inn** *44800 Little Lake Rd., 707/937-4143; 2/$$-$$$; 2-night minimum on weekends; unsuitable for children under 12; all bathtubs; some fireplaces, ocean views; full breakfast.* Built in 1879 by the town banker, this small inn has a New England country atmosphere and Early American antiques in every room. In addition to the main house, there is a cottage and water tower with rooms. Bikes are available for guests to use, and airport pickup via a '48 Chevy woodie can be arranged.

MacCallum House Inn *45020 Albion St., 707/937-0289; 2-4/$-$$$+; 2-night minimum on weekends; cribs; some refrigerators, fireplaces, ocean views, bathtubs; some shared baths; continental breakfast, restaurant.* Built in 1882 by William H. Kelley for his newlywed daughter, Daisy MacCallum, this converted Victorian home was one of the first B&Bs in the area. Its charmingly decorated rooms are furnished with antiques—many of which belonged to the original owner. Accommodations are also available in newer structures adjacent to the house. The ten rooms in the house itself tend to be best suited for couples with a baby or just one child. A continental breakfast is served buffet-style in two magnificent dining rooms in the main house. Guests are greeted with the morning paper and a crackling fire in the two fireplaces built of smooth river stone. In the evening an independent restaurant operation serves elegant seafood and game entrees in the dining rooms. Light dinners and snacks are available across the hall in the cozy **Grey Whale Bar** also operated by the restaurant. Interesting drinks include Daisy's Hot Apple Pie (a blend of apple cider, Tuaca, cinnamon, and whipped cream) and—for children—a Velvet Rabbit (a frothy mix of cream, grenadine, and strawberries served elegantly in a brandy snifter).

Mendocino Hotel & Garden Suites *45080 Main St., 800/548-0513, 707/937-0511; 2/$$-$$$+, 4/$$$+; children under 10 free; some TVs, fireplaces, ocean views, bathtubs; some shared baths; room service, restaurant.* Built in 1878, this hotel has been renovated in Victorian style. Its rooms combine modern convenience with 19th century elegance. Modern suites, located behind the hotel, offer additional lodging.

♥ **Mendocino Village Inn** *44860 Main St., 707/937-0246; 2/$$-$$$; 2-night minimum on weekends; unsuitable for children under 10; some fireplaces, bathtubs, ocean views; some shared baths; full breakfast.* Built in 1882, this Queen Anne Victorian home is known as "the house of the doctors" because it was originally built by a doctor and then bought in turn by three more doctors. All the cozy rooms are individually decorated.

Sea Gull Inn *44594 Albion St., 707/937-5204; 2/$-$$, 4/$$$; children under 2 free; some TVs, bathtubs; continental breakfast.* Built in the 1880s, this rustic, non-cutesy inn has a casual atmosphere. A mature garden, with giant fuchsias and a century-old rosemary bush, surrounds the inn.

Sea Rock Bed & Breakfast Inn *11101 N. Lansing St., 707/937-5517; 2/$$-$$$+, 4/$$$-$$$+; 2-night minimum on weekends; cribs; all TVs, ocean views; some kitchens, fireplaces; continental breakfast.* These pleasant cottage units are in a scenic location about 1/4 mile from town. Guests have access to a private cove and beach.

Sears House Inn *44840 Main St., 707/937-4076; 2/$-$$$, 4/$$$-$$$+; 2-night minimum on weekends; children under 2 free; some refrigerators, fireplaces, bathtubs; some shared baths; continental breakfast.* Accommodations are in both an 1870 Victorian house and in a circa 1915 annex. Families are welcome in the even newer cottages.

♥ **Whitegate Inn** *499 Howard St., 707/937-4892; 2/$$-$$$; 2-night minimum on weekends; unsuitable for children under 14; some fireplaces, ocean views; some shared baths; continental breakfast weekdays, full breakfast weekends.* Built in 1880, this tasteful Victorian home has been refurbished and decorated with antiques.

■ WHERE TO STAY NEARBY

Big River Lodge *on Comptche-Ukiah Rd., 707/937-5615; 2-4/$$$+; cribs; 2-night minimum on weekends; all ocean views; some TVs, kitchens, fireplaces; continental breakfast.* Located on the outskirts of town, upon a bluff overlooking a scenic llama farm and duck pond, these modern luxury motel rooms are decorated with antiques, fresh flowers, and the work of local artists. Guests may borrow bicycles.

♥ **Fensalden Inn** *33810 Navarro Ridge Rd., Albion, 7 miles south of town, 707/937-4042; 2/$$$-$$$+, 4/$$$+; 2-night minimum on weekends; unsuitable for children under 12; some refrigerators, fireplaces, bathtubs, ocean views; continental breakfast.* Originally a stagecoach way station in the 1860s, this B&B sits atop 20 tree-lined acres of headland meadow.

♥ **Glendeven** *8221 N. Highway 1, Little River, 707/937-0083; 2/$$-$$$+, 4/$$$+; 2-night minimum on weekends; unsuitable for children under 8; cribs; some fireplaces, refrigerators, bay views, bathtubs; some shared baths; full breakfast.* Built in 1867, this attractive Maine-style farmhouse overlooks the headland meadows and bay at Little River. Rooms are furnished eclectically with antiques and contemporary art, and the atmosphere is casual.

Heritage House *5200 N. Highway 1, Little River, 707/937-5885; 2-4/$$$+; closed Dec and Jan; children under 2 free; some fireplaces, bathtubs, ocean views; full breakfast and dinner included, restaurant.* Located on a craggy stretch of coast, this inn offers a luxurious escape from city living. Guests are housed in cottages furnished with antiques. Male guests are encouraged to dress in jacket and tie for meals served in the cliffside dining room. If it all looks familiar, you may have seen it before in the movie *Same Time Next Year* which was filmed here.

Little River Inn *7750 N. Highway 1, Little River, 707/937-5942; 2/$$- $$$+, 4/$$$-$$$+; cribs; 2-night minimum on weekends; some TVs, kitchens, fireplaces, ocean views.* Built in 1853, this house became an inn in 1929 and now offers cozy attic rooms, cottages, and standard motel units. A 9-hole golf course is available for guests.

Mendocino Coast Holiday Reservations *800/262-7801, 707/937- 5033; 2-4/$$-$$$+; 2-night minimum, 1-week in July & Aug; cribs; all kitchens, fireplaces; some bathtubs, hot tubs.* This vacation home rental service will arrange lodging in studios, cabins, cottages, inns, and estate homes located on the Mendocino coast.

■ *WHERE TO EAT IN TOWN*

Cafe Beaujolais *961 Ukiah St., 707/937-5614; B/L daily, D Th-Sun; closed part of Jan & Feb; highchairs, booster seats; $$; reservations suggested; no cards.* Breakfast in this converted Victorian home is the usual items prepared with unusual care—as well as such delights as homemade coffeecake, croissants, cashew granola, fruit salad with creme fraiche, and Mexican hot chocolate. Lunch includes innovative entrees and sandwiches and two popular desserts: panforte di Mendocino and a buttercream caramel bar sundae. All this plus a large selection of specialty coffees and fresh flowers decorating each plate!

Mendocino Bakery *on Lansing St., 707/937-0836; daily 8-5:30;$.* Perfect for a light lunch, this super bakery dispenses tasty homemade soup and pizza still warm from the oven. A hunk of the fragrant, fantastic gingerbread makes the perfect dessert, though some favor the chewy cinnamon twists. The bakery also makes an assortment of breads and breakfast pastries—all without mixes or preservatives. Everything is exceptional.

Mendocino Hotel *45080 Main St., 707/937-0511; B/L/D daily; highchairs, children's portions; reservations suggested; $$; AE,MC,V.* Stop in the bar to enjoy a fancy drink among stained glass and oriental carpet splendor. Then move on to the formal dining room furnished in old-fashioned oak. Fresh seafood and steak are on the dinner menu along with hamburgers and deep-dish pie desserts.

Mendocino Ice Cream Co. *45090 Main St., 707/937-5884; Sun-Th 9- 7, F & Sat to 11, in winter daily to 6; $.* People wait in long lines to get the 1/4-pound ice cream cones scooped up here. And, indeed, the award-winning ice cream is delicious. My favorite is Black Forest—rich chocolate ice cream with chocolate chips and cherry bits. The foot-long hot dogs are pretty good, too. Sodas and sandwiches round out the menu, and wooden booths are available.

Sea Gull of Mendocino *10481 Lansing St., 707/937-2100; B/L/D daily; highchairs, booster seats, children's portions; reservations suggested; $$; no cards.* The specialty here is fresh food prepared simply. Breakfasts are especially good, and choices include eggs, pancakes, and hot oatmeal. The premier choice on the dinner menu is fresh local fish items—including a cioppino and gumbo. A cheeseburger, steak sandwich, and several chicken entrees are also available. Dinners come with homemade soup or green salad, fresh vegetable, baked potato or rice pilaf, and crusty French bread. The upstairs **Cellar Bar** usually has live music in the evening and is a good choice for an Irish coffee nightcap.

■ *WHAT TO DO*

Beachcombing. Take the little path behind the church on Main Street down to the beach. While you're there, make a kelp horn. Cut the bulb off the end of a long, thin piece of fresh bull kelp. Rinse out the tube in the ocean so that it is hollow. Wrap it over your shoulder and blow through the small end. The longer the tube, the greater the resonance.

Catch A Canoe *off Highway 1 at Comptche-Ukiah Rd., 707-937-0273; daily 9:30-5:30; $10+/hr; reservations recommended.* Drifting down calm Big River affords the opportunity to picnic in the wilderness, swim in a secluded swimming hole, and observe a variety of wildlife. Canoe rentals include paddles and life jackets.

Current local events. Check the postings in the entryway to the Sea Gull restaurant.

Ford House *on Main St., 707/937-5397; daily 10-5, Nov-Mar F-M only; free; no strollers.* Inside this historic 1854 home is an interpretive center focusing on the history of the area. During whale-watching season, a short orientation film is presented. Information on interpretive programs held nearby at **Mendocino Headlands State Park** can also be obtained here then. (December through April whales migrate close to shore and can sometimes easily be seen "breaching"—jumping out of the water—from the headlands.) In good weather consider a picnic in the backyard where you can enjoy a spectacular ocean view.

Kelley House Museum *45007 Albion St., 707/937-5791; daily 1-4 June-Oct, F-M rest of year; $1 donation.* A gigantic cypress tree grows in the front yard of this home built by William H. Kelley (Daisy MacCallum's father) in 1861. The restored first floor displays a collection of photos from the 1800s and changing exhibits of local artifacts and private collections. Inquire about the schedule of walking tours. Next door is the delightful town duck pond; there are plenty of noisy geese as well.

Mendocino Art Center *45200 Little Lake St., 707/937-5818.* Movies are usually scheduled on weekend evenings. There is also an irregular schedule of Sunday afternoon concerts and plays. Call for current details. Browsing in the galleries is also a pleasant passtime.

Mendocino Cyclery *Main St., 707/937-4744; daily 10-5; $5+/hr.* Mountain bikes, 10-speeds, tandems, and beach cruisers are available along with free trail maps.

Pygmy Forest *south of town on Little River Airport Rd.* The leached soil in this unusual forest produces small, stunted trees. The 1/3-mile trail takes about fifteen minutes to walk. A brochure describing the various types of trees is available at the trailhead.

Wind & Weather *on Albion St., 707/937-0323; daily 10-5.* Located inside a picturesque old water tower, this tiny specialty shop sells barometers, weather vanes, sundials, and other paraphernalia for measuring the weather. Don't miss it.

FORT BRAGG

■ *ANNUAL EVENTS*

World's Largest Salmon Barbecue *July; 707/964-5832.* In addition to feasting on king salmon, participants can look forward to music, dancing, a variety of educational salmon displays, and a fireworks show over the ocean. Proceeds benefit the non-profit Salmon Restoration Association and help them restock Northern California salmon runs.

■ *GETTING THERE*

Located approximately 15 miles north of Mendocino.

■ *WHERE TO STAY*

Beachcomber Motel *1111 N. Main, 1/2 mile north of town, 707/964-2402; 2/$-$$, 4/$$; cribs; all TVs; some kitchens, ocean views.* This ordinary motel is in an extraordinary location just 200 feet from the beach.

Colonial Inn *533 E. Fir St., 707/964-9979; 2/$-$$, 4/$$; children under 5 free; all TVs; some fireplaces, ocean views.* Located in a quiet residential area, this huge 1912 woodframe house has tastefully decorated rooms.

♥ **The Grey Whale Inn** *615 N. Main St., 800/382-7244, 707/964-0640; 2/$$-$$$+, 4/$$$+; 2-night minimum on Sat; unsuitable for children under 12; some kitchens, fireplaces, bathtubs, ocean views; full breakfast.* This stately redwood building was a hospital from 1915 to 1971. An inn since 1976, it offers spacious, pleasantly decorated rooms. A few have private decks.

Pine Beach Inn *on Highway 1, 4 miles south of town, 707/964-5603; 2-4/$$-$$$; children under 16 free; cribs; all TVs; some bathtubs; continental breakfast Nov-Mar, restaurant Apr-Oct; 2 tennis courts (fee).* These modern motel units are located on twelve acres of private land. Facilities include a private beach and cove.

■ *WHERE TO EAT*

Cap'n Flint's *32250 N. Harbor Dr., 707/964-9447; L/D daily; highchairs, booster seats, children's portions; no reservations; $; no cards.* Popular with locals, the menu here offers various types of fish and chips, clam chowder, and the house specialty— deep-fried shrimp wontons made with a tasty cream cheese filling. Hamburgers, hot dogs, sandwiches, and interesting mixed wine drinks are also available. Though the decor is well-worn mismatched furniture, the view of picturesque Noyo Harbor is excellent.

Egghead Omelettes of Oz *326 N. Main St., 707/964-5005; B/L daily; highchairs, booster seats; no reservations; $; no cards.* This cheerful, popular, and tiny diner serves a large variety of huge omelettes. Regular breakfast items and an assortment of sandwiches are also available. Families will appreciate the privacy afforded by enclosed booths; children's portions are available upon request.

■ WHAT TO DO

The Fort Bragg Footlighters *248 Laurel St., 707/964-3806; summer only, W & Sat at 8pm; all seats $5; reservations suggested.* Gay 90s music and nonsense highlight this program for all ages.

Georgia-Pacific Tree Nursery *90 W. Redwood Ave., 707/964-5651; M-F 8-4 Apr-Sept; free.* Visitors here get a view of four million seedling trees. A nature trail and picnic tables are available. The nursery closes October 1—when the seedlings are taken out and planted.

Guest House Museum *343 N. Main St., 707/961-2840; W-Sun 10-4 Apr-Oct; $1.* Get a sense of this area's history by viewing the old logging photos and artifacts on display in this beautifully restored mansion made entirely of redwood. A steam donkey is among the displays in the manicured gardens.

Jughandle State Reserve *on Highway 1, 3 miles south of town, 707/937-5804; daily dawn-dusk; free.* A unique self-guided nature trail takes hikers through an **ecological staircase** consisting of five wavecut terraces which demonstrate how plants and soils affect one another. During the five-mile, three-hour walk the terrain changes from grass-covered headlands, to a pine and redwood forest, to a pygmy forest filled with full-grown trees only one to two feet tall. Wear sturdy shoes, and bring water and a lunch.

Mendocino Coast Botanical Gardens *18220 N. Highway 1, 2 miles south of town, 707/964-4352; daily 9-5, Oct-Mar 10-4; adults $4, under 12 free.* Enjoy a self-guided tour through 47 acres of flowering plants. This garden is known for its rhododendrons, fuchsias, and native California plants. Concerts are often scheduled in the summer. Picnic facilities are available, and a cafe serves a good selection of inexpensive breakfast and lunch items.

Ricochet Ridge Ranch *24201 N. Highway 1, 707/964-7669; daily by appt. at 10, 12, 2, & 4.* Equestrian excursions vary from by-the-hour guided rides to week-long overnight trips. They include treks on Fort

Bragg's **Ten Mile Beach** and in Mendocino's **Russian Gulch Park**. Catered trips, camping expeditions, and tours with lodging at inns can also be arranged. All this and ponies, too!

Skunk Train/California Western Railroad *foot of Laurel St., 707/ 964-6371; round trip: adults $20, 5-11 $10, under 5 free if they don't occupy a seat; schedule varies; reservations suggested.* For those of you with little skunks who love trains—voila—the Skunk Train. The train gets its name from the fact that the original logging trains emitted unpleasant odors from their gas engines. They smelled not unlike skunks. Now a steam engine usually pulls the train in the summer (the Super Skunk) and a diesel engine is used the rest of the year (the Skunk). The train travels through two deep mountain tunnels, through 40 miles of dense redwood forest, over 31 bridges and trestles, and it makes stops along the way to deliver mail. It runs between Fort Bragg and Willits, where there is a stopover for lunch. Like many town attractions, this one is owned by Georgia-Pacific Co.

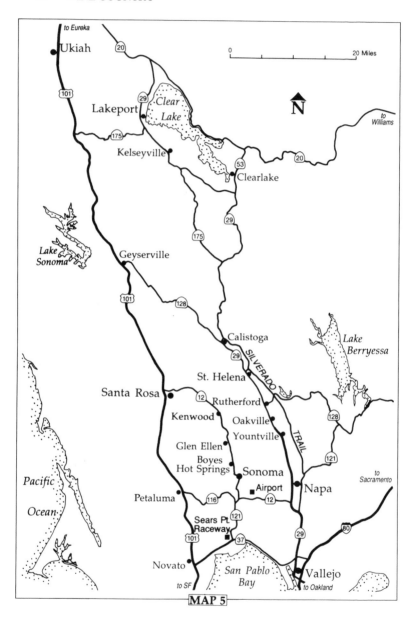

to Eureka

Ukiah · 20

101

Lakeport · 29 · Clear Lake

175

Kelseyville ·

0   20 Miles

N

to Williams

53 · Clearlake

29

175

Lake Sonoma · Geyserville ·

101 · 128

Calistoga ·

29 · SILVERADO

Lake Berryessa

St. Helena ·

Santa Rosa · 12 · Rutherford

Kenwood · Oakville ·

Glen Ellen · Yountville ·

128

TRAIL

121

Boyes Hot Springs · Sonoma ·

Pacific · Airport

Petaluma · 116 · 12

Napa ·

to Sacramento

Ocean

Sears Pt. Raceway · 121

80

101 · 37

29

Novato ·

San Pablo Bay

Vallejo

to SF

to Oakland

MAP 5

WINE COUNTRY

■ *A LITTLE BACKGROUND*

California's first wineries were appendages of the 21 Franciscan missions which were built a day's ride (by horseback) from each other in a chain reaching from San Diego to Sonoma. The wine was produced by the missions for sacramental use. Eventually the church gave up producing wine and the art passed into the realm of private enterprise.

Presently Sonoma County and Napa County are literally erupting with new small family wineries. Winemaking is becoming a hobby with many city folks who have bought themselves little vineyard retreats.

The best route for wine tasting in this area is along Highway 29 between Oakville and Calistoga. When visiting this stretch of highway, which is heavily concentrated with wineries, the problem is to remain selective in tasting and not get too heavily concentrated yourself. Experts suggest not planning to taste at more than four wineries in one day.

Young children can be difficult on a winery tour. Out of courtesy to the other tour participants (a noisy child interferes with the guide's presentation), parents might consider selecting a member of their party to stay with the children while the rest go on a tour. Or visit a winery with a self-guided tour. Most wineries allow tasting without taking a tour. It's a nice idea to bring along some plastic wine glasses and a bottle of grape juice so the children can "taste" too.

Many wineries have picnic areas. An ideal agenda is to tour a winery, taste, and then purchase a bottle of the wine you enjoy most to drink with a picnic lunch.

A new wrinkle in the pleasure of wine tasting is that many wineries now charge for tasting. Charges range from $1 to $5. Sometimes they include a free souvenir glass. Other times the charge is applied to a purchase. But the purpose seems to be to keep the less serious tasters away. A tasting fee tends to be imposed by smaller wineries with expensive vintages.

Because the Wine Country is so close to the Bay Area, this trip can easily be made into a one-day adventure.

SONOMA

■ *VISITOR INFORMATION*

Sonoma Valley Visitors Bureau *453 First St. East, Sonoma 95476, 707/996-1090.*

■ *ANNUAL EVENTS*

Kenwood World Pillow Fighting Championships *July 4th weekend; in Kenwood, 707/833-2440.* This very serious all-day competition takes place on a pipe positioned over a muddy morass into which losers as well as winners are buffeted.

■ *GETTING THERE*

Located approximately 45 miles north of San Francisco. Take Highway 101 to Highway 37 to Highway 121 to Highway 12.

■ *WHERE TO STAY*

El Dorado Inn *405 First St. West, 707/996-3030; 2/$$-$$$; cribs;*

some TVs, bathtubs; some shared baths; room service, continental breakfast, restaurant. This historic inn dates from 1840. Rooms are furnished with antiques, and some have scenic views. A restaurant operating on the ground floor features an inviting patio attractively shaded by an old fig tree.

El Pueblo Motel *896 W. Napa St., 707/996-3651; 2-4/$$; children under 2 free; cribs; all TVs, bathtubs; pool (unavail. Nov-May).* Located on the outskirts of town, eight blocks from the town square, this is a pleasant, spacious motel.

♥ **Sonoma Hotel** *110 W. Spain St., 707/996-2996; 2/$$-$$$, 4/$$$+; cribs; all bathtubs; some shared baths; continental breakfast, restaurant.* Dating from the 1870s, when it was the town theater, this three-story hotel is located on the town square and has rooms furnished in carefully selected turn-of-the-century antiques. Private bathrooms feature clawfoot tubs, and room #3 boasts a carved rosewood bed said to have once been owned by General Vallejo. The restaurant specializes in hearty country fare and serves lunch and dinner in the dining room daily except Wednesday; an old-fashioned bar adjoins. My personal experience suggests staying away from here with children under 12.

Sonoma Mission Inn & Spa *18140 Highway 12, Boyes Hot Springs, 3 miles north of town, 800/862-4945, 707/938-9000; 2/$$$-$$$+, 4/ $$$+; children under 18 free; cribs; all TVs, refrigerators, bathtubs; some fireplaces; room service, 2 restaurants; 2 heated pools, 2 jacuzzis, sauna; 2 tennis courts (fee for night lighting).* Built in the 1920s, this sedate luxury resort features pink adobe architecture and rooms cooled with old-fashioned ceiling fans. Though children are welcome, this is an adult-oriented resort; children under 18 are not allowed in the spa.

■ *WHERE TO EAT*

Big 3 Fountain *18140 Highway 12, Boyes Hot Springs, 3 miles from town, 707/938-9000; B/L/D daily; highchairs, booster seats; $; all cards.* Operated by the Sonoma Mission Inn, this airy, noisy, and casual dining room offers seating on stools at the fountain counter, at ice cream parlour tables, or in comfy booths. Toasters are right on the tables, and lemon slices pretty-up the water glasses. The menu offers traditional American fare, exceptional cottage fries, and fancy ice cream creations.

■ PICNIC PICK-UPS

Fantasie Au Chocolat *40 W. Spain St., 707/938-2020; Th-Sat 10- 9:30, Sun-W 10-5:30.* A chocoholic's dream come true, this specialty shop dispenses handmade truffles and candies as well as tortes laced with Grand Marnier. My family's favorite, however, is the indescribably delicious frosted brownie.

Sonoma Cheese Factory *2 W. Spain St., 707/938-5225; daily 9-5:30.* This crowded shop stocks hundreds of cheeses (including their famous varieties of Sonoma Jack made from old family recipes), cold cuts, salads, marvelous marinated artichoke hearts, and cheesecake flown in from New Jersey. Sandwiches are made-to-order. If you wish to eat here, a few tables are available inside and also outside on a shaded patio. The workings of the cheese factory may be viewed in the back.

Sonoma French Bakery *468 First St. East, 707/996-2691; W-Sat 8-6, Sun 7:30-noon, closed last 2 weeks of Aug.* This renowned bakery makes sourdough French bread which is so delicious that people are willing to wait in a long line to purchase it. Personally, I favor the sweet French bread. The Basque baker, hailing from the French Pyrenees, makes the bread without yeast. Flutes, rolls, croissants, gateau Basque bread, French and Danish pastries, and cream puffs are just a few of the other delights available.

Sonoma Sausage Company *453 First St. West, 707/938-8200; M-Sat 9:30-5:30, Sun 12-6.* Over 60 kinds of sausage—including hot beer sausage, Nurnberger bratwurst, smoked Hawaiian Portugese, and Kalbs leberwurst—are available here. They're all made with Old World techniques from 100% meat (no fillers), and some are smoked and ready to eat. You can also get German potato salad, sauerkraut, and herb bread.

■ WHAT TO DO

Depot Museum *270 First St. East, 707/938-9765; W-Sun 1-4:30; adults 50¢, 10-18 25¢.* Operated by volunteers from the Sonoma Historical Society, this tiny museum is housed in the restored North West Pacific Railroad Station and features changing historical and railroad exhibits. An adjacent park has a playground and picnic area. A bicycle path, which follows the old railroad track, originates here.

Sonoma State Historic Park *located off the Plaza along Spain St., 707/938-1578; daily 10-5; adults $1, 6-17 50¢; admission includes barracks, mission, and Vallejo home.* This extensive park preserves structures dating from the early 1800s, when General Vallejo, founder of Sonoma, was Mexico's administrator of Northern California. The two-story whitewashed adobe barracks once housed his soldiers; it now contains historical exhibits. Vallejo drilled his soldiers across the street in what is now the town square. Next door and across the street from the barracks, the well-preserved remnant of **Mission San Francisco Solano**, founded in 1823 and the most northerly and last in the chain of California missions, exhibits a collection of mission watercolors by Chris Jorgensen. An impressive old prickly pear cactus forest graces the mission courtyard. **General Vallejo's home**, a Victorian Gothic with original furnishings, is located about one mile east. Shaded picnic tables and another giant prickly pear garden are found there.

Sonoma Town Square Park. This old-fashioned park is great for picnics. Children may frolic at the playground and feed ducks in the tiny pond.

Toscano Hotel *20 E. Spain St., 707/938-0510; daily from 10; tours on Sat & Sun 1-4, M 11-1; by donation.* This beautifully restored mining-era hotel was built in 1858.

Train Town *20264 Broadway, 707/938-3912; daily in summer 10:30-5, weekends rest of year; adults $2.20, 2-16 $1.60.* A miniature steam locomotive winds through ten acres during the fifteen-minute ride on the **Sonoma Gaslight and Western Railroad**. It passes through forests and a tunnel and crosses a 70-foot double truss bridge and a 50-foot steel girder bridge. During a five-minute stop at a miniature mining town, where the train takes on more water, the engineer distributes food for kids to feed the ducks and swans.

Vasquez House *129 E. Spain St. in El Paseo de Sonoma, 707/938-0510; tours W-Sun 1-5; by donation.* Built in 1856, this refurbished woodframe house features a tearoom serving homemade pastries and tea.

■ WHAT TO DO NEARBY

Aero Schellville *23982 Arnold Dr., at the airport off Highway 121, 2 miles north of Sears Point Raceway, 707/938-2444; daily 9-5:30.* Ride in an authentic 1940 Stearman biplane used to train World War II combat pilots. Have your picnic *after* this excursion as the aerobatic ride is said to "top any rollercoaster ever built." Calmer scenic rides are also available, and old and antique planes may also be viewed at the airport. Call for current information.

Jack London State Historic Park *2400 London Ranch Rd., Glen Ellen, north of town off Highway 12, 707/938-5216; daily 8-dusk,*

museum 10-5; $3/car. Located in the **Valley of the Moon**, this 50-acre park contains the ruins of Jack London's dream castle **Wolf House** (reached by a pleasant one-mile trail), his grave, and a museum—**The House of Happy Walls**—built in his memory by his widow. The park, given to the state by London's nephew, provides ample room for picnicking and romping. Guided one- and two-hour horse rides and horse-drawn surry rides—some with a picnic included—are available within the park. For information and reservations contact the **Sonoma Cattle Company** *(707/996-8566).* To get in the mood for this trek you may want to read a London classic such as *The Call of the Wild* or *Martin Eden.* Or on your way to the park stop at the **Jack London Bookstore** *(14300 Arnold Dr., 707/ 996-2888),* where the owner can guide you to a good selection by London.

Morton's Warm Springs *1651 Warm Springs Rd., Kenwood, 10 miles north of town, 707/833-5511; May-Sept only, Tu-F 10-6, Sat & Sun 9-8; adults $2.75-$3.75, 2-11 $2.25-$2.75.* Two large pools and one toddler wading pool allow everyone in the family to enjoy a refreshing summer swim. Lifeguards are on duty. There are picnic tables and barbecue pits, a snackbar, and a large grassy area for sunbathing. A special teenage rec room is equipped with a juke box, Ping Pong tables, and pinball machines, and dressing rooms and lockers are available. A few rules: no cutoffs in the pools; no glass allowed; all drinks must be in cans.

Sears Point International Raceway *Highways 37/121, 800/338-SPIR, 707/938-8448; Apr-Oct only.* This is where you go to see car races. The 2.52-mile course has twelve turns. Call for current schedule and ticket prices; children under 12 are free.

■ *WINERIES*

Buena Vista Winery & Vineyards *18000 Old Winery Rd., 707/938-1266; tasting daily 10-5; self-guided tour.* Founded in 1857, this is California's oldest winery. Though it went through a period of decline when it was vacant and then used as a women's prison, it has long been restored to its original charm. It has the finest picnic area of any winery I've visited. Tables, shaded by stately old eucalyptus trees growing on the banks of a tiny brook, encircle the vine-covered entrance to the winery's limestone cellars. If kids are along, have them taste the Johannisberg Riesling grape juice. If they say "Yeah," purchase a chilled bottle for them. After tasting wines in the welcoming old Press House, select a bottle for your picnic. When it gets crowded here, the attractive vineyard parking lot is opened, and it is a short, pleasant hike in. A **Midsummer Mozart Festival** is scheduled each August; call for details.

Chateau St. Jean Vineyards and Winery *8555 Highway 12, Kenwood, 10 miles north of town, 707/833-4134; tasting daily 10-4:30; self-guided tour 10:30-4.* This relatively new winery, which specializes in white varietals, was built in 1975. The tasting room is in a 1920s chateau, and there is a grassy, shaded picnic area with fountains and several fish ponds.

Hacienda Winery *1000 Vineyard Lane, 707/938-3220; tasting daily 10-5; tours by appt.* Built in a Spanish Colonial-style of architecture, this winery has a charming tasting room. If you decide to picnic on one of the inviting tables outside, wine glasses are available for loan. If you want to feed the ducks and geese that often wander up from the nearby pond, pack appropriate provisions.

Sebastiani Vineyards *389 Fourth St. East, 707/938-5532; tasting and tours daily 10-5.* This winery has been owned continuously by the same family since 1904—longer than any other in the country. Children are thoughtfully served grape juice when their parents are tasting. While here, take time to view the world's largest collection of carved oak wine casks and an adjacent museum of Indian artifacts featuring an extensive collection of arrowheads.

Smothers Brothers Wines *9575 Highway 12, Kenwood, 707/833-1010; tasting daily 10-4:30; no tours.* Many people stop here just to see if Dick or Tommy are around. Children are served grape juice while their parents taste, and there is a small shaded picnic area with tables.

YOUNTVILLE

■ *VISITOR INFORMATION*
Yountville Chamber of Commerce *P.O. Box 2064, Yountville 94599, (no phone).*

■ *GETTING THERE*
Located approximately 60 miles north of San Francisco. Take Highway 101 to Highway 37 to Highway 121 to Highway 12 to Highway 29.

■ *WHERE TO STAY*
Burgundy House *6711 Washington St., 707/944-2855; 2/$$$-$$$+; cribs; some fireplaces, bathtubs; some shared baths; continental breakfast.* The stone walls of this former brandy distillery are 22 inches thick. Rooms in the rustic main inn are decorated with antiques, and an inspired breakfast is served—depending on the weather—in either the charming downstairs hearth room or the garden. More rooms are available down the street in the ultra-modern **Bordeaux House.**

Embassy Suites *1075 California Blvd., Napa, 800/EMBASSY, 707/253-9540; 2-4/$$$+; children under 12 free; cribs; all TVs, refrigerators, bathtubs; some fireplaces; room service, full breakfast; heated indoor pool, jacuzzi, sauna, steam room.* All the rooms in this new nation-wide lodging chain are suites. Each has a bedroom, front room with hide-a-bed, and kitchenette. Further amenities include a small bottle of wine in each room, two TVs, and complimentary evening drinks. Breakfast is the all-you-can-eat type with eggs cooked-to-order, bacon, sausage, pancakes, fried potatoes, toast, donuts, cereals, and beverages. It can be enjoyed in a pleasant indoor atrium or outside by a pond inhabited with both black and white swans.

♥ **Magnolia Hotel** *6529 Yount St., 707/944-2056; 2/$$$-$$$+; unsuitable for children under 16; some fireplaces, bathtubs; full breakfast; heated pool (unheated Nov-Apr), jacuzzi.* Located in the center of town, the twelve rooms in this rustic, three-story circa 1873 stone building are decorated with Victorian antiques. More rooms are located in several adjacent buildings. Guests are greeted with a complimentary decanter of port in their room.

Napa Valley Lodge *Highway 29/Madison, 800/368-2468, 707/944-2468; 2-4/$$$-$$$+; children under 12 free; cribs; all TVs, refrigerators, bathtubs; some refrigerators, fireplaces; continental breakfast; heated pool, jacuzzi, sauna.* This attractive modern motel is located on the outskirts of town, across the street from a park and playground. Each room has a patio or balcony, and facilities include an exercise room with weights and a spa. Bicycles are available for rent.

Napa Valley Railway Inn *6503 Washington St., 707-944-2000; 2/$$-$$$, 4/$$$-$$$+; 2-night minimum on weekends; children under 7 free; some bathtubs.* Three cabooses and six turn-of-the-century rail cars have been converted into rooms and suites. Note that there are no TVs.

Silverado Country Club and Resort *1600 Atlas Peak Rd., Napa, 15 miles south of town, 800/532-0500, 707/257-5440; 2-4/$$$+; cribs; all TVs, kitchens, fireplaces, bathtubs; room service, 3 restaurants; 1 heated, 7 unheated pools; jacuzzi, sauna, 20 tennis courts (3 with night lights).* Accommodations at this classy resort are all luxurious modern condominiums—each with a private patio or balcony. Facilities include jogging trails, bicycle rentals, and two 18-hole golf courses.

Vintage Inn *6541 Washington St., 800/351-1133, 707/944-1112; 2-4/$$$+; 2-night minimum on weekends May-Oct; children under 12 free; cribs; all TVs, refrigerators, fireplaces, bathtubs; room service, continental breakfast; heated pool, jacuzzi, 2 tennis courts.* This attractive new lodging is centrally located next to Vintage 1870. In summer, bicycles are available for guests to rent.

■ *WHERE TO EAT*

The Chutney Kitchen *6525 Washington St. (in Vintage 1870; see p.106), 707/944-2788; L daily; highchairs, booster seats, children's portions; reservations suggested; $; AE,DC,MC,V.* The perfect spot to enjoy a casual, light lunch, the menu here is composed of a variety of salads and sandwiches, homemade soup, and an assortment of desserts. Special touches include a thin slice of lemon in each water glass and a small container of the kitchen's delicious chutney on each luncheon plate. More chutneys may be tasted and purchased at the check-out area, including my favorite apricot-sour cherry-almond mixture.

The Diner *6476 Washington St., 707/944-2626; B/L/D Tu-Sun; highchairs, booster seats, children's portions; no reservations; $; no cards.* This unpretentious spot offers counter seating as well as tables *and booths.* California-ized Mexican specialties enhance the cafe menu, and all items are made with quality ingredients. Breakfast choices include the house specialty of crispy cornmeal pancakes served with smoky links, plus potato pancakes and old-fashioned oatmeal with nuts and raisins. At lunch it's hamburgers, sandwiches, and soda fountain treats. Dinners are a bit more substantial and include an excellent flauta entree and, in season, a dessert cobbler made with fresh apricots and blackberries and topped with a scoop of vanilla ice cream.

♥ **Domaine Chandon** *California Dr., 707/944-2892; L/D daily; reservations suggested; $$$; AE,MC,V.* The spacious, elegant dining room at this winery is lovely, but in good weather the terrace is the premier spot to be seated. Classic French cuisine dominates the marvelous a la carte menu. Consider trout in champagne sauce stuffed with seafood mousse, or lasagne stuffed with lobster and zucchini blossoms. The dessert selection is extensive. In addition to the winery's own sparkling wines, available by the glass, the wine list includes still varietals from neighboring vintners. See also p.106.

♥ **French Laundry** *6640 Washington St., 707/944-2380; D W-Sat; reservations essential; $$$; no cards.* This attractive old brick building was actually once a French laundry. With only one seating, the dining pace is leisurely; a stroll in the garden between courses is encouraged. The kitchen specializes in freshly prepared, innovative cuisine and serves a fixed-price five-course dinner.

Mama Nina's *6772 Washington St., 707/944-2112; L M-Sat, D daily, SunBr; booster seats, children's portions; reservations suggested; $$; MC,V.* Homemade pastas are the house specialty. Gnocchi, tagliarini pesto, and fettucine Alfredo take their turns on the menus as specials, as do dishes such as scampi and veal piccata. My favorite is the tortellini Nina—small circles of pasta filled with a mix of ground veal, Parmesan cheese, and spices and topped with a delicate sauce of cream, butter, minced chicken breast, and Parmesan cheese. Pizza and calamari are also available. Two super desserts are the sandpie (an oatmeal cookie crust filled with vanilla ice cream and topped with hot fudge sauce and chopped peanuts) and the mudpie (a chocolate cookie crust filled with coffee ice cream and topped with hot fudge sauce).

Mustards *7399 Highway 29, 707/944-2424; L/D daily; reservations suggested; $$; MC,V.* This popular bar and grill features a cool, screened porch and tables set with crisp white nappery. The atmosphere is casual and chic and the menu imaginative. Selections include salads and sandwiches plus entrees such as barbecued baby backribs, mesquite-grilled rabbit with tomato salsa and black beans,

and marinated skirt steak on grilled bread. Fresh fish specials are
also available. The thin, light onion rings are superb, and homemade
ketchup may be ordered to go with them. Garlic lovers will be
pleased with a head of roasted garlic to spread on the delicious complimentary baguette, and for dessert there are homemade ice creams
and sherbets. Varietal wines are available by the glass.

■ *WHAT TO DO*

Adventures Aloft *6525 Washington St., 707/255-8688; $145/person;
reservations necessary.* Tour the Napa Valley via hot air ballon.

Trips average one hour in the air; altitude and distance depend on which way the wind blows. Rides include an after-flight champagne brunch celebration and a flight certificate. **Napa Valley Balloons** *(800/253-2224, 707/253-2224; $145, children under 9 $72.50)* offers a similar experience.

Vintage 1870 *6525 Washington St., 707/944-2451; daily 10-5:30.* This lovely old brick building, a former winery, now houses a number of interesting specialty shops and restaurants. The **Yountville Pastry Shop** bakery offers breads, fancy pastries, and tiny quiches as well as coffee. **Cooks' Corner Deli** has picnic supplies, **Gerhards Sausage Kitchen** a variety of fresh sausages made without nitrates (which can be packed on ice to travel), and **The Chocolate Tree** ice cream concoctions and homemade candies. The fifteen-minute **Napa Valley Show**, which follows the seasons in the vineyards with slides and music, is offered daily in the Keith Rosenthal Theatre. From the children's play area outside, hot air balloons can often be viewed taking off. See also The Chutney Kitchen, p.103.

Wild Horse Valley Ranch *at the end of Coombsville Rd., Napa, 20 miles southeast of town off Highway 121, 707/224-0727; daily; reservations necessary; unsuitable for children under 7.* Breakfast ($30), lunch, and dinner ($35) rides are available, and 3 1/2-hour trail rides ($25) are scheduled for mornings and afternoons. Overnight rides are also occasionally scheduled.

■ WINERIES

Domaine Chandon *California Dr., 707/944-2280; daily May-Oct, W-Sun Nov-Apr; tours 11-5:30, tasting to 6; tasting fee.* This modern winery is reached by crossing a wooden bridge spanning a scenic duck pond surrounded by beautiful grounds. Its walls were built with stones gathered on the site, and its arched roofs and doorways are said to be inspired by the caves in Champagne, France. For tasting, visitors are seated at tiny tables covered with French floral cloths in a bar area called **Vins Le Salon**. There champagne may be purchased by the glass; a variety of champagne cocktails are also available. Complimentary bread and cheese are provided to help keep things steady. Children are allowed in the salon and may order mineral water or orange juice. See also p.104.

The Silverado Trail

Pine Ridge Winery *5901 Silverado Trail, 707/253-7500; tasting Tu-Sun 11-4; tours by appt.* The tiny tasting room here is a pleasant place to sample the premium Cabernets produced by this winery's Stags Leap regional grapes. A pleasant picnic area is situated under a young grove of tall pines, and two board swings await the kiddies.

Rutherford Hill Winery *200 Rutherford Hill Dr., Rutherford, 707/963-7175; tasting & tours daily 10:30-4:30; tasting fee.* A sylvan hillside picnic area, with spacious tables sheltered by old oaks, beckons across the street from the tasting room.

ST. HELENA

■ *VISITOR INFORMATION*

St. Helena Chamber of Commerce *P.O. Box 124, (1080 Main St.), St. Helena 94574, 707/963-4456.*

Note: St. Helena Highway, Main Street, and Highway 29 are all the same road.

■ *GETTING THERE*

Located on Highway 29 approximately 15 miles north of Yountville.

■ *WHERE TO STAY*

El Bonita Motel *195 Main Street., 707/963-3216; 2/$-$$, 4/$$-$$$; cribs; all TVs; some kitchens, bathtubs; unheated pool.* Decorated in art deco style, this motel has a shaded, grassy pool area and offers an alternative to classy, cutesy, and expensive Wine Country lodging.

Harvest Inn *One Main St., 707/963-WINE; 2-4/$$$+; 2-night minimum on weekends; cribs; all TVs, bathtubs; some fireplaces; continental breakfast; 2 heated pools, 2 jacuzzis.* Situated on a 21-acre working vineyard, this recently built English Tudor-style inn has beautifully landscaped grounds complete with a koi pool and ducks. Rooms are furnished with antiques.

Meadowood Resort & Hotel *900 Meadowood Lane, 800/458-8080, 707/963-3646; 2-4/$$$+; 2-night minimum on weekends; children under 12 free; cribs; TVs, refrigerators; some fireplaces, bathtubs; room service, 2 restaurants; heated pool (unavail. in winter), 6 tennis courts (fee).* This luxury resort allows guests an escape from reality. Facilities on the 256 acres of lush, wooded grounds include a 9-

hole golf course, children's playground, parcourse, four croquet lawns, and seven miles of hiking trails. The resort also operates a Wine School; a package—which includes classes, winery tours, meals, and lodging—is sometimes offered. Lodging is mostly in cabins, but a few hotel rooms are also available.

♥ **Sutter Home Inn** *225 St. Helena Highway, 707/963-4423; 2/$$$-$$$+; 2-night minimum on weekends; unsuitable for children under 14; all fireplaces; some bathtubs, refrigerators; continental breakfast.* Located next door to **Sutter Home Winery** *(707/963-3104; tasting daily 10-4:30; no tours),* this Victorian mansion was built by the winery's original owner in 1874. It was completely renovated in 1987 (before that it was known as the Chalet Bernensis Inn). Five antique-furnished rooms are distributed between the main house and the adjacent Water Tower and Carriage House. The inn is surrounded by a classic Victorian garden with a picnic area.

♥ **The Wine Country Inn** *1152 Lodi Lane, 707/963-7077; 2/$$$-$$$+; 2-night minimum on some rooms; unsuitable for children under 13; some refrigerators, fireplaces (usable Oct-Apr only); continental breakfast; solar heated pool (Apr-Oct), jacuzzi.* Built in the style of a New England inn, this attractive, quiet lodging is located back from the main highway on top of a small country hill. Rooms are decorated with floral wallpapers and tasteful antiques, and many have views of the surrounding vineyards and hills. A filling breakfast, served on attractive handmade crockery, includes homemade granola and breads. A particularly interesting antique shop, **The Arbor** *(1095 Lodi Lane, Th-Sun 11-5)*, is operated inside an old stone-walled building located within easy walking distance.

■ *WHERE TO EAT*

♥ **Auberge Du Soleil** *180 Rutherford Hill Rd., Rutherford, 707/963-1211; B/L/D daily; reservations suggested; $$$; MC,V.* Located off The Silverado Trail near the Rutherford Hill Winery, this elegant French restaurant has plush inside seating as well as more rustic seating outside on a veranda overlooking the valley. Three-course dinners are fixed-price; lunch is a la carte with a two course minimum. The beautifully executed dishes change regularly. A memorable luncheon I enjoyed here included quail eggs in aspic, beef strips in black truffle sauce, and hazelnut souffle. In 1985 a luxury resort was added. Sandy Walker was the architect, Michael Taylor the interior designer. Call for more information.

♥ **Miramonte Restaurant** *1327 Railroad Ave., 707/963-3970; D W-Sun, closed part of Dec & Jan; reservations suggested; $$$; no cards.* The five-course, fixed-price nouvelle dinners at this well-reviewed restaurant change each week and tend to be very unusual and interesting. The chef is celebrated for sophisticated French dishes; appetizers and fish items are particularly well-prepared. The cozy dining rooms are attractively decorated and feature beamed ceilings, antler chandeliers, and walls covered with tapestries depicting hunting scenes. In warm weather, patio seating is available.

Vines *3111 N. St. Helena Highway, 2 miles north of town, 707/963-8991; cafe: L/D W-M, $-$$; restaurant: L W-Sat, SunBr, D W-M, $$-$$$; booster seats; reservations suggested; AE,MC,V.* This new restaurant, which features on-going exhibitions of contemporary artists, is really two restaurants in one. Downstairs is a casual cafe where the menu offers sandwiches, salads, some interesting pastas, and wood-oven pizzas. Upstairs is an elegant restaurant with a more pricey menu. Offerings include such delights as fritters made with pinenuts, basil, and red pepper seeds; a trio of chilled salmon—poached, smoked, and marinated; and roast rack of lamb with a rich sauce made from soy and Thai herbs. Pizzas and pastas are also available. Desserts change daily, and the chef ends a meal upstairs by sending a spoon to each diner half-filled with a dense chocolate sauce. The extensive wine list features over 100 local vintages. Live piano music is scheduled each evening, and Sunday brunch features a jazz band. This restaurant is part of **Vintners Village**, which when completed will house tasting rooms for some of the area's smaller wineries and a delicatessen. A picnic area is available on a scenic hill in back.

■ *PICNIC PICK-UPS*

Napa Valley Olive Oil Manufacturing Co. *835 McCorkle Ave. (Charter Oak/Allison), 707/963-4173; daily 8-5.* In addition to the house cold press olive oil and homemade red wine vinegar, you can purchase everything you need for a picnic: cheese, sausage, olives, etc. This Old World-style Italian deli also offers a variety of pastas, sauces, and dried mushrooms—all placed helter-skelter in barrels and on make-shift tables. It's really quite unusual. A picnic area is available outside.

Oakville Grocery *7856 Highway 29, Oakville, 707/944-8802; daily 10-6.* Everything needed to put together a fantastic gourmet picnic can be found here. Select from a large variety of mustards, vinegars, jams, fresh fruits, imported beers, mineral waters, natural juices, cheeses, and other deli items as well as smoked poissons, cornichons, sausages, and a large assortment of enticing desserts.

■ *WHAT TO DO*

Bale Grist Mill State Historic Park *3369 Highway 29, 3 miles north of town, 707/942-4575; daily 10-5; adults $1, 6-17 50¢.* Reached via a shaded, paved streamside path, this grist mill ground grain for farmers from the 1840s through the turn of the century. The damp site and slow-turning millstones were reputedly responsible for the exceptional cornmeal produced here. Now interpretive displays are located inside the gable-roofed mill house, and the state hopes soon to restore the 45-foot waterwheel to full operation.

Barrel Builders *1085 Lodi Lane, 707/963-7914; M-F 8-5, Sat 10-2.* The wooden barrels are actually assembled in Missouri and Kentucky, but this cooperage shaves, repairs, and sells them. Redwood hot tubs and miniature vinegar casks are also available.

Dansk Designs *801 Main St., 707/963-4273; daily 9-6.* For description, see p.60.

Lake Berryessa *take Highway 128 east, 707/966-2111.* This man-made lake is over 25 miles long, 3 miles wide, and has 165 miles of shoreline. Boats and waterskis may be rented, and the swimming and fishing are excellent. Camping and resort facilities are also available.

Silverado Museum *1490 Library Lane, 707/963-3757; Tu-Sun 12-4; free.* This museum, housed in the St. Helena Public Library, contains over 7,900 pieces of Robert Louis Stevenson memorabilia—including paintings, sculptures, and manuscripts as well as his childhood set of lead soldiers. I suggest a family read-in of *A Child's Garden of Verses* or *Treasure Island* before or after this visit. The modern stucco library building, situated on the edge of a scenic vineyard, also contains the **Napa Valley Wine Library**.

■ *WINERIES*

Beaulieu Vineyard *1960 St. Helena Highway, Rutherford, 707/963-1451; tasting daily 10-4; tours 10-3.* Founded in 1900 by Frenchman Georges deLatour, this winery is known for its Cabernet Sauvignon, Chardonnay, Pinot Noir, and Sauvignon Blanc.

Beringer Vineyards *2000 Main St., just north of town, 707/963-4812; tours 10-5 June-Sept, 9:30-4 Oct-May; tasting follows tour.* This winery is noted for its Chardonnay, Cabernet, and White Zinfandel. Its Visitor's Center is located in the Tudor **Rhine House**—a beautiful oak-paneled, stained-glass-laden reproduction of a 19th century German mansion. Unfortunately, picnicking is not permitted on the beautifully landscaped grounds.

The Christian Brothers Greystone Cellars *2555 Main St., just north of town, 707/967-3112; tours 10-4:30 in summer, 10-4 in winter; tasting follows tour.* This magnificent landmark winery building is constructed of locally quarried volcanic stone. Part of **Brother Timothy's corkscrew collection** is on display, and for a $5 fee visitors may participate in a **barrel tasting** held three times daily. In addition to its commercial wines (including a noteworthy Cabernet Sauvignon, barrel-fermented Chardonnay, and Zinfandel Port), the winery still produces sacramental wines. Winery revenues are used to help operate The Christian Brothers Schools.

Freemark Abbey *3022 St. Helena Highway North, 707/963-9694; tasting daily 10-4:30; tour at 2.* The tasting room here is inside a large, lodge-like room with oriental carpets covering its hardwood floor. An operating fireplace and comfortable furniture invite a leisurely sampling. Nearby the **Hurd Beeswax Candles shop** *(M-F 10-5, Sat & Sun to 5:30)* offers open views of its factory. Be sure to see the active beehive hidden behind two wooden window covers.

Spring Mountain Vineyards *2805 Spring Mountain Rd., 707/963-5233; tasting daily 10-4; tours by appointment (weekdays at 10:30 & 2:30, weekends 10:30); grounds tours daily 11-4, on the hour.* Located off the main highway on a scenic sideroad, this winery is known for the Victorian manor house made famous in the opening scenes of TV's *Falcon Crest.* The house, a private residence, is not included on the winery tour but can be easily seen from the tasting room. Fans may be pleased to know that some of the less expensive wines (the winery is known for its pricey Chardonnays and Cabernet Sauvignons) have labels sporting pictures of "the house." Unfortunately, no picnicking is allowed on the scenic, spacious grounds.

V. Sattui Winery *White Lane, 707/963-7774; daily 9-5.* V. Sattui wines are sold only at the winery. Taste them while selecting picnic supplies from the well-stocked deli—said to have the largest selection of international cheeses on the West Coast. Then step outside and enjoy your selections in the spacious picnic area.

The Silverado Trail

Rutherford Hill Winery *200 Rutherford Hill Rd., Rutherford, 707/963-7194; tasting daily 10:30-4:30; tours at 11:30, 1, and 2:30.* The tour here includes the largest wine-aging caves in the U.S. Across from the tasting room, a wonderful hillside picnic area boasts plenty of tables sheltered by old oak trees and a pleasant view of the valley.

CALISTOGA

■ *A LITTLE BACKGROUND*

Often referred to as "the Hot Springs of the West," Calistoga is enjoying a renaissance as a popular weekend and summer retreat. The name originated from a combination of *California* and *Saratoga* (a New York spa area). For more on the town's history, I suggest reading *The Silverado Squatters* by Robert Louis Stevenson.

The town sits on top of a hot underground river. Its many unpretentious spas are geared to helping visitors relax, unwind, and get healthy in pools filled from hot springs. Most offer services such as mud baths, steam baths, and massages, and many make their mineral pools available for day use for a small fee.

Don't miss taking a **mud bath**. The mud is made from a mixture of volcanic ash (collected from nearby Mount St. Helena), peat moss, and naturally heated mineral water. After a period of nude immersion, the bather takes a mineral bath, a steam bath, and then, swaddled in dry blankets, rests and cools. Ahhh.

■ *VISITOR INFORMATION*

Calistoga Chamber of Commerce *1458 Lincoln Ave. #4, Calistoga 94515, 707/942-6333.*

■ *GETTING THERE*

Located on Highway 29 approximately 10 miles north of St. Helena.

■ *WHERE TO STAY*

Calistoga Spa Hot Springs *1006 Washington St., 707/942-6269; 2-4/ $$-$$$; 2-night minimum on weekends; children under 1 free; cribs; all TVs, refrigerators; some kitchens; room service; 3 pools, jacuzzi.* This conveniently located spa offers both motel rooms and cottages, plus three pools: a 105-degree covered jacuzzi, a 100-degree open-air mineral pool, and an interesting 85-degree Roman olympic outdoor pool. Mud baths, mineral baths, steam baths, and massage are available.

Dr. Wilkinson's Hot Springs *1507 Lincoln Ave., 707/942-4102; 2-4/ $$; 2-night minimum on weekends; children under 4 free; cribs; all TVs; some kitchens, bathtubs; 1 indoor pool, 2 outdoor pools, jacuzzi, steam room.* Operated by the Wilkinson family, this pleasant spa features an indoor 104-degree mineral pool with a view of the nearby foothills, a cooler 92-degree outdoor mineral pool, and a refreshing 82-degree outdoor swimming pool. Pools are not open to non-guests. Mud baths, mineral baths, steam baths, and massage are available. Lodging is in motel units. Cottages are also available nearby, but children are not permitted.

Mountain Home Ranch *3400 Mountain Home Ranch Rd., 6 miles from town, 707/942-6616; 2/$-$$$, 4/$$-$$$; 2-night minimum in Aug;*

closed Dec-Jan; some kitchens; continental breakfast; unheated pool (unavail. Dec-Mar), 1 tennis court. Guests at this informal rural spot stay in their choice of modern cabins with either a private deck or porch, rustic cabins for which they provide their own bedding and linens, or lodge rooms. Summer activities include swimming, hiking, fishing, movies, campfires, dancing, and supervised activities for children. Rates are higher then and include both breakfast and dinner.

Mount View Hotel *1457 Lincoln Ave., 707/942-6877; 2/$$-$$$+; 2-night minimum on summer weekends; cribs; some bathtubs; full breakfast, restaurant; heated pool (unheated Dec-Mar), jacuzzi.* This beautifully restored hotel, built in 1918 and decorated in a '30s art deco style, is a National Historic Monument. The accomplished kitchen serves breakfast, lunch, and dinner daily and offers an imaginative menu of California cuisine and really spectacular desserts. In good weather mesquite barbecues are offered in the attractive outdoor pool area, and live entertainment is often scheduled in the lounge. Special events centered around food and wine are held regularly, and packages are available.

■ *WHERE TO EAT*

Calistoga Inn *1250 Lincoln Ave., 707/942-4101; L/D daily; highchairs, booster seats; reservations advised; $$$; MC,V.* The specialty here is simply-treated seafood, and the menu changes daily. Consider grilled catfish with tomatoes and garlic, grilled thresher shark with red bell pepper sauce, or ceviche of barracuda. Duck, veal, steak, and a pasta are also usually on the menu, as are irresistable desserts such as Santa Rosa plum sorbet, and raspberries with chocolate creme fraiche. An informal **brew pub** operating in the bar area offers a Pilsner-style lager (the house specialty) and hearty pub food. Modest, inexpensive lodging is available upstairs; several adjoining rooms are suitable for families.

Cinnabar Cafe *1440 Lincoln Ave., 707/942-6989; B/L/D daily; highchairs, booster seats; $$; AE,MC,V.* Attractive and unpretentious, this spot serves reasonably priced, honest food. Breakfast is the expected items plus a large assortment of omelettes, sauteed fresh boned trout, buttermilk or buckwheat pancakes, and homemade granola. Lunch includes homemade soups and breads and a large variety of sandwiches and hamburgers. Dinner is a pricier selection of fresh fish, lobster, and prime rib.

Silverado Restaurant *1374 Lincoln, 707/942-6725; B/L/D daily; highchairs, booster seats, children's portions; $$; MC,V.* Comfortable booths with views of the sidewalk parade combine with fresh and tasty food to make this a pleasant spot to dine. Lunch is informal with a menu of hamburgers, sandwiches, omelettes, and homemade soups and desserts as well as a large selection of non-alcoholic drinks and alcoholic fruit daiquiris. Dinner is more upscale and features mesquite-grilled items.

The Village Green *1413 Lincoln Ave., 707/942-0330; B/L daily, D M,Tu,F,Sat; highchairs, boosters seats; $; no cards.* This place has been around almost forever and has an informal, unpretentious atmosphere with comfortable booths and counter seating. Short-order items dominate the menu and include hamburgers, homemade French fries with the skins still on, spaghetti, design-your-own-omelettes, and ice cream fountain goodies.

■ *WHAT TO DO*

Bothe-Napa Valley State Park *3601 Highway 29, 707/942-4575; daily 8-dusk; $3/car.* You can picnic, camp, hike, fish, and swim in the pool (summer only) in this lovely park.

Calistoga Soaring Center *1546 Lincoln Ave., 707/942-5592; daily 9-dusk; $60/1 person, $80/2; reservations suggested on weekends.* The 20-minute glider ride/sightseeing trip covers approximately ten miles. It reaches altitudes of up to 2,500 feet and speeds of up to 70-

miles-per-hour. Longer flights are available, as are introductory lessons and a *Top Gun* aerobatic glider flight for one.

Old Faithful Geyser *1299 Tubbs Lane, 707/942-6463; daily 9-dusk; adults $2.50, 6-11 $1.* One of only three geysers in the world that erupt regularly and merit the name *Old Faithful* (the other two are in Yellowstone National Park in Wyoming and on North Island in New Zealand), this geyser erupts approximately every 40 minutes and shoots 350-degree water 60 to 150 feet in the air in a show that lasts three to four minutes. The idyllic site, where chickens roam freely, is located in the crater of an extinct volcano. Plenty of picnic tables are available.

Petrified Forest *4100 Petrified Forest Rd., 4 miles west of town, 707/942-6667; daily 9-6, in winter 10-5; adults $3, under 10 free.* A self-guided 1/4-mile path leads through this unusual 502-acre forest. Open to the public since 1860, it contains petrified redwood trees over 6 million years old and as long as 126 feet. Facilities include a small museum and picnic tables.

Sharpsteen Museum and Sam Brannan Cottage *1311 Washington St., 707/942-5911; daily in summer 10-4, rest of year 12-4; free.* This exceptionally well-designed museum displays an elaborate and extensive diorama of Calistoga as it appeared in 1865, when Sam Brannan opened the town's first spa and began its career as a resort area. The beautifully furnished cottage displays the style in which wealthy San Franciscans lived when they vacationed here in the late 1800s.

Smith's Mount St. Helena Trout Farm *18401 Ida Clayton Rd., 707/987-3651; Sat & Sun 10-6, Feb-May; also F & M June-Sept.* All ages can enjoy fishing on this lake. Poles and bait are free. The charge for fish caught is determined by size; cleaning and packaging are included.

■ *WINERIES*

Chateau Montelena Winery *1429 Tubbs Lane, 707/942-5105; tasting daily 10-4; tours at 11 & 2.* Noted for its Chardonnay and Cabernet Sauvignon, this hard-to-find winery offers an unusual picnic area. Small Jade Lake holds two islets, reached via footbridge, which in turn hold miniature picnic pagodas. It is stocked with ducks and geese and even a berthed Chinese junk. Reservations must be made for the picnic facilities. Parents take note: crayons and paper are provided to entertain antsy children while you are sampling in the stone tasting room.

Sterling Vineyards

Clos Pegase Winery *1060 Dunaweal Lane, 707/942-4981; tasting daily 10:30-4:30; fee includes souvenir glass; no tours.* Because of its desert-colored, stark stucco architecture, this new winery opened in 1987 amid much controversy. Surrounded by young vineyards, with tall, thin cypress trees lining its outdoor walkway, it has a surreal quality.

Sterling Vineyards *1111 Dunaweal Lane, 707/942-5151; tasting and self-guided tour daily 10:30-4:30; gondola ride: adults $5, under 16 free.* Accessible to the public only via a four-minute gondola ride, this winery was built to resemble a Greek monastery. It features stunning and unusual white stucco, cubist architecture. Spectacular views of the Napa Valley are afforded throughout the self-guided winery tour. For tasting, visitors are seated at tables in a spacious interior room or on an outdoor terrace, and each adult is given a $2 credit toward the purchase of Sterling wines. A picnic area is available at the base of the hill.

CLEAR LAKE

■ *A LITTLE BACKGROUND*

Spring-fed Clear Lake is the largest fresh-water lake totally within California. (Lake Tahoe is partially in Nevada.) It measures 25 miles by 8 miles. The 70-mile drive around the perimeter takes 2 1/2 to 3 hours.

From the 1870s into the early 1900s, this area was world-famous for its health spas and huge luxury resort hotels. Then, for various reasons, it fell into a state of disrepair and slowly lost its acclaim. Now it is basically a reasonably-priced family resort area. Lake County's first traffic light was installed in 1982, and there are still no parking meters.

Clear Lake is situated on volcanic terrain, which gives it an unusual physical appearance and a profusion of hot springs. Many years ago the Pomo Indians lived here. They had a legend which said that if there is no snow on 4,200-foot Mount Konocti in April, the volcano will erupt. If you heed legends, be sure to check the April snowfall before you make your vacation reservations.

■ VISITOR INFORMATION

Lake County Chamber of Commerce *875 Lakeport Blvd., Lakeport 95453, 707/263-6131.*

■ GETTING THERE

Located approximately 50 miles north of St. Helena via Highway 29. This scenic route goes through the heart of the Wine Country. The rolling hills are strewn with blooming wild flowers during the spring and with brilliantly colored foliage during the fall. Make the drive during daylight; this two-lane road is tedious and dangerous to drive at night, and you also miss the lovely scenery.

An alternate route follows Highway 101 north to Highway 175 east.

■ WHERE TO STAY

Jules Resort *14195 Lakeshore Dr., Clearlake, 707/994-6491; 2-4/$-$$; 1 week minimum July-Sept; cribs; all TVs, kitchens; pool, sauna.* Stay in a pleasant old cabin, and sunbathe by a lakefront pool. Facilities include a game room, private beach, fishing pier, and launching ramp; a super miniature golf course is just across the street. This place is so popular in the summer that you have to book at least one year in advance.

Konocti Harbor Inn *8727 Soda Bay Rd., Kelseyville, 800/862-4930, 707/279-4281; 2/$$-$$$+, 4/$$$-$$$+; children under 12 free; cribs; all TVs; some kitchens, bathtubs, lake views; 2 restaurants; 2 heated pools, (unavail. Nov-May), 2 wading pools; 8 tennis courts (fee/night lights).* Nestled in the shadow of Mount Konocti on the rim of the lake, this beautifully landscaped resort enjoys a superb setting. It is reminiscent of luxury resorts in Hawaii but is a lot easier to reach and much less expensive. The list of facilities is extensive: tennis lessons, a children's playground, a teenage recreation room, a running/bike trail, feature films, a bar with live music in the evenings, a paddlewheel boat cruise (fee), a miniature golf course (fee), and a marina which rents equipment for fishing, waterskiing, and paddle boating. The resort even has its own gas station. In the summer college students are hired to run day camps for children ages 5 to 12; babysitting can ususally be arranged for younger children. Tennis, golf, and fishing packages are available. The dining room has stunning lake views, offers an Italian continental menu, and is comfortably set up for children. A coffee shop serves more informal meals.

Skylark Motel *1120 N. Main St., Lakeport, 707/263-6151; 2/$-$$, 4/ $$; all TVs; some kitchens, lake views; heated pool.* These modern motel units and cottages are located lakefront. The spacious, well-maintained grounds feature a large lawn area, swings, and a wading area in the lake.

Will-o-Point Resort *1 First St., Lakeport, 707/263-5407; 2-4/$$; cribs; all TVs, kitchens; some lake views; restaurant.* The attractive cabins at this thirteen-acre waterfront resort are bargains when rented by groups of four to eight people. Campsites and RV hookups are also available. Facilities include a fishing pier, boat ramp, bait and tackle shop, boat rentals, recreation room, and sandy beach. A public park equipped with a tennis court, waterfront playground, children's wading pool, and roped-off lake swimming area is adjacent.

■ *WHERE TO STAY NEARBY*

Wilbur Hot Springs Health Sanctuary *at Highways 16 & 20, 22 miles west of Williams, 916/473-2306; $25+/person; day use $10; reservations necessary.* Soaking in one of the four hot sulphurous springwater tubs and then plunging into the cool water of the outdoor pool is the main activity here. Clothing is optional. For the ambitious, there are also walks in the surrounding forested hills. Lodging is available in both dormitory-style shared rooms and private rooms. Evening light is provided by kerosene lamps, heat by wood-burning stoves. A communal parlor has a pool table and piano, and guests prepare their own meals in the large kitchen.

■ *WHAT TO DO*

Fishing, hunting, swimming, boating, rock hunting, golfing, and water-skiing are the big activities here.

Nice lakefront public parks and beaches are located in Lakeport and Clearlake.

■ *WINERIES*

Kendall-Jackson Winery *600 Matthews Rd., Lakeport, 707/263-5299; tasting daily in summer 11-5, call for winter hours; no tours.* This winery produces mostly whites. Sampling occurs in a rustic tasting room, and there is a large grassy play area for kids. A picnic arbor overlooking the vineyards is invitingly situated among shady walnut trees.

Konocti Winery *Highway 29/Thomas Dr., Kelseyville, 707/279-8861; tasting M-Sat 10-5, Sun 11-5; tours by appt.* Located midway between Kelseyville and Lakeport, this winery offers a grassy picnic area and a summer music festival.

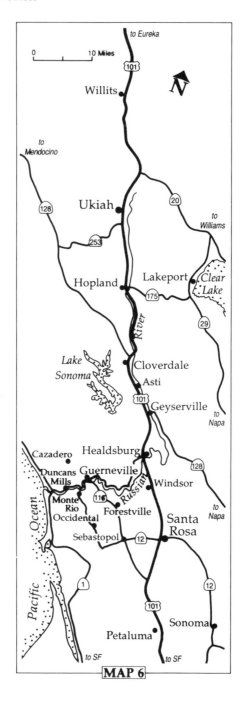

MAP 6

101 NORTH

SANTA ROSA

■ *A LITTLE BACKGROUND*

Santa Rosa is not a tourist mecca, but it is a convenient base for touring the Wine Country.

■ *VISITOR INFORMATION*

Santa Rosa Chamber of Commerce *637 First St., Santa Rosa 95404, 707/545-1414.*

Sonoma County Farm Trails *PO Box 6674, Santa Rosa 95406.* This helpful map leads you to local farms which sell directly to the consumer. For a free copy send a stamped, self-addressed legal-size envelope.

■ *ANNUAL EVENTS*

Scottish Gathering and Games *August; 415/897-4422.* The oldest and largest gathering of the clans outside of Scotland, this event features a variety of competitions—including the popular **Caber Tossing Championships** in which a piece of wood the size of a telephone pole is tossed end-over-end for accuracy.

■ *GETTING THERE*

Located approximately 60 miles north of San Francisco. Take Highway 101 all the way.

■ *WHERE TO STAY*

Sheraton Round Barn Inn *3555 Round Barn Blvd., 800/833-9595, 707/523-7555; 2-4/$$-$$$+; children under 18 free; cribs; all TVs, bathtubs; some refrigerators; room service, 2 restaurants; heated pool, jacuzzi, 5 tennis courts nearby (fee).* Sprawled on one of the few hills in town, this comfortable modern motel has jogging trails and a nearby golf course.

Vintners Inn *4350 Barnes Rd., 800/421-2584, 707/575-7350; 2-4/$$$-$$$+; children under 6 free; cribs; all TVs, bathtubs; some refrigerators, fireplaces; room service, continental breakfast, restaurant; jacuzzi.* This elegant country inn is surrounded by a 50-acre working vineyard. All rooms are decorated with European antiques. The highly acclaimed **John Ash & Co.** *(707/527-7687)* restaurant is located right next door.

■ *WHERE TO EAT*

Brass Ass Saloon *1529 Farmers Lane (in Alpha Beta Plaza), 707/575-8553; L/D daily; highchairs, booster seats; $; no cards.* Enjoy a tasty pizza or calzone (pizza turnover) in a friendly atmosphere. A variety of sandwiches, a salad bar, and a good selection of beers round out the menu. Comfy wooden booths are great when you have kids in tow, and a juke box and pool table provide entertainment.

Polka Dots *115 Fourth St., 707/575-9080; B/L/D daily; highchairs, booster seats; $$; MC,V.* Situated inside an historic brick building, the dining room here is light and airy. Tables are covered with butcher paper, and diners are encouraged to entertain themselves by doodling with a cupful of crayons. I favor breakfast because of the selection of freshly baked breads—huge cinnamon rolls, "mega" muffins, scones, biscuits—all made in the restaurant's own kitchen. Delicious "scrambles" consist of eggs scrambled to perfection with a variety of tasty ingredients. The lunch/dinner menu includes salads, sandwiches, hamburgers, and ice cream specialties.

Willie Bird's Restaurant *1150 Santa Rosa Ave., 707/542-0861; B/L/D daily; highchairs, booster seats, children's portions; $; AE,MC,V.* This casual restaurant celebrates Thanksgiving every day by serving their tasty, natural brand of turkey in varied forms. You can get the Willie Bird Special—the traditional turkey feast—or something more unusual like turkey scallopini or turkey sausage. Children's portions include a turkey hamburger and hot dog. Plenty of non-turkey items are also available.

■ *WHAT TO DO*

The Church of One Tree/Robert L. Ripley Memorial Museum *492 Sonoma Ave., 707/576-5233; W-Sun 11-4, closed Nov-Feb; adults $1, 7-17 50¢.* Believe it or not, Robert Ripley was born, raised, and buried in Santa Rosa! On display in this museum dedicated to his memory are a wax reincarnation of Ripley as well as some of his original drawings and personal effects. A few oddities mentioned in his columns are also displayed, including stuffed Siamese twin calves and a 45-inch white rhinoceros horn. The museum is located inside the Church of One Tree—built in 1873 from the wood of a single redwood tree! The museum opens onto the beautifully landscaped gardens of **Julliard Park**. A self-guided tour of the park's unusual trees may be enjoyed with a brochure available at the museum.

Howarth Memorial Park *Summerfield Rd., access from Sonoma Ave. and Montgomery Dr.; rides operate daily in summer 10-1, 2-6.* There is something for everyone in this scenic park. Children especially enjoy the playground, miniature train ride, animal farm, pony rides, and merry-go-round. There are also paddleboat, rowboat, and sailboat rentals on Lake Ralphine, plus hiking trails and tennis courts.

Kyoto Koi & Garden Center *2783 Guerneville Rd., 707/575-9223; daily 9-5.* Visitors are welcome to stroll along gravel paths in the peaceful Japanese garden located inside this commercial nursery. You can even sit for awhile beside the man-made waterfall and reflect upon nature. Japanese music sets the mood for browsing among the traditional plants and bonsai. For a quarter, you can buy feed for the colorful koi fish. Prices for the koi range from ten for $1 (feeder goldfish) to $350 and up (ten- to twenty-year-olds).

Luther Burbank Memorial Garden *Santa Rosa/Sonoma Aves., 707/576-5115; gardens open daily 8-5, free; house tours Apr-Oct, W-Sun 10-3:30, adults $1, under 12 free.* During his 50-year horticultural career, Luther Burbank developed over 800 plants. This memorial garden displays many of his achievements, including the tasty Santa Rosa plum, the ornamental Shasta daisy, and a warren of spineless cacti. Mr. Burbank is buried in an unmarked grave at the base of a towering Cedar of Lebanon which he planted at the turn of the century. Tours of his modified Greek Revival-style home last 1/2 hour.

Railroad Square *centered at Fourth/Davis Sts.* Now a national historic district, this area is filled with antique stores, restaurants, and specialty shops. The **Hotel La Rose** *(707/579-3200; 2/$$-$$$)* features turn-of-the-century charm combined with modern conveniences. The

Xcelsior Brewery *(99 Sixth St.; tasting daily 12-5)* brews its Acme Beer on the premises and offers free tours when they aren't too busy. Beer-to-go is kept chilled in an antique ice box. The **Marquee Theatre** *(15 Third St., 707/545-1906; Th-Sat at 7:30, Sun at 2; tickets $3-$7)* presents melodrama and vaudeville programs. And the **Daily Planet** *(Fifth/Davis Sts., 707/578-1205)* presents live comedy and dancing in the evenings.

Redwood Empire Ice Arena *1667 W. Steele Lane, 707/546-7147; daily, call for schedule; adults $5, 12-17 $4.50, under 12 $4, includes skates.* Since this ice arena is owned by cartoonist Charles Schulz, the Alpine decor is somewhat surprising. However, the fast-food coffee shop does have a few stained-glass windows depicting Snoopy, and there is a **Snoopy Gift Shop** *(daily 10-6)* with an extensive selection of *Peanuts* goodies. Schulz has an office on the premises and is frequently sighted by skaters.

Sonoma County Museum *425 7th St., 707/579-1500; W-Sun 11-4; adults $1, under 12 50¢.* Located inside the city's beautifully restored 1910 post office building, this museum exhibits material relating to the county's history.

Victorian Homes. Take a drive along MacDonald Avenue. Located in the older part of town, this street is the area's Beverly Hills and features lovely Victorian mansions.

GUERNEVILLE/RUSSIAN RIVER

■ *A LITTLE BACKGROUND*

Once upon a time in the '20s and '30s this was a summer resort area favored by wealthy San Franciscans who traveled here by ferry and train. Then it faded in popularity and became a pleasant and uncrowded retreat. Today, slowly recovering from a state of decay, it is regaining its former popularity. The area has also become very popular with gays, and many resorts catering exclusively to this group have opened.

Guerneville, the area's hub, is surrounded by many smaller towns. There are numerous public beaches, but many more are privately owned and not open to the public. Also, there are many unofficial nude beaches. Inquire when in town so that you may find or avoid them, depending on your attitude.

■ *VISITOR INFORMATION*

Russian River Region Visitors Center *P.O. Box 255, (14034 Armstrong Woods Rd.), Guerneville 95446, 800/253-8800, 707/869-9009.*

Russian River Wine Road *P.O. Box 127, Geyserville 95441, 707/433-6935.* This free map provides details on wineries from Forestville to Cloverdale.

■ *ANNUAL EVENTS*

Slug Fest *March; 707/869-9033.* This unusual festival features banana slug races and a recipe contest bake-off.

Bohemian Grove *last two weeks of July.* Many of the world's most powerful political, military, and corporate leaders meet at this 2,700-acre private resort. The public is not invited.

Gravenstein Apple Fair *August; in Sebastopol, 707/544-GRAV.* Held on and off since the turn of the century, this old-time country fair celebrates the Gravenstein apple which is indigenous to the area.

Jazz Festival *September; 707/887-1502.*

■ *GETTING THERE*

Located approximately 15 miles west of Santa Rosa. Take Highway 12 west to Highway 116 north.

■ *WHERE TO STAY*

Brookside Lodge and Motel *Highway 116/Brookside Lane, 707/869-2470; 2/$-$$$+, 4/$$-$$$+; children under 3 free; cribs; all TVs; some kitchens, fireplaces, bathtubs; heated pool, jacuzzi, sauna.* Accommodations are in a choice of motel rooms or cottages and facilities include a playground, recreation room, and spacious, attractive grounds.

Johnson's Beach & Resort *16241 First St., 707/869-2022; 2-4/$; closed Oct-May; all TVs, refrigerators; some river views.* Some of these rustic old hotel rooms and cabins are located right on the river. Reservations are taken only for stays of at least a week, but rooms are often available at the last minute on a first-come, first-served basis. The beach, one of the best-equipped in the area, has a slide into the water, picnic tables, and rentals of boats and beach paraphernalia.

♥ **Ridenhour Ranch House Inn** *12850 River Rd., 707/887-1033; 2/ $$-$$$; closed Dec; 2-night minimum on weekends; unsuitable for children under 10; all TVs; some fireplaces, bathtubs; some shared baths; room service, full breakfast; jacuzzi.* This historic ranch house, built of redwood in 1906, is decorated with English and American antiques, quilts, and fresh flowers. Special dinners are prepared for guests upon request. Among the facilities are a cozy living room with fireplace and a croquet lawn. Secluded beaches are just a short walk away.

Riverlane Resort *16320 First St., 707/869-2323; 2/$, 4/$$-$$$; 2-night minimum on weekends; children under 1 free; cribs; all TVs, kitchens; some fireplaces, river views; heated pool (unavail. Nov-Mar), hot tub.* Located by the river, this pleasant enclave of cabins offers a private beach, recreational equipment, and movies in the evenings.

Southside Resort *13811 Highway 116, 707/869-2690; 2-4/$-$$; 1-week minimum in July & Aug; all kitchens; some TVs, fireplaces, bathtubs, river views.* Tucked under a bridge, these cheery yellow cottages provide bright dots of color on the woodsy grounds. A private beach has a shallow wading area safe for children, and recreational facilities include a playground, game area, and evening campfires and movies. Campsites are also available.

House Rentals. Call the Visitors Center for the names of realty companies which rent private homes to vacationers.

■ *WHERE TO STAY NEARBY*

♥ **Timberhill Ranch** *35755 Hauser Ridge, Cazadero, 13 miles west of town, 707/847-3258; 2/$$$+; 2-night minimum; unsuitable for children; all refrigerators, fireplaces; heated pool (summer only), jacuzzi, tennis courts.* Ten modern cedar cottages offer a quiet retreat on this 80-acre working ranch. A six-course dinner and full breakfast are included in the room rates.

■ *WHERE TO EAT*

Cazanoma Lodge *1000 Kidd Creek Rd., Cazadero, 13 miles west of town, 707/632-5255; Mar-May, D F-Sun & SunBr; May-Sept D also on W & Th; closed Dec-Feb; highchairs, booster seats, children's portions; reservations suggested; $$; AE,MC,V.* German specialties include barbecue spareribs and a sausage platter with sauerkraut, but the really unusual item at this 1926 lodge-turned-restaurant is **catch-your-own-trout**. That's right. Customers here have the option of catching their own trout from the adjacent pond—to make sure it's really fresh. For the unimpressed, the kitchen will do the job with a net. Live music is sometimes scheduled on weekends. Medium-priced cabins and lodge rooms are also available May through September in this tranquil forest setting.

The Occidental Three *in Occidental, 10 miles south of town.* **Fiori's,** *707/823-8188;* **Negri's,** *707/823-5301;* **Union Hotel,** *707/874-3662.* All three of these restaurants serve multi-course, family-style Italian dinners. All have highchairs, booster seats, and a reasonable plate charge for small children. All are moderately priced and offer inexpensive ravioli and spaghetti dinners which include less side dishes. Reservations are suggested at prime dining times during the summer.

Skippy's Hacienda Inn *11190 McPeak Rd., Forestville, 7 miles southeast of town, 707/887-2366; D F-Sun Oct-June, also Th July-Sept; highchairs, booster seats, children's portions; reservations suggested; $$; no cards.* This comfortable restaurant has a steak and seafood menu and is famous for its jukebox filled with old tunes. All dinners include soup, salad, vegetable, potato, bread, dessert, and coffee! When making reservations ask for directions; it's difficult to find.

Topolos at Russian River Vineyards *5700 Highway 116, Forestville, 707/887-1562. Restaurant: L W-Sat, SunBr, D W-Sun, in summer L/D also on M; closed Jan; highchairs, booster seats, children's portions; reservations suggested; $$; AE,DC,MC,V. Winery: 707/887-2956; tasting daily 11-5; tours by appt.* In good weather diners are seated outdoors under grape arbors and umbrellas. In colder weather, tables are available inside an attractive old farm house. California and Greek dishes are the house specialty, but a hamburger is also available. A large selection of the winery's own vintages are available by the glass.

■ *WHAT TO DO*

Duncans Mills *10 miles west of town on Highway 116.* Once a lumber village, this town is now home to a number of cutesy shops, the attractive and inexpensive **Blue Heron Inn** vegetarian restaurant, a riverside campground with private beach, and horse rentals.

Kozlowski Farms *5566 Highway 116 North, Forestville, 7 miles southeast of town, 707/887-2104; daily 9-5.* This scenic farm has 50 acres of apple trees and 15 acres of assorted berries. In season the products may be purchased in bulk. Homemade juices, berry vinegars, wine jellies, and flavorful berry jams and apple butter made without sugar are available year-round at the farm's colorful produce stand.

Pee Wee Golf/J's Amusements *13803 Highway 116, 707/869-2887; daily in summer*. Various kiddie rides and entertainments await the family in search of cheap thrills.

Swimming. Anywhere you choose to lay your blanket on the banks of the Russian River is bound to be nice. A prime spot is under the Monte Rio bridge, where parking and beach access are free. Another choice spot is Johnson's Beach (see p.127). Canoe and paddle boat rentals and snack stands are available at both. The riverbed and beaches are covered with pebbles, so bring along waterproof shoes.

■ WINERIES

Korbel Champagne Cellars *13250 River Rd./Highway 116, 707/887-2294; tasting daily 9-4:30; tours daily 10-3, longer hours in summer; rose garden tours May-Nov, daily 9:30-3.* This winery is over a century old and produces champagne, brandy, and wine. An **Antique Rose Garden**, faithfully restored to its turn-of-the-century beauty, is filled with old-time flowers such as coral bells, primroses, and violets plus more than 200 varieties of roses.

Mark West Vineyards *7000 Trenton-Healdsburg Rd., Forestville, 7 miles southeast of town, 707/544-4813; tasting & tours daily 10-5.* Picnic benches are available on a lawn, and a deli provides snacks for purchase.

HEALDSBURG

■ VISITOR INFORMATION

Healdsburg Chamber of Commerce *217 Healdsburg Ave., Healdsburg 95448, 800/648-9922, 707/433-6935.*

■ ANNUAL EVENTS

Antique Apple Tasting *Sept-Oct;* **Sonoma Antique Apple Nursery,** *4395 Westside Rd., 707/433-6420; nursery open Tu,W,F,Sat 9-4:30 Jan-Mar, and by appt.* Are you fed up with mushy, tasteless apples? Then visit this free tasting of little-known apple varieties. Meet the spicy, flavorful, but not very pretty Spitzenburg—said by some to be the best tasting apple of all time. The crisp and tart Sierra Beauty and the sweet Stayman Winesap are also among the 20 varieties usually available for tasting. Bulk apples, a special blend of apple cider, and some potted trees are available for purchase, and orders are taken for bareroot trees to be delivered in February.

■ GETTING THERE

Located approximately 20 miles northeast of Guerneville.

■ WHERE TO STAY

Dry Creek Inn *198 Dry Creek Rd., 800/222-5784, 707/433-0300; 2-4/ $$; children under 16 free; all TVs; room service, continental breakfast, restaurant; heated pool.* Some rooms in this attractive new motel have waterbeds; all have a complimentary bottle of wine awaiting their occupants.

■ PICNIC PICK-UPS

Downtown Bakery and Creamery *308A Center St., 707/431-2719; W-M 9:30-6:30, Sun to 3.* Owner Lindsey Shere did time in the kitchen at Berkeley's renowned Chez Panisse. She also wrote the best-selling cookbook *Chez Panisse Desserts.* So the exceptional breads, pastries, and ice creams produced in her kitchen here are not a complete suprise. And what a pleasure to indulge in one of the old-fashioned milk shakes or sundaes on a hot Wine Country day.

The Salame Tree Deli *304 Center St., 707/433-7224; M-Sat 8-6:30, Sun 9-5:30; AE,MC,V.* Sandwiches are made-to-order at this old-time deli, and there is a large selection of supporting items.

■ WHAT TO DO
Boating.
Grani-Ann's Wine Country Kayaking *10070 Old Redwood Highway, Windsor, 707/838-7787; 9:30 & 2 on some summer Sundays; $29, lunch $6.50.* Swimmers of all ages may participate in these tours. The morning trip begins in Healdsburg and ends a leisurely three miles later at the **Hop Kiln Winery.** After lunch, a tour of the winery, and some tasting, the afternoon trip begins.

W.C. "Bob" Trowbridge Canoe Trips *20 Healdsburg Ave., 707/433-7247; daily 8-6 Apr-Oct; $32/canoe/day, dinner $5-$6; reservations necessary.* Trips are unguided, and children must be at least 6. The canoe fee includes life jackets, paddles, and canoe transport. An additional $1 per person provides a ride back to the starting point. An after-canoeing barbecue occurs from 4 to 7 each weekend and includes steak or chicken, vegetable, baked beans, salad, garlic bread, and beverage. Trowbridge has eight other rental sites along the river.

Swimming.
Healdsburg Memorial Beach *707/433-1625; 8-dusk; $2/car.* This is a choice spot to swim in the warm Russian River. In summer, the water temperature averages 70 to 75 degrees. A lifeguard is on duty from 10.

Healdsburg Memorial Pool *1024 Prince Ave., 707/431-3326; daily 1:30-5:30; adults $1.50, 6-17 75¢, under 6 50¢.* They keep the water warm here—between 80 and 90 degrees—and there is a wading pool for young children.

Timber Crest Farms *4791 Dry Creek Rd., 707/433-8251; M-F 8-5, also Sat in Dec 10-2.* The high-quality dried fruits available here are made without sulfur, preservatives, or additives. The usual are available as well as the unusual—tropical starfruit, red cherries, mission figs. Depending on the time of year, you can observe the fruit being harvested or prepared for packaging.

Windsor Waterworks *8225 Conde Lane, Windsor, 6 miles south of town, 707/838-7760; summer 10-8; adults $2, children $1, waterslides $2.50/half-hr.* The four 400-foot waterslides here have tunnels, 360-degree turns, and a 42-foot drop. In addition, there are swimming pools, volleyball courts, and shaded picnic facilities.

■ *WINERIES*

Dry Creek Vineyards *3770 Lambert Bridge Rd., 3 miles west of Highway 101, 707/433-1000; tasting daily 10:30-4:30; no tours.* The best time to visit here is at the annual **Spring Open House**. That's the time to bring a picnic and celebrate the season with live music and wine tasting. Call for current details. A pleasant picnic area is always available.

Piper Sonoma Cellars *11447 Old Redwood Highway, 707/433-8843; tasting & tours daily 10-5, Jan-Mar F-Sun only; tasting fee.* Celebrated for its French-style champagnes, this ultra-modern winery is softened with attractive landscaping and a lily pond. Luncheon is available by reservation in the **Cafe du Chai** dining room or out on a sunny deck. A stop here allows you to kill the proverbial two birds with one stone. Park once, taste twice. The winery listed next is located just across the way.

Rodney Strong/Windsor Vineyards *11455 Old Redwood Highway, 707/433-6511; tasting daily 10-5; hourly tours.* Visitors are seated comfortably at tables for tasting. This winery offers an unusual gift idea: wine labels personalized with a message of your choice.

Simi Winery *16275 Healdsburg Ave., 707/433-6981; tasting daily 10-4:30; tours at 11, 1, & 3.* When I visited this friendly tasting room, I was offered fresh figs with my wine samplings. A nice selection of reasonably-priced hand-blown wine glasses are for sale, as is a child's t-shirt proclaiming, "Now you SIMI...Now you don't!" A shady picnic area is situated under some ancient redwoods.

GEYSERVILLE

■ GETTING THERE

Located approximately 8 miles north of Healdsburg via Highway 101.

■ WHERE TO STAY

♥ **The Hope-Merrill House** *21253 Geyserville Ave., 707/857-3356; 2/ $$-$$$; 2-night minimum on weekends; unsuitable for children; full breakfast; pool.* This Eastlake Stick Victorian dates from 1870. It is exquisitely restored to that period with antique furnishings and even authentically duplicated wallpapers. Wine is served in the afternoons—out in the lovely pool setting when the temperature permits. Should this lovely home be booked, try the charming Queen Anne Victorian **Hope-Bosworth House.** Located across the street, it is under the same ownership.

■ WHERE TO EAT

Souverain Winery *Restaurant: 707/433-3141; L Tu-Sat, SunBr, D F & Sat; highchairs, booster seats; reservations suggested; $$; AE,MC,V. Winery: 707/433-8281; tasting & tours daily 10-4:30.* In addition to tasting, this winery features a first-rate restaurant. Menu choices for the elegant luncheon include delicious fresh soups and salads, varied entrees, fancy desserts, and, of course, a selection of the winery's vintages. In good weather diners are seated outdoors with a view of the vineyards and Mayacamas Mountains.

■ WHAT TO DO

Lake Sonoma *3333 Skaggs Springs Rd., 707/433-9483.* This scenic spot hosts all manner of water activities—fishing, boating, water skiing, swimming. A **Visitors Center** offers displays of the area's wildlife and a self-guided tour through a **fish hatchery.**

Stage-A-Picnic *707/857-3356; $40/person; Sat & Sun at 10 & 12:15, weekdays by appointment, May-Oct.* Passengers gather at the historic Hope-Merrill House to board a vintage stagecoach drawn by two draft horses. As the stage bumps along through vineyards and back roads, the driver relays information about the area's winemaking history. Stops are made at three wineries for tasting. At the last, everyone enjoys a deliciously prepared picnic lunch featuring seasonal products from local farms and orchards. Then everyone is shuttled back to their cars in an old-fashioned Model T truck. Children are charged full price, but a pony is provided for them to ride while their parents taste wines.

■ WINERIES

Geyser Peak Winery *22281 Chianti Rd., 1 mile north of town, 800/ 225-WINE, 707/433-6585; tasting daily 10-5; tours by appt.* This winery provides shaded picnic tables on a patio overlooking Alexander Valley. More picnic tables and barbecue facilities are available nearby at the winery's **Margot Patterson Doss Trail**—a self-guided nature trail. These facilities are, however, a bit difficult to find; ask for directions in the tasting room. While parents are tasting wines, children are treated to grape juice and balloons.

Pat Paulsen Vineyards *26155 Asti Store Rd., Asti, 800/262-9463, 707/ 894-2969; tasting daily 10-6; no tours.* Don't miss the chuckle of a visit to this tasting room inside what looks like a country store. Mr. Paulsen says, "My wine has been served in the White House, even if I haven't."

The Winery at Asti *26150 Asti Rd., Asti, 707/433-2333; tasting daily 10-5; call for tour times.* Formery Italian Swiss Colony, this winery has a deli stocked with picnic supplies and a shaded picnic area with tables. Children are given tastes of non-alcoholic sparkling muscat while their parents taste wines.

Trentadue Winery *19170 Geyserville Ave., 707/433-3104; tasting daily 10-5; tours by appt.* Don't miss a picnic here in the welcoming shade of the spacious grape arbor. This small family winery also sells picnic supplies in its tasting room.

HOPLAND

■ GETTING THERE

Located approximately 25 miles north of Geyserville via Highway 101.

■ WHERE TO EAT

Mendocino Brewing Company Hopland Brewery Tavern *13351 S. Highway 101, 707/744-1361; L/D daily; highchairs; no reservations; $; MC,V.* This microbrewery sells its refreshing products directly to the public. Opened in 1983, it is the first brewpub in California since prohibition. Enjoy a Blue Heron Ale (like English bitter) or the popular Red Tail Ale inside the 100-year-old brick pub room featuring vintage stamped tin walls. If children are along, opt for the pleasant garden. They can play there in a large sandbox while the adults sip suds in shade provided by hop vines. The simple, tasty pub food includes hamburgers, beer sausage, salads, and chips with salsa or guacamole. Before leaving, check out the adjacent brewhouse.

UKIAH

■ GETTING THERE

Located approximately 15 miles north of Hopland.

■ WHERE TO STAY

Orr Hot Springs *13201 Orr Springs Rd., 707/462-6277; 2/$-$$; open Th eve-M morn; children under 2 free; communal kitchen; pool, hot tubs.* In the 1800s, when this mineral springs resort was built, patrons reached it via stagecoach. Its natural rock swimming pool is filled with cool mineral spring water; bathing suits are optional in the hot tubs. Lodging is in primitive cabins or on the floor in a loft area in the lodge. Guests must bring their own food. Campsites and day use rates are also available.

■ WHAT TO DO

Grace Hudson Museum and **Sun House** *431 S. Main St., 707/462-3370; W-Sat 10-4:30, Sun from 12; tours of Sun House on the hour, 12-4; donation $2/person, $5/family.* Intricate Indian baskets and Pomo Indian games and musical instruments are among the many items displayed in this museum. Named for the prominent painter who specialized in portraits of the area's Pomo Indians, it also houses some of her personal paraphernalia. Her six-room home, the California Craftsman-style Sun House, is adjacent to the museum. Built of redwood in 1911, it has most of its original furnishings. Picnic facilities are available.

WILLITS

■ *GETTING THERE*

Located approximately 25 miles north of Ukiah.

■ *WHERE TO STAY*

Emandal Farm *16500 Hearst Rd., 16 miles northeast of town, 707/ 459-5439; open for week-long stays during Aug, weekends in spring and fall; rates vary according to age and include 3 meals/day; cribs.* On weekend visits to this 1,000-acre working cattle and pig farm, guests arrive for Friday night dinner. Families are assigned a table for the weekend and then spend some blissful hours there chowing down superb home cooking prepared with the farm's own organically grown produce. Days are filled with leisurely activies—perhaps a short hike down to a sandy beach on the magnificent Eel River for a swim, or maybe a hike up the steep mountain behind the barn to Rainbow Lake. Some folks just doze in the hammocks outside each of the rustic one-room redwood cabins dating from 1916. Others get involved with the farm chores: milking the goats, collecting eggs, feeding the pigs.

EUREKA/REDWOODS

■ *A LITTLE BACKGROUND*

Ambitious logging activity has, over time, changed the scenery here quite a bit. The best of the remaining virgin redwoods are in this area's state parks, all of which were established in the 1920s.

The winter off-season is an uncrowded (and cold) time to visit the north coast redwood country around Humboldt Bay. Pack your warmest clothing, kiss the sunshine good-

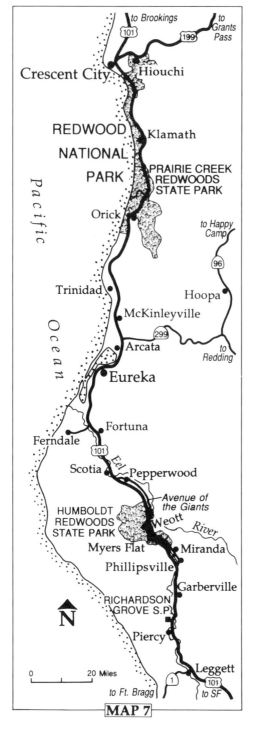

to Brookings
to Grants Pass
101
199
Crescent City   Hiouchi
REDWOOD   Klamath
NATIONAL
PARK   PRAIRIE CREEK REDWOODS STATE PARK
Pacific
Orick
to Happy Camp
96
Trinidad
Hoopa
McKinleyville
299
Ocean
Arcata
to Redding
Eureka
Fortuna
Ferndale
101
Scotia   Eel   Pepperwood
Avenue of the Giants
HUMBOLDT REDWOODS STATE PARK   Weott   River
Myers Flat   Miranda
Phillipsville
Garberville
RICHARDSON GROVE S.P.
N
Piercy
0   20 Miles
Leggett
1
101
to Ft. Bragg   to SF

MAP 7

bye, and prepare to enjoy the stunning beauty of this quiet, foggy area.

Eureka and nearby Arcata are both known for their well-preserved Victorian homes. Arcata, a smaller town and home to **Humboldt State College**, also has a number of interesting restaurants in its downtown square.

■ *VISITOR INFORMATION*

Eureka Chamber of Commerce *2112 Broadway, Eureka 95501, 707/442-3738*. Guided tours of the town are available in summer. Call for information and reservations.

Eureka/Humboldt County Convention & Visitors Bureau *1034 Second St., Eureka 95501, 800/338-7352, 707/443-5097*.

■ *ANNUAL EVENTS*

Kinetic Sculpture Race *May, Memorial Day weekend.* In this unusual competition people-powered contraptions race over dunes and rivers from Arcata to Ferndale.

■ *GETTING THERE*

Located approximately 130 miles north of Willits and approximately 280 miles north of San Francisco.

Or take the **Northcoast Daylight** *(707/442-7705; runs May-Oct; adults $75/one-way, $99/round-trip, 2-12 $38/$49).* Composed of vintage railway equipment, this train travels from Willits to Eureka along the scenic Eel River and passes through no less than 40 tunnels!

■ *WHERE TO STAY*

♥ **Carter House** *1033 3rd St., 707/445-1390; 2/$-$$$+; unsuitable for children; some bathtubs; shared baths; full breakfast.* Looking a bit ominous on its bare corner lot, this naturally darkened redwood home was built in 1982. A re-creation of the 1884 design of two San Francisco architects, it is all sweetness and light inside. Contemporary paintings and ceramics are on display throughout; all are by local artists and available for purchase. Afternoon wine and cheese is served in the pleasant parlour, and at bedtime cookies and cordials appear. Across the street, the even newer **Hotel Carter** offers tasteful lodging amenable to families.

Eagle House Victorian Inn *139 2nd St., 800/522-8686, 707/442-2334; 2/$$-$$$; children under 2 free; some TVs, refrigerators, fireplaces, bathtubs; continental breakfast, restaurant; jacuzzi.* Guests find Victorian antiques, down comforters, and complimentary wine awaiting them in their rooms. The adjacent **Eagle House Theatre** presents live theater, concerts, and comedy.

The Eureka Inn *7th/F Sts., 800/862-4906, 707/442-6441; 2-4/$$$-$$$+; children under 16 free; cribs; all TVs; some refrigerators, fireplaces, bathtubs; room service, 3 restaurants; heated pool, jacuzzi, 2 saunas.* Built in English Tudor style in 1922 and now a national historic landmark, this is *the* place to stay. It is within easy walking distance of many attractions.

Motel Row. Plenty of last-minute accommodations can usually be found along both 4th Street and Broadway.

■ *WHERE TO EAT*

Lazio's Seafood Restaurant *at the foot of C St. (near Old Town), 707/ 442-2337; B/L/D daily; highchairs, booster seats, children's portions; no reservations; $$; all cards.* Fresh seafood caught by the restaurant's own commercial fishing operation is the specialty here. Picture windows allow diners to watch the fishermen bringing in the catch. It's usually crowded, so expect a short wait.

Samoa Cookhouse *445 W. Washington (from Highway 101 take Samoa Bridge to end, turn left on Samoa Rd., take first left turn), 707/442-1659; B/L/D daily; highchairs, booster seats, children's portions; no reservations; $$; all cards.* Originally built by the Georgia-Pacific Corporation to feed its loggers, this "last surviving cookhouse in the West" offers no menu choices. Just sit down and the food starts arriving. Hearty, delicious family-style meals are served at long tables in three large, noisy dining halls. Though the menu changes daily, a typical lunch might consist of marinated three-bean salad, soup, homemade bread with butter, assorted jams and honey, cole-slaw, scalloped potatoes, deep-fried cod with tartar sauce, mixed vegetables, coffee or tea, and butterscotch pudding topped with whipped cream. A fantastic value! Most items are prepared with fresh ingredients. The only item not included in the fixed price is milk. After dining you can wander through a mini-museum. Freshly-baked loaves of bread and toy logging trucks are available for purchase and make good souvenirs of your visit. Several unmarked turnoffs from Samoa Road lead to driftwood-strewn beaches.

■ WHAT TO DO

Carson Mansion *2nd/M Sts.* Built in 1885, this is said to be the most photographed house in the United States and the "queen" of Victorian architecture. The house is now a private club and may be viewed only from the exterior.

Clarke Memorial Museum *240 E/3rd Sts., 707/443-1947; Tu-Sat 12-4; free.* An outstanding collection of local Indian baskets and artifacts and an extensive collection of pioneer relics are displayed inside this airy, high-ceilinged 1912 building. Historical photographs of the area are also on display, as are antique weapons and Victorian clothing and furniture.

Coast Oyster Co. *foot of A St., 707/442-2947; free.* Take a self-guided tour of this oyster processing plant located behind Lazio's restaurant. Hours are irregular; call for current schedule.

Covered Bridges *take Highway 101 south to Elk River Rd., then follow Elk River Rd. to either Bertas Rd. (2 miles) or Zanes Rd. (3 miles).* These two all-wood covered bridges were constructed in 1936.

Fort Humboldt State Historic Park *3431 Fort Ave., 707/445-6567; daily 9-5; free.* This was U.S. Grant's headquarters in 1854. Exhibits include locomotives, a restored logger's cabin, and displays of pioneer logging methods. At the annual **Steam Donkey Days**, held in April, there are logging demonstrations and the steam donkeys are operated. The excellent view of Humboldt Bay makes it a nice spot for a picnic.

Dolbeer steam donkey at Fort Humboldt.

Humboldt Bay Harbor Cruise *foot of C St., 707/445-1910; daily in summer at 1, 2:30, & 4; schedule varies rest of year; adults $4.50, 12-17 $3.50, 6-11 $2.50.* The one-hour cruise aboard the *M/V Madaket* (which once ferried workers to the lumber mills across the bay in Samoa) allows a view of the bustling activity and native wildlife of the bay.

Old Town *1st/2nd/3rd Sts. from C to G Sts.* This waterfront area consists of restored commercial and residential buildings. Many restaurants and interesting shops are now located here. Antique hunting is especially good. Visit the **Romano Gabriel Wooden Sculpture Garden** *(315 2nd St).* Because flowers don't grow well in the area due to the lack of sunshine, this folk art garden was constructed from vegetable crates.

Sequoia Park & Zoo *Glatt/W Sts., 707/443-7331; Tu-Sun 10-8 May-Oct, until 5 Nov-Apr; petting zoo in summer only; free.* The backdrop for this combination zoo-playground-picnic area is a 52-acre grove of virgin redwoods. Visitors may also enjoy hiking trails, gardens, and a duck pond. The bear and otter enclosures are especially nice.

101 SOUTH OF TOWN

Ferndale *15 miles south of town.* This entire town is composed of well-preserved and restored Victorian buildings. Located in farm country, the town is a State Historical Landmark. It is also an artists' colony and is filled with antique shops, galleries, restaurants, and B&B lodging. Just south of town is **Cape Mendocino**—the most westerly point on the continental U.S.

♥ **The Gingerbread Mansion** *400 Berding St., Ferndale, 707/786-4000; 2/$$$-$$$+; unsuitable for children under 10; some fireplaces, bathtubs.* Originally built in 1894 as a doctor's home, this carefully restored Victorian mansion has gables and turrets and is painted cheery colors. Rooms are furnished with Victorian antiques, and one suite features "his" and "hers" claw-foot tubs placed toe to toe. Guests are pampered with bathrobes and bubble bath, and coffee and juice is delivered to the rooms before breakfast. Bicycles and picnic baskets are available for loan, and afternoon tea is served in the parlor.

Pacific Lumber Company *on Highway 101, Scotia, 27 miles south of town, 707/764-2222; M-F 7:30-10:30am & 12:50-2:30pm; free.* Take a self-guided tour through the world's largest redwood lumber mill. Get your pass for the hour tour in the old First National Bank building, now a logging museum. Scotia is one of the last company-owned lumber towns in the West and is built entirely of redwood.

Scotia Inn *Main St., Scotia, 707/764-5683; 2/$$, 4/$$$; children under 2 free; cribs; all bathtubs; some TVs; continental breakfast, restaurant.* The hotel which stood on this site in 1888 accommodated travelers waiting for the stagecoach south. The current hotel, built in 1923, greets guests with a magnificent lobby with walls of polished redwood. Rooms are furnished with antiques, and bathrooms feature claw-foot tubs. Dinner and Sunday brunch are served in grand style in the dining room. A splurge on the Bridal Suite is worthwhile because of its impressive private jacuzzi room.

Demonstration Forest *on Highway 101, 5 miles south of Scotia; daily in summer 8-4.* To educate the public about modern forestry practices, the Pacific Lumber Company has set up self-guided tours through part of its forest.

The Avenue of the Giants, Humboldt Redwoods State Park *Weott, 707/946-2311; free.* Millions of years ago, when dinosaurs roamed the earth, gigantic redwood forests were plentiful. After the Ice Age, the redwood survived only in a narrow 500-mile strip along the northern coast of California. Before the logging days on the north coast, it is estimated the area contained 1 1/2 million acres of redwoods. Now only 100,000 acres remain—preserved by the State Parks system. Approximately half of these huge old trees are found in Humboldt Redwoods State Park, home of the Avenue of the Giants.

The Avenue of the Giants, which is actually the old Highway 101, begins just south of Pepperwood. It continues on for approximately 40 miles to Phillipsville, where it rejoins the busy newer

Highway 101. This breathtaking route parallels the freeway and the Eel River and winds through grove after grove of huge redwoods. Unusual sights along this unique stretch of road are numerous. Near Myers Flat, the **Shrine Drive-Thru Tree** has a circumference of approximately 64 feet and provides the opportunity to take an unusual picture. The **Children's Forest**, located across the south fork of the Eel River, is a 1,120-acre memorial to children. **Williams Grove** features picturesque picnic and swimming sites on the river. The 9,000-acre **Rockefeller Forest**—the world's largest grove of virgin redwoods—is near Weott. Also referred to as "the world's finest forest," it features hiking trails leading to the **Flatiron Tree**, the **Giant Tree**, and the 356-foot **Tall Tree,** as well as equestrian trails and horse rentals.

Lodging facilities are scattered along the route. A few of the best are listed here in the order found driving south to Piercy:

Miranda Gardens Resort *6766 Avenue of the Giants, Miranda, 707/943-3011; 2-4/$-$$; cribs; all TVs; some kitchens, fireplaces, bathtubs; heated pool (May-Oct), 2 tennis courts.* Lodging is in motel units or cottages. A children's playground and plenty of outdoor games—croquet, shuffleboard, and horseshoes—are provided.

Whispering Pines Motel *6582 Avenue of the Giants, Miranda, 707/943-3160; 2/$, 4/$$; cribs; all TVs; some kitchens, bathtubs; heated pool (unavail. Oct-Apr).* Shuffleboard, Ping Pong, and horseshoes keep the guests here busy.

Benbow Inn *445 Lake Benbow Dr., Garberville, 65 miles south of town, 707/923-2124; 2/$$-$$$+, 4/$$$+; closed Jan-Mar; unsuitable for infants; some TVs fireplaces, mountain views; restaurant.* This magnificent English Tudor inn, built in 1926, features blooming English gardens, rooms furnished with antiques, a cozy communal room with fireplace and library, and an elegant dining room and taproom bar. Facilities include a putting green, 9-hole golf course, lawn games, bicycle rentals, and a private beach and lake. A complimentary tea is served each afternoon, and classic films are scheduled each evening.

Richardson Grove State Park *707/247-3318; 2-4/$; unavail. Oct-Apr.* Stark, unfurnished cabins have indoor plumbing, showers, and kitchens but you must bring almost everything else, including your bed. Campsites are also available.

Hartsook Inn *900 Highway 101, Piercy, 75 miles south of town, 707/247-3305; 2-4/$-$$; closed Oct-Apr; children under 3 free; cribs; some kitchens, bathtubs; restaurant.* These cottages and motel units are scattered in a majestic 30-acre redwood setting adjoining Richardson Grove State Park. Guests may swim in the

Eel River and have use of a children's playground, lawn games, a putting green, and a lounge with games, movies, and a fireplace.

Confusion Hill *75001 Highway 101, Piercy, 707/925-6456. House: open all year, 8am-7pm; $2.50, under 6 free. Train: Apr-Sept; $2.50, under 3 free.* Visit this spot where gravity appears to be defied and water runs uphill—or take a train ride through a tree tunnel to the crest of a hill in the redwoods.

Eel River Redwoods Hostel *70400 Highway 101, Leggett, 90 miles south of town, 707/925-6469; summer and fall only.* This 32-bed facility is located on the scenic Eel River. See also p.273.

Drive-Thru Tree Park *Highway 1, Leggett, 707/925-6363; daily dawn-dusk; $2/car.* Most average-size cars can squeeze through the hole in this 315-foot high, 21-foot diameter redwood tree. Bring your camera. Nature trails and lakeside picnic areas are available.

101 NORTH OF TOWN

Bishop Pine Lodge *1481 Patricks Point Dr., Trinidad, 23 miles north of town, 707/677-3314; 2-4/$-$$; cribs; all TVs; some kitchens.* These cozy, secluded cabins are located among the redwoods. A trail leads to a bluff overlooking the ocean, and a playground—complete with a rustic treehouse—is on the spacious, well-maintained grounds. The helpful owner knows where to find both the Roosevelt elk and the best restaurants. Trinidad is a scenic fishing village with a very nice beach.

Redwood National Park *Orick, 40 miles north of town, 707/464-6101; Visitor Centers in Orick, Crescent City, and Hiouchi.* This magnificent national park encompasses 106,000 acres and three state parks. Ranger-led interpretive programs are scheduled daily May through October. During the summer, horses may be rented for rides on scenic equestrian trails; overnight pack trips may also be arranged. Inquire at the Visitors Center about inner tube and kayak float trips on the Smith River. Also ask about Family Adventure Packs to aid in your explorations.

Tall Trees Grove Shuttle Bus *707/488-3461; daily June-Sept, call for schedule; adults $3, 5-15 $1.* In summer a bus takes visitors to a trailhead leading to the Tall Trees Grove, which contains the world's tallest tree (367.8 feet) as well as the second, third, and sixth tallest trees. The entire excursion takes about four hours; the walk covers 2 2/3 miles. The rest of the year it is an 8 1/2-mile walk each way.

Prairie Creek Redwoods State Park *on Highway 101, Orick, 707/488-2861; daily 9-5; free.* The eight-mile gravel road to **Gold Bluffs Beach** and **Fern Canyon** passes through a beautiful forest into an area of fern-covered cliffs. This park tends to be foggy and cold and is a refuge for one of the few remaining herds of native Roosevelt elk.

Requa Inn *451 Requa Rd., Klamath, 60 miles north of town, 707/482-8205; 2-4/$-$$; closed Jan & Feb; some bathtubs; continental breakfast, restaurant.* Comfortable, pleasantly decorated rooms are available at this restored historic hotel. The dining room has a surf & turf menu; children's portions are available at half-price. Fishermen particularly favor this location at the scenic mouth of the Klamath River, and in the center of Redwood National Park just 30 miles south of the Oregon border.

Redwood Hostel *14480 Highway 101, Klamath, 707/482-8265.* This northernmost link in the California coast hostel chain is located within the national park boundaries. Located in the historic circa 1890s **DeMartin House**, it has a full kitchen and features spectacular ocean views. See also p.273.

Trees of Mystery *on Highway 101, Klamath, 707/482-5613; daily in summer dawn-dusk, 10-4 rest of year; adults $5, 6-12 $2.50.* Visitors to this grove of redwoods are greeted by a 50-foot tall Paul Bunyan and a 32-foot tall Babe. Then they pass through a tunnel made from a hollowed-out log and visit a well-maintained group of unusual trees. At the **End of the Trail Indian Museum** they may peruse a large collection of Indian artifacts.

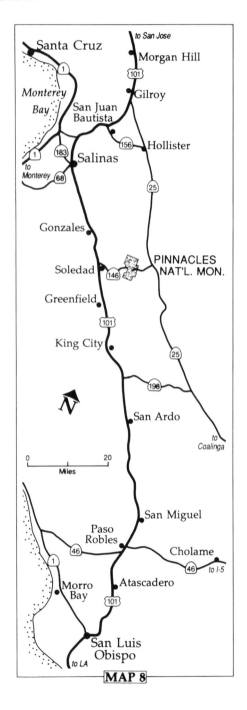

MAP 8

101 SOUTH

SAN JUAN BAUTISTA

■ *A LITTLE BACKGROUND*

Once the largest city in Central California, this town is now a sleepy remnant of that time. It's hard to believe that at one time seven stage lines operated out of the town and that there were numerous busy hotels and saloons. Now a few Mexican restaurants and an assortment of boutiques and antique shops lure visitors.

San Juan Bautista State Historic Park *(408/623-4881; 10-5 daily; adults 50¢, 6-17 25¢)* is the main attraction. Within it is **Mission San Juan Bautista**. Founded in 1797, it is the fifteenth and largest in the chain of 21 California missions. The park's assortment of restored buildings allows visitors to see what life was like in this area in the early 1800s. The **Castro Adobe** sits behind the park headquarters in a picturesque park perfect for picnicking. If everything looks familiar, it may be because you've seen it all before in the movie *Vertigo*.

■ *VISITOR INFORMATION*

San Juan Bautista Chamber of Commerce *P.O. Box 1037, San Juan Bautista 95045, 408/623-2454.*

■ ANNUAL EVENTS

Early Days at San Juan Bautista *June; 408/623-4881.* Visitors see re-enactments of 19th century townspeople performing everyday tasks such as baking bread in a hornito oven and hand-dipping candles. The restored **Plaza Hotel**'s famous bar is opened for business, and a Santa Maria-style barbecue is held in the Old Mission olive grove.

Christmas *December; 408/623-2444.* An early California folk opera, **La Pastorela**, is presented in the Old Mission Church by the local acting company El Teatro Campesino. Also scheduled are a candle-light tour of the mission and **Los Posadas**—a traditional parade in which Mary and Joseph are portrayed seeking shelter.

■ GETTING THERE

Located approximately 100 miles south of San Francisco. Take Highway 101 east.

■ WHERE TO STAY

Bed & Breakfast San Juan *315 The Alameda, 408/623-4101; 2/$$; children by prior arrangement only; children under 2 free; some shared baths; full breakfast.* This 125-year-old Gothic Revival country home is on the National Register of Historic Places and is just a short walk from town.

■ WHERE TO EAT

Jardines de San Juan *115 Third St., 408/623-4466; L/D daily; high-chairs; reservations suggested; $$; MC,V.* What a wonderful fair-weather experience to sit outside in the brick courtyard here under a sheltering umbrella. Among the profusely flowering gardens, diners sip icy cold margaritas and dip freshly fried, crisp tortilla chips in tasty salsa while perusing the menu. Excellent flautas con guacamole consist of shredded beef rolled in a deep-fried tortilla and topped with guacamole. The predictable, and popular, tacos and enchiladas are also available. After 5 p.m. regional specialties join the menu. Red snapper Veracruz is available on Fridays, drunken chicken on Sundays. Limited amounts of these specialties are prepared, so diners must call to reserve their portion. Live music is scheduled on the outdoor stage each Sunday afternoon.

San Juan Bakery *319 Third St, 408/623-4570; daily.* This old-fashioned bakery makes a wonderful sourdough French bread, a down-soft buttermilk bread, and an assortment of delicious breakfast pastries. I always buy a bag of cookies to enjoy back in the car. Picnic supplies are also available.

SALINAS

■ *A LITTLE BACKGROUND*

Known as "the salad bowl of the nation," the Salinas Valley is where John Steinbeck spent his formative years. Many of his novels are set here. In fact, the first working title for *East of Eden* was "Salinas Valley." Salinas is one of the biggest cities in the valley.

■ *VISITOR INFORMATION*

Salinas Visitor and Convention Bureau *P.O. Box 1170, (119 E. Alisal), Salinas 93902, 408/424-7611.*

■ *ANNUAL EVENTS*

California Rodeo *July; 408/424-7355.* First presented in 1911, this outdoor rodeo is ranked fourth largest in the world. It is especially noted for its trick riders, clowns, and thoroughbred racing. Prize money totals over $200,000—attracting the best of the cowboys to the competitions.

Steinbeck Festival *August; 408/758-7314.* Bus and walking tours, films, lectures, and panel discussions are all part of the festivities.

■ *GETTING THERE*

Located approximately 20 miles south of San Juan Bautista.

You can also take Amtrak from Oakland and San Jose and return the same day. Call 800/872-7245 for more information.

■ *WHERE TO EAT*

The Steinbeck House *132 Central Ave., 408/424-2735; seatings at 11:45 & 1:15 M-F; highchairs, booster seats; reservations suggested; $; MC,V.* In 1902 John Steinbeck was born in the front bedroom of this beautifully renovated Victorian house. Now a volunteer group owns the house and operates it as a gourmet luncheon restaurant. Serving seasonal produce grown in the Salinas Valley, the restaurant's three-course fixed-price menu changes daily and includes items such as spinach sausage en croute and green chili quiche. Drinks and dessert are extra. Though the dining rooms are elegantly decorated (Steinbeck memorabilia fills the walls), the atmosphere is casual. Comfortable travel attire is acceptable. Children are welcome and may share portions with their parents or siblings. After lunch, a cellar gift shop invites browsing—and perhaps selecting a souvenir book by Steinbeck. From here it's just a short walk down the Victorian-bedecked street to the **Steinbeck Library**.

John Steinbeck and his sister Mary on Jill—the inspiration for The Red Pony.

GONZALES

■ *GETTING THERE*

Located approximately 20 miles south of Salinas.

■ *WHAT TO DO*

The Monterey Vineyard *800 S. Alta St., 408/675-2481; tasting and tours daily 10-5.* This attractive modern winery building features 25-foot stained glass windows.

PINNACLES NATIONAL MONUMENT

■ *GETTING THERE*

Located approximately 20 miles southeast of Gonzales. Exit 101 in Soledad, then take Highway 146 east.

■ *A LITTLE BACKGROUND*

Formed by ancient volcanic activity, this scenic area is home to—yes—pinnacles and spires. It is particularly surprising to come across, as this area is otherwise flat. Spring and fall are the best times to visit for hiking and camping; spring is a particularly popular time because of the stunning display of wildflowers. At other times the temperatures can be uncomfortable. A day use fee of $3 per car is charged. For more information call 408/389-4462.

SAN MIGUEL

■ *GETTING THERE*

Located approximately 65 miles south of Soledad.

■ *WHERE TO STAY*

♥ **The Ranch** *3625 Cholame Valley Rd., 805/463-2320; 2/$$; unsuitable for children under 5; children 5-11 free; some bathtubs; some shared baths; continental breakfast; unheated pool, jacuzzi.* Located in the hills, this ranch is said to be where early California bandit Joaquin Murrietta was finally captured. Guests can ride horses or pony-carts, fish, hunt for Indian artifacts, and hike. There are, of course, cookouts, and you're welcome to help with ranch chores. Adults are preferred.

■ *WHAT TO DO*

Mission San Miguel Arcangel *801 Mission St., 805/467-3256; daily 10-5.* Founded in 1797, the present mission building was constructed in 1816. The delicate neoclassical paintings are especially noteworthy.

PASO ROBLES

■ *GETTING THERE*

Located approximately 5 miles south of San Miguel.

■ *WHERE TO EAT*

A&W Rootbeer Drive-In *2110 Spring St., 805/238-0360; children's portions; daily 10am-11pm; no cards.* An oasis on this long, usually hot drive, this A&W stand is right out of the '50s. A waitress appears when you turn on your car lights, and food is served on a tray which attaches to your partially rolled-down car window. Choices are simple: hamburgers, hot dogs, French fries, onion rings, and *cold* root beer.

■ *WHAT TO DO*

James Dean Memorial *on Highway 46, in Cholame, 25 miles east of town, 805/238-1390.* Depending on your mood, this can be an interesting or bizarre side trip. This is where the legendary James Dean died in his Porsche in 1955. An obelisk shrine, constructed and maintained by a Japanese national who comes to pay homage twice a year, is located in front of the town's post office.

Wine Tasting. For a free brochure/map to the area's wineries, call the **Paso Robles Chamber of Commerce** at 805/238-0506.

SAN LUIS OBISPO

■ *VISITOR INFORMATION*

San Luis Obispo County Visitors & Conference Bureau *1039 Chorro St., San Luis Obispo 93401, 800/634-1414, 805/543-1323.*

■ *GETTING THERE*

Located approximately 30 miles south of Paso Robles.

■ *WHERE TO STAY*

Embassy Suites *333 Madonna Rd., 800/EMBASSY, 805/549-0800; 2-4/ $$$; cribs; all TVs, refrigerators, bathtubs; room service, full breakfast, restaurant; heated indoor pool, jacuzzi, sauna, exercise room.* For description, see p.102. This branch is located adjacent to a large shopping mall with a series of fast-food outlets.

Madonna Inn *100 Madonna Rd., 805/543-3000; 2-4/$$$-$$$+; cribs;*

all TVs; some fireplaces; restaurant. Begun in 1960 and built one room at time, this motel now has 109 guest rooms. Many are uniquely (some might say weirdly) decorated—like the Cave Man Room with its stone walls and the Barrel of Fun in which all the furniture is made from barrels. A photo file at the check-in desk is available to help you decide. If you're not spending the night, consider stopping for a snack in the flamboyant coffee shop or dining room, and don't miss the restrooms.

Motel Inn *2223 Monterey St., 805/543-4000; 2-4/$; pool.* Opened on December 12, 1925, this is the world's very first motel. One-story adobe units are scattered about the attractive grounds. Well-maintained grassy areas and gardens add to the general appeal.

■ *WHERE TO EAT*

Farmers' Market *held downtown in the 600 and 700 blocks of Higuera St.; Th 6:30-9pm.* You can buy your dinner fully prepared or pick up the fixings to do it yourself. This market is known for delicious barbecued items, and there is free live entertainment.

■ *WHAT TO DO*

California Polytechnic State University (Cal Poly) *on Grand Ave., 805/756-2487; tours M,W,F at 10 & 2; free.* Tours of this attractively situated campus begin at the Administration Building and include a visit to the campus nursery and chicken farm.

Gum Alley *next to 733 Higuera.* For over a decade gum chewers have been depositing their product on these brick walls. Some have even taken the time to make designs. A vulgar, tacky eyesore to some, it is a cheap thrill for gum aficionados and most children. Don't find yourself stuck here without a stick. Stock up with different colors of gum before your visit, and remember that Double Bubble is reputed to stick best.

Hot Springs. On the way to or from the coast, consider a stop at either **Sycamore Mineral Springs** *(1215 Avila Beach Dr., 805/595-7302),* where you can rent an outdoor hot tub by the hour or spend the entire night in a room with a private spa, or at **Avila Hot Springs** (805/595-2359), where you can rent inner tubes to use in a warm pool.

Mission San Luis Obispo de Tolosa *Monterey/Chorro Sts., 805/543-6850; daily 9-4; by donation.* Built in 1772, this is referred to as "the Prince of Missions" and features a museum and fragrant rose garden. A charming chapel is still used for services. An adjacent park offers shady trees, grass, and paths hugging a stream; inviting open-air cafes surround it. Nearby are the **Judge Walter Murray Adobe** *(M,W,F 12-4)* and the **County Historical Museum** *(696 Monterey St., 805/543-0638; W-Sun 10-4; free).*

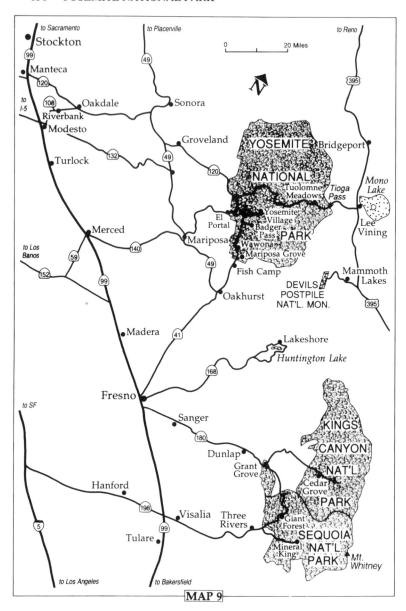

MAP 9

YOSEMITE NATIONAL PARK

■ *A LITTLE BACKGROUND*

Yosemite Park is a place of rest. A refuge...in which one gains the advantage of both solitude and society...none can escape its charms. Its natural beauty cleanses and warms like fire, and you will be willing to stay forever... —John Muir

And if you did stay forever, you would be priviledged to enjoy the spectacular beauty of the park's dramatic seasonal changes. Most visitors see this grand national park in the summer, when it is at its busiest with congested roads and accommodations filled to capacity. All this makes it hard to focus on what you came for—the scenic, natural beauty of the High Sierra. If you want to catch a glimpse of the Yosemite described by Muir, consider a visit in the off-season: in fall when the colorful foilage change is spectacular; in winter when snow blankets the valley floor; in spring when the falls are at their fullest.

Yosemite was designated a national park in 1890. Among its scenic wonders are **El Capitan**—the largest piece of exposed granite in the world—and **Yosemite Falls**—the highest in the Northern Hemisphere.

Remember that falls and rivers can be dangerous as well as beautiful; keep a good grip on children when hiking.

A $5 admission fee is collected at all park entrances, and visitors are given an activities newsletter and map.

■ *VISITOR INFORMATION*

National Park Service *Yosemite National Park 95389, 209/252-4848.*

■ *ANNUAL EVENTS*

Bracebridge Dinner *December 22,24,&25.* Spending Christmas at The Ahwahnee hotel and attending this memorable dinner is a pleasure not many get to enjoy. This expensive experience costs $85 per person and requires that participants apply for reservations a full year in advance. Applications are so numerous that guests must be chosen by lottery. Since 1927 the fare at the three-hour dinners has been seven courses of elegant Christmas dishes. Pageantry, carols, and jesters entertain diners between courses.

■ *GETTING THERE*

Located approximately 240 miles east of San Francisco. Take Highway 80 to Highway 580 to Highway 205 to Highway 120. To minimize the need for chains in winter, consider taking low elevation Highway 140 in from Merced.

■ *STOPS ALONG THE WAY*

Numerous cafes and produce stands are located along Highway 120. Fast-food heaven is in Oakdale, and there are several cafes in the rustic mountain town of Groveland. In the summer the **Groveland Motel** *(209/962-7865)* offers inexpensive lodging in carpeted tepees.

Oakwood Lake Resort *874 E. Woodward Rd., Manteca, 209/239-2500; May-Sept, call for schedule; all day pass $12.95, under 5 free.* The main attraction here is the nine fiberglass waterslides. Most feature over 60 feet of enclosed tunnel and several 360-degree turns. A special slide for small children and the timid is available at no charge. More daring is required for the Rapids Ride, which is maneuvered on an inner tube, and the Rampage Ride, in which riders sit on a plastic toboggan and drop 63 feet down a steep slide and then skim across the water. Resort facilities include a swimming lagoon, hot tubs, an outdoor roller skating rink, playgrounds, barbecue and picnic areas, and overnight camping. Special rates for shorter visits, picnic use, and camping are available.

Riverbank and Stanislaus County Cheese Companies *from Modesto take Highway 108 to Riverbank.* **Riverbank** *6603 Second St., 209/869-4533; daily 9-5; tours M-F by appt.* **Stanco** *3141 Sierra Ave., 209/869-2558; daily 9-6; no tours.* Specialty cheeses made by these two companies include teleme and assorted varieties of cheddars and Jacks. Picnic supplies are also available. A riverside picnic may be enjoyed in town at **Jacob Myers Park**, located at First Street across the Burneyville Ferry Bridge. *1- 20 9-848- 8126*

Hershey Chocolate Company *1400 S. Yosemite Ave., Oakdale, 209/ 847-0381; tours M-F 8:15-3; free.* Half-hour tours allow visitors to see and smell such delights as kiss-wrapping machines and chocolate being mixed in huge vats. After the tour all visitors receive a sweet treat.

Knight's Ferry Covered Bridge *turnoff is about 12 miles east of Oakdale off Highway 108.* Built in 1863 and measuring 330 feet long, this bridge is the longest and oldest covered bridge west of the Mississippi. It is closed to cars now, but pedestrian traffic is still permitted. A park with picnic tables, hiking trails, and a cold swimming hole is on the freeway side of the Stanislaus River. On the other side is a rustic Gold Rush-era town with a general store and another park.

■ WHERE TO STAY

PARK LODGING

It is especially difficult to obtain room accommodations in the summer and on holiday weekends. Reservations are essential. Call 209/252-4848 for information or to make reservations at any park hotel. Rates for two range from $16.65 to $149.50. Children under three stay free in their parents' room; cribs are available. A bargain Midweek Ski Package is available in the winter.

In the Valley

The Ahwahnee *$$$+; pool, tennis courts.* This very sedate luxury hotel is also a national historic landmark. Some cottages are available.

Campgrounds *$; Apr-Oct, several open year-round.* Make reservations through Ticketron.

Curry Village *$-$$; pool.* Accommodations and facilities are similar to Yosemite Lodge, but inexpensive tent-cabins are also available.

Yosemite Lodge *$-$$; pool.* Accommodations vary from old cabins without plumbing to luxurious modern hotel rooms.

Elsewhere

High Sierra Camps *$$*. Five camps provide tent accommodations complete with linens and two meals. Reserve no later than January for the following summer.

Tuolumne Meadows Lodge *$*. This facility is located at the eastern entrance and is all tent-cabins.

Wawona Hotel *$$; open Apr-Nov & Christmas vacation; pool, tennis courts, 9-hole golf course.* This 1876 Victorian hotel is located at the southern entrance (Highway 41) near the Mariposa Grove of Big Trees, 30 miles from the valley. A national historic landmark, it is the oldest resort hotel in the state.

White Wolf Lodge *$*. Located at Tioga Pass, 31 miles from the valley.

NON-PARK LODGING

The Redwoods *in Wawona, 209/375-6256; 2/$$-$$$, 4/$$$-$$$+; 2-night minimum; children under 2 free; cribs; all TVs, kitchens; some fireplaces, bathtubs.* These rustic, modern homes and cottages are furnished with linens and kitchenware. The property is located six miles inside the southern entrance to the park.

Tree House Hostel *in Midpines, 209/742-6318; Apr-Nov only.* Located on Highway 140, about 35 miles west of the park, this cabin has seven beds. See also p.273.

■ *WHERE TO EAT*

All of these valley facilities are open daily and equipped with highchairs and booster seats.

The Ahwahnee *209/372-1489; B/L/D daily; children's portions; reservations essential for dinner.* The best time to dine in the rustic splendor of this elegant dining room is during daylight hours. Only then can you take full advantage of the spectacular views of the valley offered by the 50-foot-tall floor-to-ceiling windows. Dinner is expensive, and men are expected to wear a sport or suit jacket and women to dress accordingly. Guests of the hotel get first choice at dining times, so otherwise be prepared for either an early or late seating. Children fit in best at breakfast or lunch. Dinner ski buffets are presented weeknights January through March.

Curry Village and Yosemite Lodge Cafeterias *B/L/D daily.* Meals here are quick and inexpensive.

Four Seasons Restaurant *Yosemite Lodge; B/D daily; children's portions.* The dinner menu offers good old American fare—steak, fried chicken, fish, and hamburgers.

Mountain Room Bar *Yosemite Lodge.* This is the place to get rid of the kinks developed on the long drive in.

Mountain Room Broiler *Yosemite Lodge; D only.* The walls in this stunning room are papered with striking black and white photo murals, and floor-to-ceiling windows look out on **Yosemite Falls.** The menu features salmon, lobster, and well-aged broiled steak as well as artichokes, sauteed fresh mushrooms, and hot cheese bread.

Picnic. Request a box lunch from your hotel kitchen the evening before you need it, or pick up supplies at **Degnan's Deli** in the Village.

■ *WHAT TO DO*

The Ansel Adams Gallery *in the Village.* Exclusive special edition photographs from this well-known photographer may be purchased here.

Bicycle Rentals *Yosemite Lodge (209/372-1208; daily 9-5) and Curry Village (209/372-1200; daily 8-8) Apr-Oct; $3.50/hr.* A bicycling map and information about ranger-led bike tours may be obtained when you rent your bike. Child carriers are available.

Bus Tours *209/372-1240; valley floor $11, grand tour $26.75.*

Glacier Point *an hour drive from the valley.* From this spot you can enjoy a 270-degree view of the high country, or you can look down 3,242 feet for a bird's-eye view of the valley. Several trails lead

down to the valley. Consider arriving in the morning (get the one-way ticket on the **Glacier Point Bus Tour**) so that you can spend the rest of the day hiking back down.

Hiking. Participate in a ranger-guided walk or take any of the many self-guided trails. Check in the park stores for maps.

Indian Cultural Museum *next to the **Village Visitor Center**; W-Sun 9-12 & 1-4.* Visitors learn about the Awanichi Indians through artifacts, cultural demonstrations, and recorded chants. A reconstructed Indian village is located behind the museum. It features a self-guided trail pointing out plants used by the Indians for food, clothing, and shelter.

Inner Tube Float Trip. Scenic and calm is the area on the Merced River between Pines Campground and Centinnel Bridge. Raft rentals are available in June and July.

Junior Ranger Program. This program is available in the summer for children in third grade and above. Reservations are necessary. Consult the free *Yosemite Guide* for details.

Mariposa Grove of Big Trees *on Highway 41, 35 miles from the valley; tours 8-7 May-Oct; adults $2.50, children $1.50.* Several hundred giant sequoias are located in this 250-acre grove. Open-air trams take visitors on guided tours. In winter, this is a choice spot for cross-country skiing.

Movies. Scenic movies and slide shows are scheduled some evenings. Check the *Yosemite Guide* for times and locations.

Pioneer History Center *on Highway 41, 25 miles from the valley, 209/375-6321; daily 9-5.* This village of restored pioneer buildings is reached by walking across an old **covered bridge**. In the summer history comes to life with demonstrations of soap making, yarn spinning, rail splitting, and other pioneer crafts. Sometimes there are stagecoach rides and old-fashioned square dancing.

Rock Climbing Lessons *Curry Village (209/372-1244) and Tuolumne Meadows (summer only; 209/372-1335).* Learn rock climbing at **Yosemite Mountaineering School**, one of the finest in the world. Basic classes are held daily year-round and cost $30. Beginners are taught safety essentials for dealing with the area's granite rock and can expect to climb as high as 80 feet in the first lesson. Snow and ice climbing are strangely offered only in the summer. Children must be at least 14 to participate.

Valley Stables *guided 2-hr horse trips leave at 8,10,&1; $20/person; half-day mule trips/$27, all-day/$45.* Said to have the largest public riding stock in the world, this concession can also arrange custom pack and fishing trips. Burros and ponies may be rented by parents for their young children to ride; parents must lead ($7/hr). As an alternative to hiring a babysitter, consider the 9:30 to 3:30 **burro picnic** for children ages 7 to 12 ($25).

Winter Activities. See pp.256 and 257.

Yosemite Mountain Sugar Pine Railroad *on Highway 41 in Fish Camp, an hour drive from the valley, 209/683-7273; call for schedule; adults $5-$7, 3-12 $2.75-$3.75.* The cars on this narrow-gauge steam railway are carved out of logs. Passengers may stopover at the midway point of the scenic four-mile ride to picnic or hike. Moonlight rides, which include a steak-fry and campfire program, are scheduled Saturday nights in summer. Quaint Jenny rail cars operate on the same route as the train. This railroad is not affiliated with Yosemite National Park.

SEQUOIA AND KINGS CANYON NATIONAL PARKS

■ *A LITTLE BACKGROUND*

Though located just south of Yosemite National Park, these two scenic national parks are often overlooked. It's a shame because they, too, offer spectacular scenery and are much less crowded.

Their main attraction is the enormous sequoia trees, with their vibrant cinnamon-colored bark, located in Sequoia Park's **Giant Forest**. The largest is the **General Sherman Tree** which towers 275 feet high, measures 36 1/2 inches in diamenter, and is 3 to 4,000 years old—higher than Niagara Falls, as wide as a city street, and already middle-aged when Christ was born! It is said to be the largest living thing on this planet. **Mt. Whitney** is also located in Sequoia Park and at 14,495 feet is the highest point in the United States outside of Alaska. It is a two- to three-day hike to its peak.

Admission to the parks is $5 per car.

■ *VISITOR INFORMATION*

Sequoia and Kings Canyon National Parks *Three Rivers 93271, 209/ 565-3341.*

■ ANNUAL EVENTS

Caravan to Nation's Christmas Tree *December; 209/875-4575.* Since 1925 the **General Grant Tree** has been the site of a special Christmas service. In honor of its official status as the Nation's Christmas Tree, a wreath is placed at its base by members of the National Park Service. A car caravan leaves from the tiny town of Sanger and then reassembles nearby at the tree's base. Seats are available by reservation on a chartered bus.

■ GETTING THERE

Located approximately 250 miles southeast of San Francisco. Take Highway 80 to Highway 580 to Highway 99 south to Highway 180 east. In winter take Highway 198 through Visalia to Giant Forest, where most snow activities are centered.

■ WHERE TO STAY

Park Lodging *209/561-3314; 2-4/$-$$; cribs; some kitchens, fireplaces, private baths; restaurant.* At Sequoia, lodging includes both spartan and deluxe cabins as well as motel rooms. Kings Canyon has similar facilities, but they are generally less luxurious and there are fewer of them. Arrangements can be made to backpack into a camp facility with furnished tents. Campsites are available on a first-come, first-served basis. In the summer Lodgepole Campground may be reserved through Ticketron. Another option is to hike eleven miles into the High Sierra tent-cabin camp at Bearpaw; dinner and breakfast are included, and reservations are necessary. The best way to make lodging reservations is to call for a park brochure which explains the various options in detail. If interested, inquire about ski packages.

If you are unable to get lodging at the park facilities, several privately-owned lodgings are nearby:

Montecito-Sequoia Lodge See pp.255 and 262.

Wilsonia Lodge *209/335-2311.* For winter activities, see also p.256.

Further away:

Muir Trail Ranch *Lakeshore, 90 miles east of Fresno on Highway 168, 209/966-3195 (winter), no summer phone; $670/person/week; closed Oct-May; unsuitable for children under 6; all meals included.* One week is the minimum stay at this remote ranch in the High Sierra. Guests leave their cars behind and take a half-hour boat ride across Florence Lake. There they mount horses and ride into camp. Soaks in the natural hot springs pass for baths, and rates include meals, lodging in a tent-cabin, horses, and the boatride. Log cabins are extra.

Snowline Lodge *44138 E. Kings Canyon Rd., Dunlap, 8 miles from the parks, 209/336-2300; 2-4/$$; some kitchens, fireplaces; restaurant.* Both motel units and cabins are available on this 450-acre ranch located adjacent to **Sequoia National Forest**.

■ WHAT TO DO

Bicycle Rentals *in Cedar Grove.*

Caves.

> **Boyden Cavern** *in Kings Canyon, 209/736-2708; tours daily, May-Oct 11-4, June-Sept 10-5; adults $4, 6-12 $2; no strollers.* This cave is located in spectacular 8,000-foot-deep **Kings River Canyon**—the deepest canyon in the United States. Guided tours take about 45 minutes.

> **Crystal Cave** *in Sequoia; schedule varies, May-Sept only; adults $2, 6-11 $1.* This 50-degree marble cavern is reached via a 1/2 mile trail. The guided tour takes about an hour.

Fishing. The most popular spots are along Kings River and the forks of the Kaweah River.

Horse Rentals *in Cedar Grove, Wolverton, General Grant Grove, and Mineral King.*

Swimming/Sunbathing *at Bikini Beach.*

Trails. Over 900 miles of hiking trails are in these parks.

Unusual Trees. Most of these trees are encountered on the drive along the 46-mile **General's Highway**, which connects the two national parks. This highway is usually closed by snow December through May.

> **Auto Log.** Drive your car onto it for a photograph.

> **Room Tree.** Climb a ladder and enter down through a burn hole into the "room" and then exit through another burn hole.

> **Senate Group and House Group of Sequoias.** These are the most symmetrically formed and nearly perfect of the sequoias. They are reached via an easy trail beginning at the General Sherman Tree.

> **Tunnel Log.** Drive your car inside this tunnel carved through a tree which fell across the road in 1937.

Visitor Centers *at Lodgepole and Grant Grove; daily in summer 8-5, rest of year from 9; free.* See exhibits on the area's wildlife as well as displays on the Indians and sequoias. Inquire here about the schedule of nature walks and evening campfire programs.

Winter Activities. See pp.254 to 256.

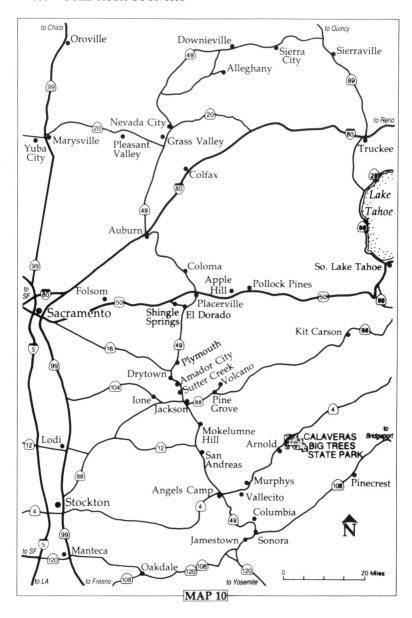

MAP 10

GOLD RUSH COUNTRY

■ *A LITTLE BACKGROUND*

The Mother Lode, as this area is also sometimes referred to, stretches along the entire route of Highway 49, south from Mariposa and north through Nevada City ending in Downieville. (On the other hand the Mother Lode *vein*, which runs from Northern California to South America, surfaces in the area between Jamestown and Auburn— where the primary gold vein was located.)

The main Gold Rush towns can all be visited by driving along Highway 49, but there are also many scenic sideroads to explore leading to towns with intriguing names like Fiddletown and Rescue.

This area provides history, adventure, and scenic beauty. Not yet heavily promoted and packaged, it also provides many low-key and inexpensive vacation joys for the hype-weary traveler. A thorough visit could take weeks, but a satisfying visit takes only a few days. If you are going for just a weekend, don't attempt to drive the entire route. Visit one portion and then go back another time to see the rest.

Because the area is steeped in history, I recommend doing a little reading for some background information. Two books about the area which are good for reading out loud are *The Celebrated Jumping Frog of Calaveras County* by Samuel L. Clemens (Mark Twain) and *The Luck of Roaring Camp* by Bret Harte.

Currently there is said to be another gold rush on. Many nervous people are staking claims, so it doesn't hurt to be cautious if you are interested in doing some prospecting yourself. As far as your prospects for success, Mark Twain once said, "A gold mine is a hole in the ground with a liar at the entrance."

■ *GETTING THERE*

Located approximately 135 miles east of San Francisco. Take Highway 80 to Highway 580 to Highway 205 to Highway 120 to Highway 49.

JAMESTOWN

■ *WHERE TO STAY*

Jamestown Hotel *Main St., 209/984-3902; 2/$$-$$$, 4/$$$; unsuitable for children under 7; continental breakfast, restaurant.* Built in the

1850s and recently remodeled, this hotel is furnished with Victorian antiques and cozy patchwork quilts. Many spacious suites with sitting rooms are available. Lunch and dinner are served daily in the nicely appointed dining room downstairs. The eclectic menu offers prime rib, seafood, chicken, veal, and pasta. Total consideration is given to children: highchairs, booster seats, children's portions, and even hamburgers are available. An attractive saloon adjacent to the dining room specializes in fancy drinks.

■ *WHERE TO EAT*

The Smoke Cafe *18228 Main St., 209/984-3733; D Tu-Sun; highchairs, booster seats, children's portions; no reservations; $$; no cards.* Located inside an old false-front building with tall ceilings and embossed tin walls, this friendly spot serves tasty Mexican chow. Specialties include pollo de mole poblano and chile verde. A hamburger is also available.

■ *WHAT TO DO*

Gold Prospecting Tours *18172 Main St., 209/984-GOLD; tours daily 9-5; 1-hr family tour $35.* Operating out of an old livery stable, this business organizes prospecting trips appropriate for children as well as adults. It is claimed gold has been found on every trip, and the rule is "finders, keepers." Once taught the basics, participants are guided to sites where they can continue panning on their own. All equipment is supplied. All-day trips and trips by river raft or helicopter can also be arranged.

Railtown 1897 State Historic Park *Fifth Ave., 209/984-3953; Sat & Sun, Apr-Oct; call for timetable; adults $7.50, 3-12 $3.50; roundhouse tours: daily 10-4; adults $2, 3-12 $1.25.* The Mother Lode Cannonball, an historic steam train, takes passengers on a one-hour, twelve-mile round trip to Lime Spur. Several special trips are also available on occasion. The **Wine & Cheese Zephyr** operates in spring and fall. Riders are served varietal wines, cheeses, fruits, and sourdough French bread. The kids get apple cider, and strolling musicians entertain everyone. The **Twilight Limited** operates in summer. Riders get cocktails and snacks en route and a steak barbecue back at the station. Tours of the old **roundhouse**, where the trains were maintained, are also available.

SONORA

■ *A LITTLE BACKGROUND*

This bustling town is a popular stopover spot for skiers and other travelers on their way to vacation cabins and recreation. Because it is a crossroads, it has been built up more than most Gold Rush towns and is far from quiet. But if you get off the main thoroughfares, you'll find a taste of the old Sonora—Victorian homes, quiet streets, and a bit of a country feeling.

■ *VISITOR INFORMATION*

Tuolumne County Visitors Bureau *P.O. Box 4020, (55 West Stockton), Sonora 95370, 800/446-1333, 209/533-4420.*

■ *WHERE TO STAY*

Gunn House Motel *286 S. Washington St., 209/532-3421; 2/$-$$, 4/ $$; 2-night minimum some weekends; cribs; all TVs, bathtubs; some refrigerators; continental breakfast; pool (heated in summer only).* Built in 1850, this two-story adobe house was once the residence of Dr. Lewis C. Gunn. Rooms are restored and furnished with antiques. The cozy office is staffed with helpful personnel, and a cocktail lounge is located by the pool.

■ *WHERE TO EAT*

Europa Coffee Shop *275 S. Washington St., 209/532-9957; B/L/D daily; highchairs, booster seats; no reservations; $; no cards.* Popular with local residents, this casual spot is open round-the-clock, offers an extensive choice of dinner entrees, and is well-known for homemade pies. Almost everything is made from scratch and cooked to perfection. Bargain-priced complete dinners include homemade soup, salad, a canned or frozen vegetable (I said *almost* everything), bread and butter, coffee, and dessert. Many children will be happy to see a hamburger and grilled cheese sandwich also on the menu.

■ *WHAT TO DO*

Autumn Colors Drive. Take Highway 108 about fifteen miles east for a dazzling tour of fall leaf colors.

Tuolumne County Museum and History Center *158 W. Bradford Ave., 209/532-1317; M,W,F 9-4:30, Tu,Th,Sat 10-3:30, Sun in summer 10-3:30; free.* Located inside a jail built in 1866, this museum displays various relics from the Gold Rush era.

COLUMBIA STATE HISTORIC PARK

■ *A LITTLE BACKGROUND*

In her prime, with over 6,000 people calling her home, Columbia was one of the largest mining towns in the southern Mother Lode. Her nickname, "Gem of the Southern Mines," was reference to the $87 million plus in gold mined there (a figure calculated when gold was $35 an ounce).

Since 1945 this reconstructed Gold Rush town has been a State Historic Park. It is open daily from 9 to 5 and admission is free. Streets are blocked off to all but foot traffic and an occasional stagecoach. A museum introduces visitors to the town's history, and related exhibits are scattered among the many restored historic buildings.

In fact, the whole town is basically a living museum. Pri-

vate concessionaires operate modern versions of businesses one would have found here in the 1800s. Cold mugs of beer and old-fashioned rootbeer-like sarsaparilla are poured in the town saloon, and classic melodrama is performed on a subterranean stage in what used to be a "palace of pleasure." A blacksmith eeks out a living practicing his craft in a ramshackle shed, and a candy kitchen uses 100-year-old recipes and antique equipment to turn out such old-time favorites as horehound, rocky road, and almond bark. Customers in the photography studio don Gold Rush-era clothing for portraits taken with vintage camera equipment but developed with modern quick-develop processes. And haircuts are still being given in what is reputed to be the oldest barbershop in the state. Visitors may even tour a still-operating gold mine and learn to pan for gold in a salted sluice.

In case Columbia looks familiar to you, *High Noon* and episodes of *Little House on the Prairie* were filmed here.

■ *VISITOR INFORMATION*

Columbia State Historic Park *P.O. Box 151, Columbia 95310, 209/ 532-4301.*

■ *ANNUAL EVENTS*

Easter Parade and Egg Hunt
Fire Muster *May.*
Miners Christmas *first 2 weekends in December.*

■ *WHERE TO STAY*

City Hotel *Main St., 209/532-1479; 2/$$, 4/$$$; children under 2 free; cribs; all shared baths; room service, continental breakfast, restaurant.* This 1856 hotel provides overnight lodging in keeping with the town's flavor. The restored rooms are furnished with Victorian antiques from the collection of the California State Parks Department. Eager-to-please students from the Columbia College Hospitality Management program dress in period clothing and supplement the full-time staff by performing such esoteric duties as fluffing pillows and, in the beautifully appointed French restaurant downstairs, de-crumbing tables. Guests are encouraged to congregate in the parlor in the evening for sherry and to entertain each other with conversation and games. To make their trek down the hall to the bath more civilized, guests are loaned a wicker basket packed with shower cap, slippers, robe, soap, and shampoo. A former chef at Ernie's in San Francisco runs the kitchen and prepares elegant cuisine for lunch and dinner. Reservations are suggested, and children are welcome. The cozy **What Cheer Saloon** adjoins.

Columbia Gem Motel *22131 Parrotts Ferry Rd., 1 mile from park, 209/586-6466; 2-4/$-$$; children under 12 free; cribs; all TVs; some bathtubs.* Typical motel room decor greets guests inside tiny cottages scattered in an attractive pine tree setting.

Fallon Hotel *Washington St., 209/532-1470; 2/$$-$$$, 4/$$$-$$$+; children under 2 free; cribs; mostly shared baths; continental breakfast.* This historic hotel, dating from 1857, has undergone a $4 million renovation and is now beautifully restored to Victorian grandeur. Many of the furnishings are original to the hotel. It is operated in similar style as the City Hotel and is under the same management. Special lodging/dinner/theatre packages are available.

■ *WHAT TO DO*

Fallon House Theatre *209/532-4644; summer performances only; reservations advised.* This historic theatre has been in operation since the 1880s. Plays have been performed here by the University of Pacific repertory theatre company since 1949. Call for current schedule.

MURPHYS

■ *A LITTLE BACKGROUND*

A map to the town's buildings and sights is available from merchants and at the check-in desk in the hotel. Across the street from the hotel, the **Old Timers Museum** operates inside the oldest stone building in town. Dating from 1856, it now houses Gold Rush-era memorabilia.

■ *WHERE TO STAY*

♥ **Dunbar House, 1880** *271 Jones St., 209/728-2897; 2/$$; unsuitable*

for children under 10; 1 fireplace; some shared baths; full breakfast.
This restored Italianate-style home was the location for the TV series
Seven Brides for Seven Brothers. The five rooms are furnished with
antiques, and smoking is not permitted.

Murphys Hotel *457 Main St., 209/728-3444; 2-4/$-$$; children under
13 free; cribs; some TVs; some shared baths; continental breakfast,
restaurant.* The rooms in this old hotel, built in 1856, are said to
have provided lodging for such Gold Rush-era luminaries as U.S.
Grant, J.P. Morgan, Mark Twain, Horatio Alger, John Muir, and
Black Bart—each of whom has a room he actually stayed in named
after him. It is now a National Historical Monument. Modern motel
rooms, with no legends attached, are available adjacent to the hotel.
Though the hotel rooms are immeasurably more interesting, they
have one big drawback: The noisy hotel bar, reputed to be the best in
the Mother Lode, is kept jumping until the wee hours by townspeople and travelers alike. If you want to sleep, opt for a less interesting
but quiet motel room. In the winter, inquire about special skier rates.
The reasonably priced restaurant located on the main floor of the
hotel serves breakfast, lunch, and dinner daily and is also popular
with locals. The portions tend to be large and consist of hearty,
made-from-scratch American country fare like fried chicken, hamburgers, and steaks. Complete facilities are available for children.

■ WHERE TO EAT

The Peppermint Stick *454 Main St., 209/728-3570; daily spring &
summer, closed Tu rest of year; booster seats, children's portions;
no reservations; $; no cards.* This building was constructed in 1893
and served the town as an ice house. Now it is a cheerful ice cream
parlor serving old-fashioned sodas and cleverly named sundae concoctions. Sandwiches, soups, and homemade candies are also available, and everything can be packed to go.

■ WHAT TO DO

Black Bart Players *209/728-3956; weekends in Apr & Nov, 8pm; reservations suggested; tickets $5.* This little theatre group does musi-
cals, melodramas, mysteries, comedies, and classics. Call for current
schedule.

Calaveras Big Trees State Park *on Highway 4, Arnold, 15 miles east
of town, 209/795-2334; daily dawn-dusk; $2/car.* This ancient forest
houses the mammoth and now rare sequoia variety of redwood. The
Big Trees nature trail is a choice trek for families with young children. Other trails are also available, as are campsites and picnic and

barbecue facilities. In warm weather, the Beaver Creek Picnic Area is a good wading area for children. Picnic provisions can be picked up in town, where there are delis, markets, and restaurants. Ranger-led snowshoe walks and cross-country ski tours are scheduled in winter (see p.177).

Mercer Caverns *off Highway 4, 1 mile north of town, 209/728-2101; June-Sept daily 9-5, rest of year Sat & Sun 11-4; adults $4, 5-11 $2; no strollers.* Discovered over 100 years ago in 1885, this well-lit 55-degree limestone cavern takes about a half-hour to tour. It is said to be the longest continually operating commercial canvern in the state.

Moaning Cavern *on Parrotts Ferry Rd. west of town, Vallecito, 209/736-2708; daily 9-6 in summer, 10-5 in winter; adults $4.50, 6-12 $2.25; no strollers.* The 45-minute tour ascends a 100-foot spiral staircase into the largest public cavern chamber in California. The cavern was first discovered by Indians, many of whom are thought to have fallen to their death here. It was then used as a burial site. In fact, the oldest human remains in the U.S. have been found here. A more expensive three-hour **rappel tour** is available which allows a 180-foot rope descent into the cave; reservations are necessary. Camping is permitted at the cavern; call for further details.

Stevenot Winery *2690 San Domingo Rd., 1 mile past Mercer Cavern, 209/728-3436; tasting & tours daily 10-5.* Located in a canyon on the site of the first swimming pool in Calaveras County, this relatively new winery (circa 1976) is housed in a series of old buildings.

The rustic tasting room has a sod roof and split-log walls. Picnic tables are sheltered under a grape arbor and feature a view of the vineyards.

Moaning Cavern rappel tour.

ANGELS CAMP

■ *VISITOR INFORMATION*

Calaveras County Chamber of Commerce *P.O. Box 111, (753 S. Main St.), Angels Camp 95222, 209/754-1821.*

■ *ANNUAL EVENTS*

Jumping Frog Jubilee *third weekend in May; 209/736-2561.* Visitors are invited to bring their own frog to enter in this historic contest, but rental frogs are available on site. In 1986 Rosie the Ribbiter set the world's record by jumping 21 feet 5 and 3/4 inches. She earned her jockey $1,500. The prize money is usually won by frog jockies who are serious about the sport and bring 50 to 60 frogs. A rental frog has never won. The **Calaveras County Fair** is part of the fun and features carnival rides, livestock exhibits, a rodeo, a destruction derby, and fireworks.

■ *PICNIC PICK-UPS*

Informal picnic areas may be found by the river. Scenic **Utica Park** has picnic tables and a children's play area. **Angels Bakery** *(1277 Main)* has cheese and salt breadsticks, garlic bread, and fruit bars among its baked goods. The **Pickle Barrel Deli** *(1225 Main)* will pack picnic supplies to go and has tables should you decide to stay.

■ *WHAT TO DO*

Angels Camp Museum *753 S. Main St., 209/736-4444; M-F 9-5, Sat & Sun 10-3; adults 50¢.* Of special interest here are the extensive rock collection and assemblage of old wagons and buggies.

SAN ANDREAS

■ *WHERE TO STAY*

Black Bart Inn and Motel *55 St. Charles St., 209/754-3808; 2-4/$;*

cribs; some TVs, bathtubs; some shared baths; restaurant; unheated pool. Rooms are available in the old hotel or in a more modern motel located adjacent.

■ *WHAT TO DO*

Calaveras County Historical Museum *30 N. Main St., 209/754-4203; daily 10-4; adults 50¢, under 13 25¢.* Items on display upstairs in this restored 1867 courthouse include Indian and Gold Rush artifacts. Among the nicely organized exhibits are life-size room displays of a Gold Rush-era general store and a miner's cabin. Downstairs, in a rustic courtyard planted with native California flora, you can see the jail cell Black Bart once occupied.

California Caverns at Cave City *off Mountain Ranch Rd., 10 miles east of town, 209/736-2708; June-Oct daily 10-4, in Nov Sat & Sun only; adults $4.50, 6-12 $2.25; no strollers.* This cavern was first opened to the public in 1850. The lighted, nearly level trail follows the footsteps of John Muir, Mark Twain, and Bret Harte. The tour runs 1 1/4 hour. Another more strenuous **spelunking tour** through the unlighted portion of the cavern is available by reservation only. This $49 tour "involves climbing rocks and a 60-foot ladder, squeezing through small passages, crossing 200-foot-deep lakes on rafts, and viewing breathtaking formations unequalled in any other cavern in the West." Reservations are necessary, and participants must be in good health, not pregnant, and at least 12 years old.

MOKELUMNE HILL

■ *WHERE TO STAY*

Hotel Leger *Main St., 209/286-1401; 2/$-$$, 4/$$-$$$; closed part of Jan; children under 2 free; cribs; some fireplaces, bathtubs; some shared baths; restaurant; unheated pool.* Once considered among the most luxurious of Gold Rush hotels, this 1879 lodging still has comfortable rooms—many with sitting areas and all with tasteful period furniture. A dining room and old-time saloon, complete with player piano, are located on the ground floor. Sometimes plays are scheduled in the **Court House Theatre.** Call for current schedule.

JACKSON

■ *VISITOR INFORMATION*

Amador County Chamber of Commerce *P.O. Box 596, (30 S. Highway 49), Jackson 95642, 209/223-0350.*

■ *ANNUAL EVENTS*

Gold Dust Days *first part of April.* Participate in free gold panning lessons and field trips.

Italian Picnic *first weekend in June; Italian Picnic Grounds at the Amador County Fair Grounds in Plymouth.* For over 100 years the public has been invited to this festive event. There are kiddie rides for the children, dancing for the adults, and a parade (in Sutter Creek) and barbecue for everyone.

■ *WHERE TO STAY*

Broadway Hotel *225 Broadway, 209/223-3503; 2/$, 4/$$; children under 4 free; cribs; some TVs, bathtubs, 1 refrigerator; some shared baths; continental breakfast; jacuzzi.* Located just a few blocks from downtown, this former miner's hotel is furnished with antiques. Swings and a sandbox await young children.

Country Squire Motel *1105 N. Main St., 209/223-1657; 2-4/$; cribs; all TVs; continental breakfast.* Located out in the country adjacent to the old Kennedy Gold Mine site, this comfortable motel housed one of the last private gambling casinos in California. It was closed in 1952. Some of the units are restored and some are motel-modern. Gold panning may be practiced year-round in the backyard "crick," and ducks and sheep roam freely on farm land across the way. There is plenty of grass for children to romp on.

National Hotel *2 Water St., 209/223-0500; 2/$, 4/$$; dining facilities; Sat night reservations must include D & B reservations in dining room.* This hotel claims to be the oldest in continuous operation (since 1862) in California. Room decor is modest, as are the prices. Prior guests have included two Presidents (Garfield and Hoover) and John Wayne. A cozy cellar dining room serves dinner Friday through Sunday and breakfast on Sunday. Lunch is served Wednesday through Sunday in the bar.

■ *WHERE TO STAY NEARBY*

♥ **The Heirloom** *214 Shakeley Lane, Ione, 12 miles from town, 209/ 274-4468; 2/$$; unsuitable for children under 10; some fireplaces; some shared baths; room service, full breakfast.* Being located in a town that was once known as Bed Bug could be a bit of a disadvantage for some lodgings. This B&B is so charming, however, that this history is easily overlooked. Resembling a colonial mansion, this circa 1863 building is situated down a country lane. It is right on Sutter Creek and has large, grassy grounds. Two of the rooms are in an adjacent sod-roof cottage. A full French country breakfast is served each morning.

Roaring Camp Mining Co. *Pine Grove, 209/296-4100; $280/week for a prospectors cabin, each extra person $65-$105; closed Oct-Apr; modern bath house; restaurant.* Guests make the one-hour trip into a remote canyon via truck; cars are left behind. They stay in this former mining camp in rustic prospector cabins without electricity and must bring all their own gear and food. Recreation consists of swimming, fishing, and panning for gold in the Mokelumne River, as well as hiking and perhaps collecting rocks. Guests may keep up to one ounce of found gold; anything over one ounce per cabin must be split with Roaring Camp. A saloon, short order restaurant, and general store are available when guests get tired of roughing it. On Wednesday evenings a group of transient guests is trucked in for a riverside steak cookout; weekly guests are invited to join this event at no charge. For stays of less than a week, call the Monday before you wish to go. Weekly stays run Sunday to Sunday. Shorter four-hour day tours are also available.

■ *WHERE TO EAT*

Right on Main *134 Main, 209/223-0611; L daily; highchairs, booster seats; $; no cards.* This old-fashioned ice cream parlor/candy store has been serving up sweet confections since the turn of the century. Nowadays you can also get soup, sandwiches, and freshly ground coffee.

Wells Fargo Restaurant *Water St., 209/223-9956; B/L/D daily; highchairs, booster seats; $; MC,V.* Daily dinner specials include such all-American items as baked shortribs, roast lamb, roast pork, baked ham, and breaded veal. The restaurant is known for its steaks, chicken, and ribs. Well-prepared, generous portions keep even the locals coming back. Hot and cold sandwiches and hamburgers are also available at dinner. An adjacent saloon dates back to the mid-1800s.

■ *WHAT TO DO*

Amador County Museum *225 Church St., 209/223-6386; W-Sun 10-4; free.* This museum is located inside an 1859 red brick house with a brightly painted wooden train engine (formerly used as a prop on TV's *Petticoat Junction*) permanently parked in front. Scale models of the Kennedy Mine tailing wheels and head frame and the North Star Mine stamp mill are on display and operated hourly(fee). Call for schedule.

Kennedy Mine Tailing Wheels *on Jackson Gate Rd; dawn to dusk; free.* Four huge 58-foot-diameter wheels, originally built in 1912 to carry waste gravel from the nearby mine, may be viewed by taking a short walk on well-marked trails on either side of the road. Two of the wheels have already collapsed. Better hurry to see this site before time takes its toll on the other two. The abandoned Kennedy Mine may be seen from the site of wheels 1 and 2. Picnic tables are available.

Wine Tasting. Many wineries are located in this area, with a heavy concentration occuring around the nearby town of Plymouth. Contact the Chamber of Commerce for a free map/brochure.

SUTTER CREEK

■ *A LITTLE BACKGROUND*

Seven gold mines were once located on this quiet Main Street. Now it is lined with modern gold mines—antique shops.

■ *SPECIAL EVENTS*

Christmas B&B Tour *December; P.O. Box 305, Sutter Creek 95685, 209/296-3519.*

■ *WHERE TO STAY*

♥ **Sutter Creek Inn** *75 Main St., 209/267-5606; 2/$-$$$; 2-night minimum on Sat; unsuitable for children under 15; some fireplaces; full breakfast.* Have you been longing to spend the night in a bed suspended from the ceiling by chains? You can fulfill that and other yearnings here (the guests really *swing* here), and maybe even see a friendly ghost. Opened as an inn in 1964, this 1859 Greek Revival structure was one of the first B&Bs in the state. In the morning guests are served brandy and coffee by the fireplace, and then at 9 a.m. sharp a full sit-down breakfast is served in the dining room and kitchen. Spontaneous entertainment, in the form of lectures and concerts, sometimes occurs in the parlor, and croquet and hammocks beckon from the gardens. Handwriting analysis and massages are available by appointment. The more expensive rooms are in an adjacent carriage house.

■ *WHERE TO EAT*

Bellotti Inn *53 Main St., 209/267-5211; L/D daily; highchairs, booster seats, children's portions; reservations suggested; $$; no cards.* Located inside an historic building, this well-established saloon and restaurant serves huge Italian family-style dinners with veal, chicken, and steak entrees. A la carte items and a hamburger are also on the menu. Inexpensive rooms are available in the hotel.

Sutter Creek Palace *76 Main St., 209/267-9852; L/D W-Sun; highchairs, booster seats, children's portions; reservations suggested; $$; MC,V.* Entry to this western-style saloon, dominated by a large bar, is through old-time swinging corner doors. The menu fare is interesting, and sometimes on the weekends there is live entertainment.

VOLCANO

■ *A LITTLE BACKGROUND*

The scenic, rural drive here from Sutter Creek is ill-marked and poorly paved and best maneuvered during daylight. And it's been my experience that directions and information obtained around here can often be vague or misleading, leaving plenty of room for error. A good map can be worth its weight in gold.

Because this tiny town is built in a depression on top of limestone caves, it is green year-round. Sleepy and quiet now, during the Gold Rush it was a boom town well-known for its boisterous dance halls and saloons. It also opened the state's first public library.

■ *WHERE TO STAY*

St. George Hotel *16104 Volcano-Pine Grove Rd., 209/296-4458; 2-4/ $-$$, on weekends $$$ but includes B & D; closed Jan-Feb; 1 bathtub; some shared baths; restaurant.* This solidly constructed hotel offers a choice of rooms in either the main hotel, built in 1862, or in an annex built almost a hundred years later in 1961. For safety reasons families with children under 12 must stay in the newer and charmless annex located around the corner, their consolation being that they get a private bathroom. In the hotel there is a cozy memorabilia-crammed bar and parlour area, with fireplace and games, to relax in. Dinner is served in an adjacent dining room Wednesday through Saturday, and reservations are necessary. Breakfast is served on weekends, and a special chicken dinner is served on Sunday from 1 to 6.

■ *WHERE TO EAT*

Jug and Rose Confectionery *Main St., 209/296-4696; B/L W-Sun, in winter F-Sun; highchairs, children's portions; reservations suggested; $; no cards.* Famous for all-you-can-eat sourdough pancake breakfasts, this charming spot has been in business since 1855. In the Gold Rush days it was located in a different spot and known as The Stone Jug Saloon. A prior owner had the saloon ruin moved to its present site stone by stone. Sourdough pancakes are served with warm spice syrup, strawberries and sour cream, and blackberry topping, and children's orders are made in animal shapes. (The pancakes have only been served since 1958, when Sourdough Jack visited from Alaska with his crock of sourdough.) Lunch brings homemade soups, sandwiches, and pie to the menu. Teatime goodies and exotic sundaes lure afternoon customers. How about a Moss Rose Sundae (homemade rose petal syrup on vanilla ice cream topped in season with an antique-variety rose) a Sierra Split (three flavors of ice cream, wild blackberry topping, and banana), or a Plain Jane for scardy cats? All items are served with fresh flower garnishes. A scaled-down version of the old-fashioned ice cream parlor-style tables and chairs is available for kids, along with a basket full of toys to entertain them.

■ *WHAT TO DO*

Daffodil Hill *on Shake Ridge Rd., 3 miles north of town, 209/296-7048; Mar-Apr; by donation.* Originally planted in the 1850s by a Dutch settler, then added to and maintained by Grandma McLaughlin, this six-acre garden boasts more than 300 varieties of daffodils. More bulbs are planted every year by her grandchildren and great grandchildren. Currently over 300,000 bloom together each spring, making for a spectacular display. A few tulips and hyacinths are mixed in, too. Peacocks, chickens, and sheep wander the grounds, and there is a picnic area with tables. One of the best things about this seasonal extravaganza of bloom is that it is completely non-commercial.

Indian Grinding Rock State Historic Park *14881 Pine Grove-Volcano Rd., Pine Grove, southwest of town, 209/296-7488; closed Jan-Mar; museum: Sat-W 10-5; $2/car.* The largest of the grinding rocks—a huge flat bedrock limestone measuring 175 feet by 82 feet—has over 2,100 mortar holes and approximately 300 **petroglyphs** (rock carvings). All were made by Miwok Indians who ground their acorns and other seeds here with pestles. A reconstructed **Miwok Village** contains a ceremonial roundhouse, a hand-game house, several cedar bark tepees, and an Indian football field. There is also a self-guided nature trail and a museum which orients visitors with a slide show and interpretive displays. Picnic facilities are available, and visitors may also secure campsites or arrange to camp in one of the authentic bark houses. A **"Big Time" Miwok Celebration** is scheduled each September.

"Old Abe" Volcano Blues Cannon. Located in the center of town in a protected shelter, this cannon—without firing a shot—helped win the Civil War. Cast of bronze and brass in Boston in 1837 and weighing 737 pounds, it somehow reached San Francisco and was smuggled to Volcano in 1863. It was used by the town to control renegades who were drawn there in search of quick wealth. For the complete story, ask around town. And don't believe everything you hear.

Park. Scenic stone ruins, rocky terrain, and a gurgling stream provide a picturesque backdrop against which to enjoy a picnic or just a few moments of quiet contemplation.

Sing Kee's Store. Built in 1857 and formerly a general store, this building is now a gift shop.

Volcano Pioneers Community Theatre Group *209/223-0587; Apr-Oct, F & Sat at 8pm, occasionally Th & Sun; tickets $6; reservations necessary.* The first little theater group to form in California was the Volcano Thespian Society in 1854. Children are welcome at performances in the intimate 50-seat **Cobblestone Theater**.

AMADOR CITY

■ *A LITTLE BACKGROUND*

With a population of 130, this is said to be the smallest incorporated city in the state.

■ *WHERE TO STAY*

Mine House Inn *14125 Highway 49, 209/267-5900; 2/$-$$, 4/$$; children under 2 free; continental breakfast; unheated pool (unavail. Oct-Apr).* Formerly a mine office, this attractive restored brick building now houses guest rooms furnished with Gold Rush-era antiques. Each room is named for its original function: the Mill Grinding Room, the Vault Room, the Retort Room. In the morning, just push the buzzer and coffee is delivered to the door (children get hot chocolate). One Easter when my family was staying here, we arranged for an Easter basket to arrive in this same mysterious manner. Our son still hasn't figured out how that one was pulled off.

■ *WHERE TO EAT*

Buffalo Chips Emporium *Highway 49, 209/267-0570; B/L daily, closed M & Tu in winter; highchairs; $; no cards.* Some folks just buy a cone here and then sit outside on one of the weathered benches to leisurely watch the busy world drive by. Others prefer to sit inside what was once the town's Wells Fargo Bank and indulge in a fancy fountain item.

The Cellar *10 Main St., 209/267-0384; L Sat & Sun, D Tu & F-Sun; highchairs; $$; MC,V.* Located in the stone-walled cellar of a former bakery, this unusual restaurant serves fondue, sandwiches prepared with homemade sourdough bread, and homemade soups and desserts. Children may be interested to know that both a peanut butter & jelly sandwich and chocolate fondue are on the menu.

DRYTOWN

■ *A LITTLE BACKGROUND*

Once the home of 27 saloons, Drytown is now known for its equally abundant antique shops.

■ *WHAT TO DO*

Piper Playhouse *209/245-3812; May-Sept, F-Sun; tickets $9; reservations necessary.* Raucous melodramas are the bill of fare. Call for current schedule.

SHINGLE SPRINGS

■ *WHERE TO EAT*

Sam's Town *Highway 50/Cameron Park, 916/677-2273; B/L/D daily.* This is a funky combination restaurant/honky-tonk piano bar/general store/memorabilia museum/pinball arcade. The outside grounds are littered with covered wagons, and the inside floors are littered with peanut shells discarded by happy revelers. Food runs the gamut from a hamburger and soda to prime rib and champagne.

EL DORADO

■ *WHERE TO EAT*

Poor Red's *Highway 49, 916/622-2901; L M-F, D M-Sun; highchairs, booster seats; no reservations; $; MC,V.* Judging just from the outside, which looks to be an unsavory bar, I would easily have passed this spot by. But then I would have missed the experience of dining on exquisite ham, ribs, chicken, and steak—all cooked over an open oakwood pit and served in generous portions. Because this restaurant is very popular and also very small, weekend dinner waits can run over an hour. Some patrons pass that time downing Gold Cadillacs at the old-time horseshoe bar; some pass it staring at the mural behind the bar depicting the town as it appeared in the late 1800s; and some pass it feeding the jukebox. Others beat the wait by ordering take-out.

PLACERVILLE

■ *A LITTLE BACKGROUND*

Placerville was once known as Hangtown because hangings here were so common. This is where the Hangtown Fry (eggs, bacon, and oysters) originated. Mark Hopkins, Philip Armour, and John Studebaker all got their financial starts here as well.

■ *VISITOR INFORMATION*

El Dorado County Chamber of Commerce *P.O. Box 268, (542 Main St.), Placerville 95667, 916/626-2344.*

■ *ANNUAL EVENTS*

Reenactment of Pony Express *July; in Pollock Pines, 916/644-3970.*

Apple Hill *September-December; P.O. Box 494, Camino 95709.*
Located on a mountain ridge east of town, the route for the Apple Hill tour follows an historic path originally blazed out in 1857 by Pony Express riders. In the fall, various farms along this route sell eighteen varieties of tree-fresh apples at bargain prices as well as homemade apple goodies like apple cider, spicy apple butter, and caramel apples. Many of the farms have picnic facilities; some also have hiking trails, fishing ponds, pony rides, and train rides. A number of Christmas tree farms are also located here. For a free map to the farms, send a legal-size stamped, self-addressed envelope.

■ *WHERE TO EAT*

The Sundae Times *3025 Sacramento St., 916/621-1921; daily 11am-11pm; highchairs, booster seats, children's portions; $; MC, V.* It seems like it is hot as blazes every time my family hits this lively boom town. So we were happy to see this cheerful, air-conditioned spot on our most recent visit. We sat on ornate wire chairs at cute little tables and cooled our palates with generous hot fudge sundaes. In addition to a large selection of ice cream concoctions, there are soups, salads, and sandwiches. A grilled peanut butter & jelly sandwich lurks among the special children's items.

■ *WHAT TO DO*

Boeger Winery *1709 Carson Rd., off Highway 50 at Schnell School Rd., 916/622-8094; tasting and tours daily 10-5.* The old stone cellar tasting room is part of the original winery which was operated from the 1860s through the 1920s. Shaded stream-side picnic tables beckon.

El Dorado County Historical Museum *100 Placerville Dr., 2 miles west of town at the El Dorado County Fairgrounds, 916/626-2250; W-Sat 10-4, Sun 1-4; free.* Historic exhibits in this "great hall" include a Wells Fargo stagecoach and a wheelbarrow made by John Studebaker in the days before he manufactured cars.

Gold Bug Mine *on Bedford Ave., in Bedford Park, 1 mile north of town, 916/622-0832; daily 8:30-dusk; free.* Visitors can walk through a 1/4-mile-long lighted mine shaft, picnic at stream-side tables, and hike in this rugged 61-acre park.

Mama's Llamas. See p.270.

Sierra Vista Winery *4560 Cabernet Way, 916/622-7221; tours & tasting Sat & Sun 11-5.* Enjoy a magnificent view of the Sierras while picnicking at this pleasant winery. Bring lawn toys for children.

COLOMA

■ *A LITTLE BACKGROUND*

This is where James Marshall discovered gold in 1848.

■ *WHERE TO STAY*

Sierra Nevada House III *835 Lotus Rd., 916/622-0777; 2/$$, 4/$$$; cribs; some bathtubs; room service, continental breakfast, restau-*

rant. Built near the ruins of two former hotels of the same name, which burned to the ground in 1907 and 1926, this is an authentic reconstruction. Some rooms are in the older hotel and some are in a newer motel addition. A soda fountain dispenses short-order items as well as a special soda made from a turn-of-the-century recipe. Delicious homemade dinners with all the trimmings are available in a casual dining room. If food was this good here during the Gold Rush, the miners must have lost plenty of gold while they sat here eating instead of panning. Complete family amenities are provided.

♥ **The Vineyard House** *on Cold Springs Rd., 916/622-2217; 2/$-$$; unsuitable for children under 16; all shared baths; continental breakfast, restaurant.* Rumored to be haunted by its 19th century proprietors, this comfortable inn's wine cellar and jail cell now serve as a bar with live music on Friday and Saturday nights. Homemade dinners are served daily in the four dining rooms. Entrees include chicken and dumplings, beef stroganoff, fish, and prime rib. Children's portions are available, as are highchairs and booster seats.

■ *WHAT TO DO*

Marshall Gold Discovery State Historic Park *on Highway 49, 916/622-3470; park: daily 10-dusk, $3/car; museum: daily 10-5, adults 50¢, 6-17 25¢.*

This lovely 265-acre park encompasses 70% of the town. It contains a reconstruction of the original Sutter sawmill (where the Gold Rush began) as well as picnic facilities, nature trails, Gold Rush-era buildings and artifacts, and a museum. An exact replica of the piece of gold Marshall found is on disply in the museum (the original is at the Smithsonian in Washington, D.C.). The mill is sometimes operated; call for schedule.

AUBURN

■ *VISITOR INFORMATION*

Auburn Area Visitors and Convention Bureau *512 Auburn Ravine Rd., Auburn 95603, 800/433-7575, 916/885-5616.*

■ *WHERE TO EAT*

Auburn Hotel *853 Lincoln Way, 916/885-8132; D daily; highchairs, booster seats, children's portions; reservations suggested; $$; MC,V.* The seven-course family-style Basque dinners served here are popular with both locals and travelers. Call for current menu. A coffee shop is open for breakfast and lunch, and inexpensive rooms are available upstairs.

Cafe Delicias *1591 Lincoln Way, 916/885-2050; L/D W-M; highchairs; $; CB,D,MC,V.* Located in one of the town's oldest buildings, this cafe-atmosphere Mexican restaurant serves especially good flautas and homemade tamales. Mexican wedding cake makes a great dessert but is, unfortunately, often unavailable.

■ *WHAT TO DO*

Placer County Historic Museum Complex *museum: 1273 High St. in the Gold Country Fairgrounds, 916/885-9570; house: 291 Auburn-Folsom Rd., 916/885-0264; Tu-Sun 10-4; adults $1, 6-16 50¢, fee good for both locations.* Built of logs and stones, this old-time museum emphasizes mining exhibits but also displays local Maidu Indian artifacts and an extensive doll collection. Docent-led tours are available of the nearby Greek Revival-style **Bernhard House**, built in 1851 and furnished with Victorian antiques.

GRASS VALLEY

■ *A LITTLE BACKGROUND*

This was once the richest gold mining region in the state.

■ *VISITOR INFORMATION*

Nevada County Chamber of Commerce *248 Mill St., Grass Valley 95945, 800/752-6222, 916/273-4667.* It's worth visiting this office in person because of its location inside a replica of the historic home once occupied by scandalous Gold Rush personality Lola Montez.

■ *ANNUAL EVENTS*

Bluegrass Festival *July; 916/273-6217.*

Cornish Christmas Street Faire *December.* Experience an old-time Christmas at this event celebrating the traditions of the Cornish miners who settled this Gold Rush town. Visitors can dance in the downtown streets, which are closed to traffic, and ride in a horse-drawn carriage.

■ WHERE TO STAY

Alta Sierra Resort Motel *135 Tammy Way, 800/992-5300, 916/273-9102; 2/$-$$, 4/$$-$$$+; cribs; all TVs, bathtubs; some refrigerators.* Finding this rustic modern motel is a little like going on a treasure hunt. Just keep following those signs down that winding country road, and when you finally do find it, you'll probably agree it is somewhat of a treasure. Woodsy, spacious rooms overlook a small lake and picturesque, grassy grounds. Guests have complimentary access to a pool (summer only), golf course, tennis courts, and inexpensive dining at a country club located across the street.

Domike's Inn *220 Colfax Ave., 916/273-9010; 2/$-$$; children under 6 free; cribs; all bathtubs; 1 TV; some shared baths; full breakfast.* Located in the heart of the old section of town, this Queen Anne-style Victorian was built in 1890. Now it serves as a B&B.

♥ Holbrooke Hotel *212 W. Main, 916/273-1353; 2/$-$$$+; unsuitable for children under 12; all TVs; 2 fireplaces, some bathtubs; continental breakfast, restaurant.* Established in 1851, this grand hotel was meticulously restored and reopened in 1984. Past guests include four Presidents (Grant, Garfield, Cleveland, and Harrison). Current guests can step back in time in its beautifully decorated rooms featuring goodies like claw-foot tubs and brass beds. An old-time saloon and elegant restaurant with full family amenities operate on the main floor, and the hotel is conveniently located in the center of town.

Sivananda Ashram Vrindavan Yoga Farm *14651 Ballantree Lane, 916/272-9322; 2/$; all shared baths; meals included.* The bell rings at 5:30 each morning to wake guests. Attendance at scheduled meditation and yoga disciplines is mandatory. In between guests are fed vegetarian meals and given plenty of free time to enjoy the natural surroundings of the 60-acre farm. Guests bring their own sleeping bags and are assigned to the separate men's or women's dorms. Small huts are available for couples and families, and during the summer guests may bring their own tents.

■ WHERE TO EAT

Mrs. Dubblebee's Pasties *251 S. Auburn, 916/272-7700; daily 10-5:30; $; no cards.* Located inside a pristine white Victorian home, this unusual take-out eatery specializes in pasties. These meat and potato turnovers were once popular lunch fare among the area's Cornish miners. They carried them down into the mines in their pockets. At lunchtime they reheated their pasties on a shovel held over candles in their hard hats. Fruit turnovers and drinks are also available. How about a hasty tasty pasty picnic? (Actually, pasty rhymes with *nasty*.) You can also stay and eat them on the front porch. More pasties are available at **Marshall's Pasties** *(203 Mill St., 916/272-2844)* and at **King Richard's** *(217 Colfax Ave., 916/273-0286)*.

Tofanelli's *302 W. Main St., 916/273-9927; B/L daily, D M-F; high-chairs, booster seats, children's portions; $; MC,V*. Every kind of breakfast item imaginable is on this menu—including design-your-own-omelettes, whole wheat pancakes and waffles, and a large selection of teas. Salads, sandwiches, and a variety of hamburgers—including a tofuburger and a veggieburger—join the menu at lunch. All this and an attractive brick and oak decor, too.

■ *WHAT TO DO*

Bridgeport Bridge *take Highway 20 west about 8 miles to Pleasant Valley, turn right (north) and follow the south fork of the Yuba River 5-6 miles*. Built in 1862 and in use until 1971, this is the longest (233 feet) single-span wood-covered bridge in the world. It is now a State Historical Landmark. It is not currently maintained and its condition is shaky, so be careful should you decide to walk across it.

Empire Mine State Historic Park *10791 E. Empire St., 916/273-8522; daily 10-dusk; guided tours daily in summer at 1:30 & 3:30; adults $1, 6-17 50¢*. Once the largest and richest hard rock mine in the state, the Empire Mine was operated for over a century from 1850 to 1956. Now it is a 784-acre state park. Of special interest are the stone **Bourn Mansion** *(Sat & Sun 12 to 4)*, designed by Willis Polk

in the style of an English country lodge, and the formal gardens and fountains which surround it. The mining area illustrates many facets of the business and allows visitors to look down a lit mine shaft. There are also 22 miles of self-guided back country hiking trails.

Memorial Park *Colfax/Central Aves., 916/273-3171.* This is a good spot to picnic, get in a game of tennis, swim in the public pool, wade in the creek, or let the kids romp at the well-equipped playground.

North Star Mining Museum and Pelton Wheel Exhibit *Allison Ranch Rd./McCourtney Rd., 916/273-4255; May-Oct Tu-Sun 11-5; adults 50¢, under 18 free.* This rustic stone building, which was once the North Star Mine Power House, houses a collection of old photographs, mining dioramas and models, and a 30-foot-diameter Pelton water wheel dating from 1896 and weighing ten tons. A grassy picnic area is located across adjacent Wolf Creek.

NEVADA CITY

■ A LITTLE BACKGROUND

Said to be the best privately preserved and restored small city in the state, this picturesque mining town is also said to contain residential and commercial buildings representative of all the major 19th century architectural styles. Scenically situated on seven hills, the town boasts a particularly fine assortment of lovely gingerbread-style Victorian homes.

■ VISITOR INFORMATION

Nevada City Chamber of Commerce *132 Main St., Nevada City 95959, 916/265-9019.*

Sierra County Chamber of Commerce *P.O. Box 555, Downieville 95936, 916/289-3619.*

■ ANNUAL EVENTS

Spring in the Sierra House and Garden Tour *April; 916/265-5804.* Planners of this tour emphasize history, quality, and interest. So, unlike a stylish decorator showhouse, this tour offers a look at homes decorated by people who actually live in them.

International Teddy Bear Convention *April; 916/265-5804.* Bears from all over the world come out of hibernation for this warm, fuzzy event. Bearaphernalia and bear necessities and luxuries abound, and all kinds of bears are available for adoption.

4th of July Parade. Held in Nevada City on even years and in Grass Valley on odd, this is a real old-fashioned celebration. As might be expected, it ends with a fireworks extravaganza.

Constitution Day Parade *September.* The signing of the U.S. Constitution is honored with marching bands, drill teams, floats, fire engines, and horsemen. Pre-parade activities include a reenactment of the signing and a demonstration of colonial dancing.

Fall Colors *mid-October through mid-November.*

Victorian Christmas *the four Wednesday evenings before Christmas.*

■ *WHERE TO STAY IN TOWN*

♥ **Grandmere's Inn** *449 Broad St., 916/265-4660; 2/$$$-$$$+, 4/ $$$+; 1 TV, 1 refrigerator, some bathtubs; full breakfast.* Built in 1861, this three-story Colonial Revival home is on the National Register of Historic Places. It is beautifully decorated in French country style, with antique pine furnishings and gorgeous floral fabrics, and is conveniently located at the Top of Broad Street—one of the town's earliest residential areas. Family accommodations are available only in an expensive guest suite.

National Hotel *211 Broad St., 916/265-4551; 2/$-$$$, 4/$$-$$$; cribs; some shared baths; pool; restaurant.* Located on the town's main street, this claims to be the state's oldest continuously operating hotel. Built in 1856, it features high ceilings, cozy floral wallpapers, and old-time furniture. Families of four can be accommodated in two separate rooms with a bath between. The plush, old-fashioned dining room offers a moderately-priced lunch and Sunday brunch; steak and lobster dinners are more pricey.

Northern Queen Motel *400 Railroad Ave., 916/265-5824; 2-4/$-$$$; all TVs, VCRs, refrigerators; some kitchens, wood-burning stoves; pool, jacuzzi.* Located on the outskirts of town beside Gold Run Creek, this pleasant modern motel also has a few cottages. Facilities include a stocked trout pond as well as picnic tables and grills. Some waterbeds and a video library are also available. This motel operates the **Nevada City Historical Trolly Tour of Victorian Homes** *(daily at 9:30am; tickets $2).*

Piety Hill Inn *523 Sacramento, 916/265-2245; 2/$$, 4/$$-$$$; 2-night minimum on weekends; children under 5 free; cribs; all TVs, refrigerators; 1 bathtub; continental breakfast; jacuzzi.* This old-fashioned motel court has been cutesied up with floral wallpapers and antique furnishings. One- and two-room cottages are available.

♥ **Red Castle Inn** *109 Prospect, 916/265-5135; 2/$$-$$$, 4/$$$+; 2-night minimum on Sat Apr-Dec; unsuitable for children under 10;*

some woodstoves; some shared baths; full breakfast. This beautifully restored and plushly furnished Gothic Revival home was built in 1860. Said to be one of only two of this style left on the West Coast, it features gingerbread and icicle trim and has old-fashioned double brick walls. Its hilltop location affords good views of the town, making it a prime spot to be staying on parade days.

■ *WHERE TO STAY NEARBY*

Herrington's Sierra Pines *Highway 49, Sierra City, 60 miles north of town, 916/862-1151; 2/$-$$, 4/$$; cribs; all TVs; some kitchens, fireplaces; room service, restaurant (closed Nov-Mar).* Located on the north fork of the Yuba River, this is a combination of motel units and cottages. It also features a trout pond and a restaurant known for its fresh rainbow trout and baked goods.

Kenton Mine Lodge *3 Foote Crossing Rd., Alleghany, 40 miles north of town in a quiet canyon at the end of a 3-mile dirt road, 800/634-2002, 916/287-3212; $30/person/night; children under 6 free, special rates for older children; cribs; some kitchens, wood-burning stoves; some shared baths; meals available at additional cost.* In case you haven't heard, there's a gold rush on. Miners are heading for the hills again, and one of the most favored areas surrounds the tiny Sierra town of Alleghany. City-slickers are advised to be careful around here, though, as many miners camp on top of their claims and some have been known to get mean when confronted with trespassers. To assure your safety and warmth while trying your luck at panning for gold, consider spending a weekend at this remote, semi-refurbished mining camp dating from the 30s. Though vivid imaginations have been known to run wild here (several guests have commented that the winding forest road from Nevada City is not unlike the one seen at the beginning of the horror movie *The Shining*), once the freaked-out city traveler relaxes and acclimates to the unaccustomed peace and tranquility, apprehensions dissolve. Guests sleep in weathered cabins or bunkhouse rooms and are fed home-cooked meals, served family-style at long tables in the Cookhouse. Gold panning equipment may be borrowed for use in gurgling Kanaka Creek, which runs through the camp. An abandoned gold mine and stamp mill on the site provide for some interesting exploring. Campsites are also available.

Packer Lake Lodge *Packer Lake Rd., Sierra City, 916/862-1221; 2-4/$-$$$; closed Nov-May; cribs; some kitchens, potbelly stoves; some shared baths; restaurant.* Located at the end of the road in a remote corner of the Sierra Nevadas, this rustic resort has eight housekeeping cabins with sundecks overlooking Packer Lake. Cabin rental includes the use of a rowboat. Six sleeping cabins are available by the night.

Salmon Lake Lodge *Sierra City, 415/771-0150 (reservations phone is in San Francisco); 2-4/$; closed Nov-Apr; 1-week minimum in July & Aug; all kitchens, fireplaces; all shared baths.* Located in the glaciated high country of Sierra County, this remote resort has been in continuous operation for almost a century. Guests park their cars at the east end of Salmon Lake and are transported by barge across the lake. There they sleep in rustic tent-cabins and are given access to an assortment of boats. Guests provide their own bedding, kitchen utensils, and supplies. The experience is a lot like camping but with the added amenities of electricity and a kitchen. To ease cooking chores, guests are invited twice each week to a catered barbecue held on an island in the center of the lake.

Sierra Shangri-La *Highway 49, Downieville, 45 miles north of town, 916/289-3455; 2/$-$$, 4/$$-$$$; 2-night minimum; cribs; some kitchens, wood-burning stoves; cribs.* There is little to do here except commune with nature. Guests can relax, do some fishing and hiking, and enjoy the sight and sound of the Yuba River rushing past their cabin door. Some units are perched right over the river, allowing guests to fish from their deck.

■ WHERE TO EAT

The American Victorian Museum Dining Room *325 Spring St., 916/265-5804; SunBr & special events; highchairs, booster seats; reservations essential; $$; all cards.* Located in the historic Miners Foundry, where machine parts and architectural iron were once manufactured for use throughout the world, this is the only museum in the United States devoted to collecting, preserving, and exhibiting art and artifacts from the Victorian period (1840 to 1900). Acting as a cultural center for the community, the museum hosts theater productions, concerts, lectures, and special events in its huge circa 1856 Old Stone Hall—one of the largest free-span rooms in the area. The interesting meals served here are an unexpected bonus. Call for current menu and performance schedule.

Apple Fare *307 Broad St., 916/265-5458; L/D daily; highchairs, booster seats; no reservations; $; MC,V.* This pleasant, casual spot is popular with families and locals. Homemade soups and an assortment of sandwiches are on the lunch menu. Apple goodies include an apple-tizer (a creamy cheese and apple dip served with apple wedges and crackers) and cold apple cider. Don't miss a slab of fresh baked pie—the smooth French silk chocolate and lemon chess are especially good.

Cafe Les Stace *311 Broad St., 916/265-6440; B Sat & Sun, L/D W-M; highchairs, booster seats, children's portions; $; MC,V.* The eclectic menu in this mellow spot consists of tasty, fresh foods including hamburgers, steaks, spaghetti, and Mexican items.

Friar Tuck's *111 N. Pine St., 916/265-9093; D Tu-Sun; highchairs, booster seats, children's portions; reservations suggested; $$; all cards.* Operating in a building dating from 1857, this cozy restaurant offers a variety of casual fondue items—even chocolate dessert fondue. The extensive menu also offers grilled fresh fish, chicken, and steak. The wine list, stocked by the restaurant's adjacent wine shop, runs the gamut from inexpensive local labels to expensive rare vintages; varietals are available by the glass. Non-drinkers and children can get high on a Princess Leia or Darth Vader—updated versions of the old-time Shirley Temple and Roy Rodgers. Relaxing live guitar music is piped throughout the catacomb-like interior furnished with comfortable, large wooden booths. A 19th century pub bar hails from Liverpool, England.

■ WHAT TO DO IN TOWN

Firehouse Museum *214 Main St., 916/265-5468; Tu-Sun 11-4; adults 50¢.* Located inside an 1861 firehouse, this museum is said to be haunted. Visitors may view a Chinese altar and snowshoes made for a horse. More pioneer memorabilia is found in the annex **Bicentennial Museum**.

Nevada City Winery *321 Spring St., 916/265-WINE; tasting & tours daily 12-sunset.* Housed now in an old foundry building where gold mining tools were once cast, this winery is located only two blocks from where it began a century ago.

Nevada Theatre *401 Broad St., 916/265-8587; live theatre on most F & Sat evenings; tickets $4.50-$8.* Opened in September of 1865, this is said to be the oldest theater building in California. It has been refurbished to appear as it did when it first opened. The theatre is very small and all seats are close to the stage, making it an excellent spot to expose children to a live production. The audience is usually filled with locals, and they bring their children when the production is appropriate. Movies are often scheduled for Sunday afternoons. Call for current production information.

■ WHAT TO DO NEARBY

Campbell Hot Springs/Consciousness Village *1 Campbell Hot Springs Rd., Sierraville, off Highway 89, 80 miles north of town,*

916/994-8984; baths open M-F 8am-10pm; adults $5, under 12 free.
Swimsuits are optional in the indoor and outdoor hot tubs at this
secluded spa—in operation since the 1850s. A cool, natural mineral
water swimming pool rounds out the facilities. Rebirthing and con-
scious breathing seminars are sometimes scheduled, and a vegetarian
restaurant serves breakfast and dinner. Rooms in a lodge dating from
1909 are available; rates include two vegetarian meals and unlimited
use of the springs.

Independence Trail *off Highway 49, 5 miles north of town, 916/265-
3650; free.* Basically level and easy for baby strollers and children to
navigate, this one-mile nature trail passes Transitional Zone
vegetation.

Malakoff Diggins State Historic Park *23579 N. Bloomfield Rd., off
Highway 49, 17 miles northeast of town, 916/265-2740; museum:
daily May-Sept 10-4, Sat & Sun rest of year; $3/car.* Inhabited by
over 1,500 people in the 1800s—when it was the biggest hydraulic
gold mining operation in the world—**North Bloomfield** is now a
ghost town. Several buildings have been restored, but there are no
commercial stores. The park Historic Center has an interpretive display on hydraulic mining, and nowadays visitors may hike on old
logging roads and fish in a small stocked lake. Picnic facilities are
available. Campsites may be reserved (see p.272), and two primitive
cabins may be rented inexpensively through the park.

Oregon Creek Swimming Hole *on Highway 49, 18 miles north of
town.* Located in the middle fork of the Yuba River, this popular spot
has sandy beaches, deep swimming and shallow wading spots, and
picnic facilities. A **Tahoe National Forest** campground is also
located here.

Sierra County Historic Park and Museum *on Highway 49, Sierra
City, 60 miles north of town, 916/862-1310; W-Sun 10-5 June-Sept,
Sat & Sun in Oct, closed Nov-May; adults $1/tour, 50¢/museum,
under 13 free.* Take a 45-minute guided tour through the reconstructed 1850s **Kentucky Mine and Stamp Mill**; all the original
machinery is still intact. The museum is located inside a reconstructed woodframe hotel dating from the 19th century.

SACRAMENTO

■ *A LITTLE BACKGROUND*

It is fiery summer always, and you can gather roses, and eat strawberries and ice-cream, and wear white linen clothes, and pant and perspire at eight or nine o'clock in the morning.

— Mark Twain

Sacramento has been the state capital since 1854. Most of the major historic attractions are concentrated in the downtown area.

■ *VISITOR INFORMATION*

Sacramento Convention & Visitors Bureau *1421 K St., Sacramento 95814, 916/442-5542.*

Old Sacramento Visitors Center *130 J St., Old Sacramento 95814, 916/443-7815.*

■ *ANNUAL EVENTS*

Dixieland Jazz Festival *May, Memorial Day weekend; 916/372-5277.*

California State Fair *August; 916/924-2000.* There's something for everyone at the oldest state fair in the West and the largest agricultural fair in the U.S. Pleasures include monorail and carnival rides, thoroughbred racing, educational exhibits, and the world's largest waterslide. Special for children are a petting farm, pony rides, and a nursery where baby animals are born each day.

■ GETTING THERE

Located approximately 80 miles north of San Francisco. Take Highway 80 all the way.

By Cruise Ship. Exploration Cruise Lines *(800/426-0600; fare $329-$529)* offers a four-day, three-night cruise through the Delta to Sacramento. Passengers sleep aboard a shallow-draft ship in stateroom accommodations; informal family-style meals are included. Stops are scheduled in Sausalito, Stockton, Sacramento, and Locke.

By Ferry. The Delta Travel Agency *(916/372-3690; fare $108, reduced rates for children)* offers a two-day cruise from San Francisco through the Delta region to Sacramento. The trip operates on Saturdays June through October. It includes round-trip boat tickets, bus transfers, and hotel accommodations in Sacramento. One-day and one-way trips are also available.

By Train. Amtrak trains leave for Sacramento daily from San Jose, San Francisco (via bus connection to Oakland), and Oakland. Special family fares and an overnight hotel package are available. Call 800/872-7245 for fare and schedule information and to make reservations.

Scenic Route by Car. Take Highway 80 to Highway 24 to Walnut Creek, Highway 680 to Concord, Highway 4 to Antioch, Highway 160 to the outskirts of town, then Highway 5 into Sacramento.

■ STOPS ALONG THE WAY

California Rail Museum *located between Fairfield and Rio Vista (exit Highway 80 at Highway 12, then drive east), 707/374-2978; Sat & Sun 12-5; adults $3, 12-17 $2, 3-11 $1.* Located between two sheep pastures in the middle of a flat, arid no-man's land, this very special museum displays and actually operates its collection of historic electric streetcars and steam train engines. Among the dozen or so operating electric cars are both an articulated car (hinged so it can go around corners) which ran on the Bay Bridge from 1939 to 1958 and a bright red car from the Peninsular Railway. Several cars operate each weekend and run along a 1.5-mile stretch of track with overhead electric trolley wires. Cars are operated by the same volunteers who spent countless hours restoring them. Stationary cars, waiting for repairs, can be viewed in several large barns. An oasis-like picnic and play area is available to visitors, and a bookstore with a past (check out the plaque above the bench in front) offers a large collection of railroad books and paraphernalia. All fees collected are used to restore and maintain the streetcars. (It costs between $25,000 and

$50,000 to restore a car and, because the labor is volunteer, it can take as long as ten years!)

The Nut Tree *Highway 80/Highway 505, Vacaville, 707/448-1818; B/ L/D daily; highchairs, booster seats, children's portions; reservations suggested; $$; AE,MC,V.* There is plenty to do here besides eat. For a small fare a colorful miniature train transports passengers around the spacious grounds. Numerous shops are stocked with interesting merchandise, including a toy store with a good selection of children's travel games and books. Nearby there are free rocking horse rides, climbing structures for kids (and wooden benches for the old folks), and sometimes puppet shows. An outside snack bar serves a memorable frosted orange slush, a good hot dog, and an assortment of other short-order items. The striking restaurant inside is more expensive and features a large glass-enclosed area housing a variety of plants and brightly-colored, exotic birds. The food is as tasty as the architecture is dramatic. Parents of babies will be interested to know that Gerber's baby food is on the menu!

■ *WHERE TO STAY*

Modern motels abound. Call your favorite chain for reservations or contact the Convention & Visitors Bureau for a list.

■ *WHERE TO EAT*

Buffalo Bob's Ice Cream Saloon *110 K St., Old Sacramento, 916/441-4788; L/D daily; highchairs, booster seats; $; no cards.* A variety of sandwiches (including grilled cheese and peanut butter & jelly) and hot dogs are available here, as is old-time sarsaparilla to wash it all down. Ice cream concoctions dominate the menu and include exotic sundaes such as Fool's Gold (butter brickle ice cream topped with butterscotch and marshmallow, whipped cream, almonds, and a cherry) and Sierra Nevada (peaks of vanilla ice cream capped with hot fudge, whipped cream, almonds, and a cherry).

Fanny Ann's Saloon *1023 2nd St., Old Sacramento, 916/441-0505; L/D daily; no reservations; $; no cards.* A raucous ambiance and funky decor provide the makings for instant fun. Children and adults alike enjoy the casual atmosphere and American-style fare: half-pound hamburgers, assorted styles of nine-inch hot dogs, giant French fries, and large bowls of homemade soup. A variety of sandwiches and salads are also available. Place your order with the cook at the window in back and then relax with a game of pinball or a downright cheap drink at the old bar. When I inquired whether there were booster seats, the cheerful hostess replied, "I'll hold the kids on my lap."

Los Padres *106 J St., Old Sacramento, 916/443-6376; L/D daily, B Sat & Sun; highchairs, booster seats, children's portions; no reservations; $$; AE,MC,V.* The lovely old brick walls of this nicely appointed restaurant are decorated with paintings of the California missions. The Early California/Mexican cuisine includes nachos (tortilla chips topped with refried beans and melted cheddar cheese), quesadillas (small corn tortillas topped with melted Jack cheese and guacamole), and a green enchilada (corn tortilla filled with king crab and guacamole and topped with green sauce and sour cream). Fresh tortillas and European pastries and breads are made in the restaurant's downstairs bakery, where food for take-out is also available.

■ *WHAT TO DO*

American River Parkway. This is basically 23 miles of water fun. For a free map and more information call 916/366-2066.

Bike Trail. The paved **Jedediah Smith National Recreation Trail**

runs for 23 miles along the American River.

Fishing. The best month for salmon and steelhead is October. Favorite spots are the Nimbus Basin below the dam and Sailor Bar. A state license in required.

Inner Tubing. A good area is from Sailor Bar to the Watt Avenue Bridge.

Nature Walks. The **Effie Yeaw Nature Center** *(in* **Ancil Hoffman Park**, *3700 Tarshes Dr., Carmichael, 916/489-4918; daily 9-5)* has two self-guided nature trails.

Raft Trips. Trips begin in the **Upper Sunrise Recreation Area** located north of the Sunrise Boulevard exit off Highway 50. During summer several companies rent rafts and provide shuttle bus return.

Swimming. For a refreshing swim in the river or loll in the sun on its sandy banks, take the Watt exit off Highway 50.

California Almond Growers Visitor Center *1701 C St., 916/446-8409; tours M-F at 9,10,1,& 2; free.* A one-hour tour of the world's largest almond factory includes almond tasting and a 25-minute film about the history of almonds.

California State Capitol Building *Capitol Mall/10th St., 916/324-0333; tours M-F 9-4, Sat & Sun 10-4; free.* In 1981 the Capitol was remodeled to the tune of $68 million in what is said to be the largest restoration project in the history of the country. The main reason for the project was to make the building earthquake safe. Restored now to its turn-of-the-century decor, it is quite a showcase. Specialized tours stress the architectural restoration, the history, and the legislative process (January to September only—when the legislature is in session). Tickets may be picked up in the basement a half-hour before the tour. A small museum with a ten-minute orientation film entertains visitors while waiting, and a short-order cafeteria is available for meals and snacks. Tours of the surrounding grounds—home to hundreds of varieties of trees and flowers—are scheduled in summer.

Crocker Art Museum *216 O/3rd Sts., 916/449-5423; Tu 1-9, W-Sun 10-5; adults $2, 7-17 $1.* The oldest art museum in the West, this 1874 Victorian building houses a gallery of special exhibitions in addition to a permanent collection of European and American paintings. Cultural events such as lectures, films, and Sunday afternoon concerts are often scheduled; call for current information. Picnic tables are available in a lovely park across the street.

Music Circus *15th/G Sts., adjacent to the Sacramento Civic Theater,*

916/441-3163; nightly during July & Aug; tickets $17-$18.50, children half-price some performances. This is said to be the only tent theater west of the Mississippi. It seats 2,500 and presents summer stock musicals suitable for the entire family. Call for current schedule.

Old Governor's Mansion *16th/H Sts., 916/324-0539; tours on the hour daily 10-4; adults $1, 6-17 50¢.* Built in 1877, this fifteen-room Victorian mansion was bought by the state in 1903 for $32,500. During the next 64 years it was home to thirteen governors and their families. Now it serves as an interesting museum.

Old Sacramento. Bordering on the Sacramento River, Old Sacramento was the kickoff point for the gold fields. It was the western terminus for both the Pony Express and the country's first long distance telegraph, and the country's first transcontinental railroad started here.

Said to be the largest historic preservation project in the West, it is a 28-acre living museum of the Old West. Vintage buildings, wooden sidewalks, and brick streets recall the period from 1850 to 1880. Restaurants and shops as well as historic exhibits make it an entertaining and educational spot to visit.

Guided tours of the town begin at the train depot weekends at 11:30 and 1:30. For more information call 916/445-4209.

An open-air motorized cable car runs between here and the Capitol area. Also, several horse-drawn vehicles may be hired for shorter rides.

California State Railroad Museum *111 I St., 916/448-4466; daily 10-5, in summer to 9; adults $3, 6-17 $1 (ticket admits visitor to Central Pacific Passenger Station on same day).* This gigantic three-story building houses the largest railroad museum in the U.S. Inside there are 21 beautifully restored railroad cars and engines on display. A film, slide show, and assorted interpretive displays tell the history of American railroading, and a large collection of toy trains—including a pastel train designed especially for little girls—are on display. Nearby the **Central Pacific Passenger Station** *(930 Front St.),* a reconstructed train depot, provides visitors the opportunity to step back in time to 1876—an era when riding the train was the chic way to go. A tour wand is provided which picks up recorded descriptions of displays, and on summer weekends visitors can ride a steam train to **Miller Park**.

Old Eagle Theatre *925 Front St., 916/446-6761; performances F & Sat at 8pm; tickets $7.* A reconstruction of California's first theater building built in 1849, the Eagle now presents Gold Rush-era

plays and musicals. Children's programs are also sometimes scheduled. Call for current production information and for schedule of free tours.

Sacramento History Center *101 I St., 916/449-2057; daily 10-5; adults $2.50, 6-17 $1.* Located inside a replica of Sacramento's first public building, a three-story brick structure, this museum houses an extensive collection of gold specimens, old photos, and historic farm equipment. The 113-foot free-standing fiberglass flagpole in front is said to be the tallest such in the entire country.

Schoolhouse *Front/L Sts., 916/483-8818; M-F 9:30-4, Sat & Sun 12-4.* This one-room school is now a museum. Kids may play on the old-fashioned board swings in the yard.

Sacramento Science Center and Junior Museum *3615 Auburn Blvd., 916/449-8255; M-F 9:30-5, Sat & Sun 12-5; adults $2, 3-15 $1.* Of special interest to children, this museum features a live animal hall, walk-through aviary, self-guided nature trail, and hands-on exhibits. A picnic area is available.

Silver Wings Aviation Museum on **Mather Air Force Base** *east of town off Highway 50, Rancho Cordova, 916/364-2908; M-F 10-4, Sat & Sun 12-4; free.* The history of aviation is documented with an assortment of exhibits. The only surviving American 1934 Corben Superace with a Model A engine—painted a shiny blue and black and in mint condition—is on display. Small visitors can sit in a half-size scale model of a World War I German Junker CL1, and every-one can examine an LR-11 rocket engine of the type in Chuck Yeager's plane when he broke the sound barrier. A collection of over 200 wooden models hangs overhead, and short aviation films run continuously.

Sutter's Fort State Historic Park *2701 L St., 916/445-4209; daily 10-5; adults $1, 17 and under 50¢.* A reconstruction of the settlement founded in 1839 by Captain John A. Sutter, this is the oldest restored fort in the West. Exhibits include carpenter, cooper, and blacksmith shops as well as prison and living quarters, and a cannon is fired daily at 11 and 2. Hand-held audio wands are loaned to visitors for self-guided tours. The **California State Indian Museum** *(2618 K St, 916/445-4209; daily 10-5; adults $1, 6-17 50¢)* is located adjacent. Established in 1940 and recently rebuilt, it has continuously chang-ing exhibits on Indian culture. The bark clothing samples are particu-larly interesting, as is the permanent basket collection featuring col-orful Pomo feather baskets. Films and puppet shows are often presented on weekends; call for details. A duck pond across from the museum makes a great picnic spot.

Towe Ford Museum *2200 Front St., 916/442-6802; daily 10-6; adults $4, 13-17 $2, 5-12 $1.* Opened in 1987, this museum houses 150 Ford cars. Every year and model from 1903 to 1953 is represented.

William G. Stone Navigation Lock Visitor's Overlook *at end of South River Rd. (take West Sacramento exit off Highway 80), 916/ 371-7540; daily dawn to dusk; free.* Operated by the U.S. Army Corps of Engineers, this is the only ship navigation lock in California. It passes smaller craft such as barges and tug boats. Its operating schedule is dependent on ship traffic. However, you can usually count on usage by recreational boats on fair weather weekends.

William Land Park *Freeport Blvd. between 13th Ave. and Sutterville Rd.* This 236-acre park has a supervised playground, wading pool, kiddie rides, pony rides, and fishing for children under 16. It also has a 9-hole golf course and:

Fairytale Town *916/449-5233; daily 10-5, Sat & Sun only Dec & Jan; adults $1.50, 3-12 75¢.* Nursery rhymes and fairy tales come to life in this amusement park.

Sacramento Zoo *3930 W. Land Park Dr., 916/449-5166; M-Sun 9-4; adults $2.50, 3-12 $1.* The orangutan grotto, golden eagle flight cage, and areas for the cheetahs, lions, and tigers are noteworthy. **Camel rides** are available at additional charge.

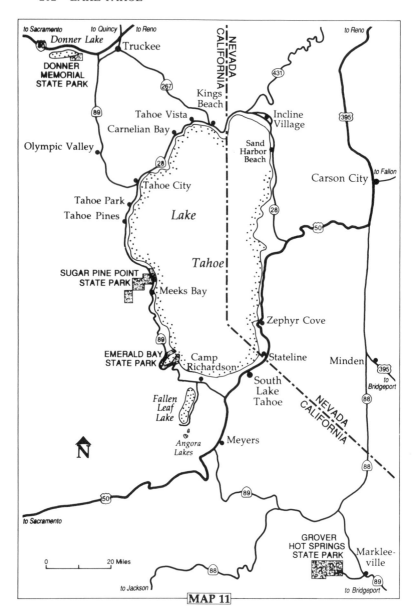

MAP 11

LAKE TAHOE

SOUTH LAKE TAHOE

■ *A LITTLE BACKGROUND*

...At last the Lake burst upon us—a noble sheet of blue water lifted six thousand three hundred feet above the level of the sea, and walled in by a rim of snowclad mountain peaks that towered aloft full three thousand feet higher still!

It was a vast oval. As it lay there with the shadows of the great mountains brilliantly photographed upon its surface, I thought it must surely be the fairest picture the whole earth affords...

—Mark Twain

Lake Tahoe lies half in California and half in Nevada. It is the largest (192 square miles surface) and deepest (1645 feet) Alpine lake in North America and the second largest in the world. At 6,227 feet above sea level, its crystal clear, deep blue summer waters provide a striking contrast with the extensive green forests and majestic mountains encircling it.

Once a remote Sierra lake, Tahoe is now a popular and well-equipped vacation area offering a wide range of recreational activities along with its spectacular scenery. Swimming, hiking, boating, tennis, bicycling, horseback riding, river rafting, camping, fishing, water-skiing, and backpacking are among the summer outdoor activities you can look forward to. In winter there is excellent skiing.

On the Nevada side gambling is another big attraction. Most lodgings provide transportation to the casinos and have discount casino coupons for their guests.

Children may go into a casino with adults but are not

allowed to "loiter" (not even babies in backpacks!) or play
the slot machines. Fortunately, childcare is relatively easy
to find in this area. Many lodging facilities maintain a list
of local sitters. Childcare centers which take drop-ins are
listed in the Yellow Pages. **Tender Loving Care** *(916/541-
5197)* is city-licensed and provides sitters over the age of 35
for a minimum of four hours at $5 per hour plus transporta-
tion. There is a small extra charge for more than one child,
and $1 more per hour is charged on weekends and holidays.
Said to have more slot machines than any other casino in
the world, **Harrah's** also has a **supervised recreation center** for children 6 to 14. It operates year-round from 9 a.m.
to 11 p.m.; admission is $2.50, and there is a five-hour
maximum. Children do need extra money for some of the
facilities, which include a movie theater and video and
snack machines. For older children, a gigantic video arcade
is located just outside the center. Sure beats sitting on the
curb reading comic books like I did when I was a kid. For
further information call 800/648-3773 or 702/588-6611
x447.

■ *VISITOR INFORMATION*

Lake Tahoe Visitors Authority *P.O. Box 16299, South Lake Tahoe
95706, 916/544-5050, 800/822-5922 (lodging reservations service),
916/577-3550 (winter road and weather conditions).*

■ *GETTING THERE*

Located approximately 200 miles north of San Francisco. Take Highway 80 to Highway 50 to the lake.

■ *STOPS ALONG THE WAY*

California Rail Museum. See p.204.

The Nut Tree. See p.205.

Sacramento. See p.203.

Folsom *25 miles east of Sacramento.* Described as a community "in
touch with its past; in charge of its future," this town makes a pleasant stop. Try the **Folsom Zoo** *(Natoma/Stafford, 916/355-7200; Tu-*

Sun 10-4; free) where you'll see native animals, a few exotics, and the largest captive wolf pack in Northern California. **The Candy Store Gallery** *(605 Sutter St., 916/985-2927; W-Sun 11-5),* a standout among the many boutiques and antique shops lining historic Sutter Street, displays the work of some well-known irreverent artists. You'll find Robert Arnesons but no candy. For more information contact the **Folsom Chamber of Commerce** *(200 Wool St., 916/ 985-2698).*

Sam's Town. See p.188.

Poor Red's. See p.188.

Placerville. See p.189.

■ *WHERE TO STAY*

LAKEFRONT

Inn By the Lake *3300 Lake Tahoe Blvd., 800/535-0330, 916/542-0330; 2/$$-$$$+, 4/$$$-$$$+; 2-night minimum on weekends; children under 13 free; cribs; all TVs, bathtubs; some kitchens, lake views; continental breakfast; heated pool, 2 jacuzzis, sauna.* Located in a grove of pine trees across the street from the lake, this attractive modern motel offers comfortable, quiet rooms and a free shuttle to the casinos and ski areas.

Royal Vahalla *4104 Lakeshore Blvd., 800/822-5922, 916/544-2233; 2-4/$-$$$+; cribs; all TVs; some kitchens, lake views; heated pool.* Pick from one-, two-, or three-bedroom units. Guests have use of a private beach.

Sail In Motel *861 Lakeview Ave., 800/822-5922, 916/544-8615; 2-4/$-$$$; all TVs; some lake views.* Located off the beaten path, this attractive and comfortable motel is right on the beach and close to a park.

Tahoe Beach and Ski Club *3601 Lake Tahoe Blvd., 800/822-5962, 916/541-6220; 2-4/$$-$$$+; all TVs, kitchens; some lake views; restaurant; heated pool, hot tub, sauna.* Located one mile from the casinos, this lakeside hotel provides a shuttle. An added ammenity is 400 feet of private beach.

Tahoe Marina Inn *800/822-5922, 916/541-2180; 2-4/$$-$$$+; cribs; all TVs, kitchens; some fireplaces, lake views; heated pool, sauna.* These motel units are located right on the edge of the lake.

Timber Cove Lodge *Highway 50/Johnson Blvd., 800/528-1234, 916/*

541-6722; 2/$-$$, 4/$$-$$$; cribs; all TVs; some lake views; restaurant; heated pool, jacuzzi. This motel has a private beach, marina, and pier.

CONDOS AND HOMES

Accommodation Station *916/541-2355; $$-$$$+; 2-night minimum, 5-night minimum during holidays; all kitchens, fireplaces; some TVs.* Privately-owned condominiums, cabins, and homes may be rented through this agency. Price is determined by the number of bedrooms and type of accommodation. **Lake Tahoe Accommodations** *(800/544-3234, 800/228-6921, 916/544-3234; 4-night minimum)* is a similar service.

Lakeland Village *on Highway 50, 800/822-5969, 916/541-7711; 2/$$-$$$+, 4/$$$-$$$+; usually a 2-night minimum; cribs; all TVs, kitchens, fireplaces; some lake views; 2 pools, wading pool, jacuzzi, 2 saunas, 2 tennis courts (fee).* Though located on a bustling highway, this condominium complex manages to retain a secluded, restive feeling. Many of the units are lakefront; all are within a short walk. Amenities include a recreation room and playground. During the Christmas holidays, sleigh rides are available through the resort's nineteen wooded acres.

OTHER

Casinos. The major casinos offer large numbers of luxury hotel rooms. Call for details. **Caesars** 800/648-3353, **Harrah's** 800/648-3773, **Harvey's** 800/648-3361, **High Sierra** 800/648-3322.

Motel Row. Highway 50 into town is littered with more motels than is to be believed.

Zephyr Cove Resort *760 Highway 50, Zephyr Cove, Nevada, 4 miles north of Stateline, 702/588-6644; 2/$-$$$, 4/$$-$$$; cribs; some TVs, kitchens, fireplaces, bathtubs; restaurant.* Located in a lovely forested area by the lake, these rustic cabins and lodge rooms are run by the Forest Service and provide a convenient yet out-of-the-way spot to stay. Facilities include a beach, marina with boat rentals, stables, and arcade. Campsites are also available. Book early; cabins are usually rented-up a year in advance!

■ *WHERE TO EAT*

Cantina Los Tres Hombres *765 Emerald Bay Rd., 1/4 mile north of the Y, 916/544-1233; L/D daily; highchairs, booster seats, children's* *portions; no reservations; $$; all cards.* There is almost always a wait to be seated in this popular spot, but don't let that keep you away. My family often passes the time sitting in the bar. We order a pitcher of margaritas for the adults, some soft drinks for the kids (mine are fond of the tasty nina coladas), and some nachos (tortilla chips mixed with green chiles, melted cheese, and chorizo and topped with sour cream and guacamole) for all of us. Then we settle into the noisy, happy surroundings and munch and sip. We have found that sometimes our hunger is satisfied by this tactic, and we are ready to leave before we are called to a table. When we do stick around to dine, we've been overwhelmed by the wonderful selections on the menu: chimichangas, crab enchiladas, carnitas (pork roast), a large variety of giant burritos, and fresh fish on Fridays. The menu has changed a lot over the years, but it just keeps getting better. So far, I've never had enough room left to try the deep-fried ice cream for dessert.

Casinos. For some of the best and least expensive food in this area, try the casino restaurants and buffets. Most offer bargain prices and family amenities; none accept reservations. My favorites are:

Caesar's Cafe Roma *800/648-3353; B/L/D daily; highchairs, booster seats.* This coffee shop is open round-the-clock.

Harrah's Forest Buffet *702/588-6611; B & L M-Sat, SunBr, D daily; highchairs, booster seats, children's portions.* Located on the 18th floor, this classy restaurant provides spectacular lake and mountain views and outstanding food at a reasonable price.

Harvey's Carriage House *800/648-3361; B/L/D daily; highchairs, booster seats.* Don't miss the delicious fried chicken dinner. The casino also has an ice cream parlor and video arcade/shooting gallery to entertain children.

Top of the Tram *top of Ski Run Blvd., 916/544-6263; summer: L M-Sat, Sun Br, D daily; winter: L & SunBr only; children's portions; reservations suggested; $$; tram: adults $9, under 13 $5.* A bright red aerial tram lifts diners 2,000 feet above Lake Tahoe to enjoy magnificent views while dining. Call for the current menu.

■ WHAT TO DO

Amusement Centers. These spots are open daily in summer and as the weather permits in winter.

Magic Carpet Golf *2455 Lake Tahoe Blvd., 916/541-3787.* Choose either 19 or 28 holes of miniature golf. This is the kind of colorful course that has goodies like giant plaster dinosaurs and a new theme at each hole.

Tahoe Amusement Park *2401 Lake Tahoe Blvd., 916/541-1300.*
Facilities include a variety of kiddie rides and a giant slide.

Angora Lakes Trail *on Spring Creek Rd., off Highway 89.* Take the
road to Fallen Leaf Lake (visit the lake there to see the falls) and
then turn left at the sign to Angora Lakes. It is a half-mile hike from
the end of the road to the lakes, where you should be able to find a
quiet spot to picnic and swim.

Beaches/Biking. The **Pope-Baldwin Recreation Area** *(on Highway 89
between the Y and Emerald Bay, 916/573-2600; daily 8-6; $2/car)* is
lined with good beaches. This same stretch of highway has a number
of bike rental facilities and a nice bike trail.

Boating.

Lake Tahoe Cruises *at foot of Ski Run Blvd., 916/541-3364; call for
schedule; adults $9, under 12 $4.50.* The big new **Tahoe Queen**
paddlewheeler offers two-hour cruises to Emerald Bay. The boat
has a large window area in the floor for underwater viewing. Call
for information on the sunset dinner/dance cruise and the winter
ski shuttle to Squaw Valley.

M.S. Dixie *760 Highway 50, Zephyr Cove, Nevada, 4 miles north of Stateline, 702/588-3508; Apr-Dec, call for schedule; adults $11, 3-14 $4; reservations required; no strollers.* Actually used on the Mississippi River in the 1920s, this paddlewheel steamer cruises to Emerald Bay. Dinner cruises with live music for dancing are also available.

Woodwind *760 Highway 50, Zephyr Cove, Nevada, 702/588-3000; May-Oct, call for schedule; adults $10, 2-12 $5; reservations advised.* Only 24 passengers fit on this 41-foot trimaran with glass bottom viewing window. A sunset champagne cruise is also available, and small boats and yachts may be rented.

Rentals of various kinds of boats are available at **Ski Run Marina** *(916/544-0200)* and **South Shore Marina** *(916/541-1137 & 541-2155)* in Tahoe Keys, and at **Timber Cove Marina** *(916/544-2942)*.

Water-skiing/Wind Surfing Lessons and Rentals also are available at Ski Run Marina.

Casino Shows. Big name entertainment is always booked into these showrooms. Be sure to call ahead for reservations to the dinner or cocktail shows. Seats are unassigned, and the rumor goes that for a good seat you should tip the maitre d' (the person who greets you, not the captain—who takes you to your seat and who should also be tipped). A $5 tip per person along with a request for a seat facing the stage should do it. If you are a couple and the room isn't crowded, or if you are a group of four, ask for a booth. When the room is crowded, couples are doubled up at tables, so part of the experience is sharing dinner or drinks with someone you've never seen before and probably will never see again. The best seats are held for late arrivals, so plan to arrive about 15 minutes before a cocktail show and about 1 1/2 hours before a dinner show.

Caesars Cascade Showroom *800/648-SHOW, 702/586-2000; no age restriction on children accompanied by an adult.*

Harrah's South Shore Room *800/648-3773; highchairs and booster seats available; children 6 and older preferred.*

High Sierra Theater *800/648-3322; must be 21 or older.*

Drive Around the Lake. A leisurely drive around the 72-mile perimeter of Lake Tahoe takes about three hours. Allow all day, though, as there are many tempting places to stop for picnicking, resting, swimming, and exploring.

Grover Hot Springs State Park *35 miles southeast of town, Markleeville, 916/694-2248; daily 10-9; adults $1, under 18 50¢.* Beautifully situated in a valley meadow ringed by pine-covered slopes, these two pools are filled by nonsulfurous springs. A small one is 102 degrees, a larger one 80 degrees. They are well-maintained, and lifeguards are on duty. The number of bathers permitted is limited, so sometimes there is a wait. Picnic facilities, campsites, and short trails are also available. In winter this is a popular apre's ski destination.

Horseback Riding.

Camp Richardson Corral and Pack Station *on Highway 89 North, Camp Richardson, 916/541-3113; daily June-Oct; guided rides $12.50/hr; no children under 6.* Breakfast rides leave at 8 a.m. ($25); for later risers, Sunday brunch rides leave at 10 ($27.50). Steak barbecue dinner rides ($25) are also available. Fishing trips, overnight pack trips, and spot pack trips may all be arranged, and sleigh rides are available during winter. Reservations are necessary.

Stateline Stables *at end of Park Ave. off Highway 50, Stateline, 916/541-0962; daily in summer; $14/hr.* Some gentle horses are available for children.

Lake Tahoe Historical Society Museum *3058 Highway 50, 916/541-5458 & 544-2312; Tu-Sat 11-4; free.* The history of Lake Tahoe's south shore is chronicled here.

Lake Tahoe Visitor Center *on Highway 89 north of Camp Richardson, 916/541-0209; daily 8-6 June-Sept, Oct call for schedule; free.* Enjoy campfire programs, guided nature tours, and self-guided trails. View mountain stream life from an underwater perspective in the **Taylor Creek Stream Profile Chamber**; visit in October to see the annual run of the Kokanee salmon.

Tahoe Trout Farm *1023 Blue Lake Ave., off Highway 50, 916/541-1491; daily 10-7 June-Aug; charged by size of fish caught.* Though there is, of course, no challenge to catching trout here, there are some compelling reasons to give it a try. No license in required, bait and tackle are furnished free, and there is no limit. You are virtually guaranteed to go home with tasty dinner fare. Young children, who frustrate easily, are fairly sure to succeed at catching a fish. Do bear in mind, however, that some children will be appalled at just the idea of catching a fish—let alone eating it.

Tallic Historic Site Estates *off Highway 89, 3 miles north of Highway 50, 916/573-2600; museum: daily 10-3 in summer; tours: Th-Sun from 1; free.* Three 19th century mansions and 23 cottages are situated on this 74-acre site. Special cultural and historical programs are sometimes scheduled.

Vikingsholm Castle *reached by a scenic 1-mile walk from the parking area on Highway 89, in* **Emerald Bay State Park**, *916/541-3030;*

tours daily 10-4 June-Sept; adults $1, 6-17 50¢. Butterflies, waterfalls, and wildflowers await you on the steep, dry trail descending to this magnificent 39-room, sod-roof Swedish home. Built completely by hand using native materials, it was completed in one summer. Picnic tables are available, and there is a sandy beach where swimming is permitted.

Winter Activities. See pp.245-246.

NORTH LAKE TAHOE

■ *VISITOR INFORMATION*

Greater North Lake Tahoe Chamber of Commerce *P.O. Box 884, (950 N. Lake Blvd.), Tahoe City 95730, 916/583-2371.*

Tahoe North Visitors & Convention Bureau *P.O. Box 5578, (950 N. Lake Blvd.), Tahoe City 95730, 800/TAHOE-4-U (reservations service), 916/583-3494.*

■ *GETTING THERE*

Located approximately 210 miles north of San Francisco. Take Highway 80 to Truckee, then Highway 267 south to the lake.

You can also get here by train. The Chicago-bound Amtrak train leaves Oakland daily at 12:30 p.m. and arrives in Truckee at 6 p.m. Call 800/872-7245 for fare and schedule information and to make reservations.

■ *STOPS ALONG THE WAY*

California Rail Museum. See pp.204-205.

The Nut Tree. See p.205.

Sacramento. See pp.203-211.

Auburn. See p.192.

Grass Valley. See pp.192-196.

Nevada City. See pp.196-201.

■ *WHERE TO STAY*

CONDOS ON THE LAKE

Rates vary tremendously depending on how many people are in the party, how many nights the stay is for, and what time of year it is. Call for current details.

Brockway Springs *101 Chipmunk Ave., Kings Beach, 916/546-4201; pool, children's wading pool, sauna, hot springs, private beach, lakefront beach club and recreation center, tennis courts.* All units have massive stone fireplaces and balconies overlooking the lake.

Chinquapin *3600 Northlake Blvd., Tahoe City, 916/583-6991; cribs; TVs, kitchens, fireplaces, bathtubs; room service; heated pool (unavail. Oct-May), sauna, 3 private beaches, boating facilities, fishing pier, 1-mile paved beachfront path, 7 tennis courts.*

Coeur du Lac *Incline Village, Nevada, 800/GO-TAHOE x BRAT, 702/831-3318; recreation center, heated pool, indoor jacuzzi, saunas, private beach.* This attractive complex is located one block from the lake.

Star Harbor *Tahoe City, 916/583-5594 & 583-3625; heated pool, sandy beach, lagoon, pier, 2 tennis courts.*

CONDOS FURTHER OUT

Carnelian Woods *5005 N. Lake Blvd., Carnelian Bay, 916/546-5924 (call collect for reservations); 1/4 mile from lake; recreation center with pool (summer only), saunas, sports facilities, bicycle rentals, 1-mile parcourse, 3 tennis courts, 2-mile cross-country ski course, snow play area.*

Granlibakken *end of Granlibakken Rd., Tahoe City, 800/543-3221, 916/583-4242; 1 mile from lake; children under 2 free; cribs; all TVs, bathtubs; some kitchens, fireplaces; full breakfast (Dec-Apr); heated pool, children's wading pool (both summer only); jacuzzi, sauna, jogging trail, 6 tennis courts, ski and snow play area.* See also p.247.

Kingswood Village *on Highway 267, Kings Beach, 916/546-2501 (call collect for reservations); 3/4 mile from lake; saunas, access to private lakefront beach club, recreational game area, pool, tennis courts.*

Northstar-at-Tahoe *on Highway 267, Truckee, 800/822-5987, 916/587-0200; 6 miles from the lake; pool, jacuzzi, parcourse, exercise room, 18-hole golf course, stables, 10 tennis courts; supervised children's recreation programs for ages 2-10 in July & Aug (fee).* Northstar has been described by the Sierra Club as a "model development." Hotel rooms and homes are also available for rental. A complimentary shuttle bus makes it unecessary to use your car within the complex. See also p.248.

LAKEFRONT MOTELS

Beesley's Cottages *6674 N. Lake Blvd., Tahoe Vista, 916/546-2448, off-season 213/328-3272; 2-4/$$-$$$; closed Oct-May; cribs; all TVs; some kitchens, lake views.* In addition to housekeeping cottages, a few motel units are also available. Facilities include a private beach and playground.

Golfing at Northstar.

The Dunes Resort *6780 N. Lake Blvd., Tahoe Vista 916/546-2196; 2/$-$$$+, 4/$$$-$$$+; cribs; all TVs; some kitchens, fireplaces, lake views.* Both motel units and cottages are available here, and weekly rates are discounted. Facilities include a private beach.

Lakeside Chalets *5240 N. Lake Blvd., Carnelian Bay, 916/546-5857; 2-4/$$-$$$; children under 7 free; all TVs, refrigerators, fireplaces, bathtubs; some lake views.* Facilities include a pier and sundeck.

Mourelatos' Lakeshore Resort *6834 N. Lake Blvd., Tahoe Vista, 800/553-1555, 916/583-5334; 2/$-$$$, 4/$$-$$$+; cribs; all TVs; some kitchens, lake views.* These woodsy cottages and motel units are situated in a pine forest that opens to a private beach on the lake.

Villa Vista Resort *6750 N. Lake Blvd., Tahoe Vista, 916/546-3333; 2/$-$$, 4/$$-$$$+; closed Oct-Dec & Apr-May; 2-night minimum in cottages; children under 1 free; cribs; all TVs, refrigerators; some kitchens, fireplaces, bathtubs, lake views; heated pool (unavail. Oct-May).* Both motel units and cottages are available. Facilities include a sandy beach and a deck overlooking the lake.

OTHER

Hyatt Lake Tahoe Casino *on Lakeshore, Incline Village, Nevada, 800/228-9000, 702/831-1111; 2-4/$$$-$$$+; children under 18 free; cribs; all TVs, bathtubs; some fireplaces; room service, continental breakfast, 3 restaurants; heated pool, jacuzzi, 2 tennis courts.* A special mid-week package costs just $50 to $60 per person and includes two nights lodging in the modern hotel, two keno credits, four lucky bucks, two passes to the health club, two cocktails, and a bonus book of extras.

Motel Row. Last-minute lodging can often be found among the numerous motels and cabins lining the lake in Kings Beach and Tahoe Vista. Your chances are best, of course, on weekdays.

The Tahoe Escape *3000 N. Lake Blvd., Tahoe City, 916/583-0223; 2-4/$$-$$$+; 2-night minimum; cribs.* This service handles over 150 private condominium properties located on the north and west shores.

■ *WHERE TO EAT*

Alexander's Restaurant *Olympic Valley, 916/583-2555; tram: daily 10-5; adults $7, under 17 $5.* This restaurant is located on the slopes of the Squaw Valley ski area and is reached via a tram ride. Call the restaurant for dining details. A lovely hike to Shirley Lake begins at the tram building. Hikers pass waterfalls and huge boulders as they follow Squaw Creek about 2 1/2 miles to the lake.

Cantina Los Tres Hombres *8791 N. Lake Blvd., Kings Beach, 916/ 546-4052.* For description see pp.217-218.

Hacienda del Lago *760 N. Lake Blvd., in Boatworks Shopping Center, Tahoe City, 916/583-0358; D daily; highchairs, booster seats, children's portions; no reservations; $; MC,V.* Be careful. People tend to pass the standard wait drinking margaritas at the lakeside bar. Anesthetized by these potent, tangy drinks, it is quite easy to over-indulge here on the large portions of tasty Mexican food. The menu includes a variety of burritos and chimechangas (deep-fried burritos), served topped with generous amounts of sour cream and guacamole, and enchiladas, served topped with a sprinkling of green onions and chopped fresh tomatoes. A huge berdura salad consists of a crispy-fried flour tortilla bowl filled to the brim with salad goodies. For those who know when to stop, there are a la carte portions. For those who don't, there are desserts of flan or caramel custard topped with whipped cream.

Lake House Pizza *120 Grove St., Tahoe City, 916/583-2222; L/D daily; highchairs, booster seats; no reservations; $; AE,MC,V.* This casual spot offers a stunning view of the lake and a choice of sitting inside or outside on a deck. Menu choices include pizza, sandwiches, salads, steaks, and exceptionally good homemade potato chips. **The Great American Omelette Company** *(916/583-2225)* is located upstairs and serves a breakfast menu daily until 2 p.m.

Sunnyside Restaurant *1850 W. Lake Blvd., Tahoe Park, 916/583-7200.* In the past it has been hard to beat a summer meal here outside on the huge deck—watching the sailboats on the lake or listening to live jazz on Sunday afternoons. This restaurant has a history of regularly changing its menu format and phone numbers, so you're on your own to check out the current status.

Tahoe City Bakery *in the Lighthouse Center, Tahoe City, 916/583-8918; daily 6-5:30.* Fresh donuts, cinnamon bread, and other bakery goods may be eaten on the premises or taken out.

Water Wheel *11l5 W. Lake Blvd., Tahoe City, 916/583-4404; D daily, L also in summer, closed M Mar-May & Sept-Nov; booster seats; reservations necessary; $$; MC,V.* Diners here are treated to a river view and some of the tastiest Chinese Szechwan cuisine in Northern California. Hailing from Taipei, Taiwan, chef Nelson has a way with a wok and whips up old family recipes to delight his loyal customers. The portion of the menu devoted to spicy Szechwan dishes appears flawless. Highly recommended are the beef Szechwan (beef in a marvelous crunchy sauce of minced woodear, water chestnuts, and green onions), twice-cooked pork (a colorful arrangement of brilliant chartreuse cabbage, bright orange carrot rounds, and pork in a spicy hot sauce redolent of sesame oil and garlic), and Szechwan spicy pork (shredded pork with minced water chestnuts, mushrooms, garlic, and peppers in a flavorful sauce and served with little pancakes). Indeed, the entire menu holds promise. Several window tables overlooking the Truckee River are tucked behind the bar, where Lily mixes drinks that are almost as tasty as the food.

♥ **Wolfdale's** *640 N. Lake Blvd., Tahoe City, 916/583-5700; D W-M, L also in summer; reservations essential; $$; AE,MC,V.* Talented owner/chef Douglas Dale combines French and Japanese cooking techniques to produce excellent fresh fish and meat entrees—all served with homemade herb bread. Appetizers and desserts are also generally very good. There are two seatings for dinner in the plush dining room; lunch is served on a deck overlooking the lake.

■ *WHAT TO DO*

Best Beaches.

Commons Beach *stairway is across from 510 N. Lake Blvd., Tahoe City.* This family beach boasts a lakefront playground.

Sand Harbor Beach *in Nevada 4 miles south of Incline Village; $4/ car.* This is a perfect beach. The sand is clean and fine, lifeguards are usually on duty, and there is plenty of parking.

William Kent Beach *south of Tahoe City.* Parking is difficult, but this small, rocky beach is worth the hassle.

Bike Trails begin in Tahoe City and follow the north shore to Tahoe Pines. Rentals are available in Tahoe City.

Donner Memorial State Park *on Highway 40, 2 miles west of Truckee, 916/587-3841; open June-Oct, $2/car;* **Emigrant Trail Museum:** *daily 10-4, adults $1, 6-17 50¢.* Located on Donner Lake, this park is a monument to the tragic Donner Party stranded here by blizzards in 1846. Picnic facilities, lake swimming, hiking trails, nature programs, and campsites are available. The museum features exhibits on the area's history.

Fanny Bridge/Truckee River Bridge *junction of Highways 89 and 28 (the Y), Tahoe City.* You'll know you're here when you see all those fannies lined up. Spectators gather here to view and feed the giant trout that congregate beneath the bridge. (They like to eat bread and crackers.) The only outlet from the lake, this dam has gates which control the flow of water into the river.

Fishing Charters. Get the names of captains and a fishing license at
one of the local sporting goods shops. Captains usually supply bait
and tackle.

Gatekeeper's Museum *130 W. Lake Blvd., in* **William B. Layton
Park,** *Tahoe City, 916/583-4976; daily 11-5 June-Sept only; by
donation.* Operated by the North Lake Tahoe Historical Society, this
museum is located inside a replica of a 1910 log cabin originally
inhabited by a succession of keepers whose job it was to raise and
lower the gates of the dam. Displays include Indian artifacts and
Lake Tahoe memorabilia. The 3 1/2-acre lakeside park is equipped
with picnic tables and barbecue facilities.

Ponderosa Ranch *on Tahoe Blvd., Incline Village, Nevada, 702/831-
0691; daily 9:30-5 May-Oct; adults $5.50, 5-11 $4.50.* Created especially for filming scenes for the TV show *Bonanza*, this ranch is now
open to the public for tours. Visitors get a bumpy ride from the parking lot up the hill to the ranch and then a guided tour. After the tour,
there is time to explore and visit the petting farm and what is said to
be the world's largest collection of antique farm equipment. Fast-
grub is available, and the tin cups in which beer and soft drinks are
served make great souvenirs. Call for information about the breakfast haywagon ride which includes admission to the ranch.

Truckin' on the Truckee/River Rafting/Inner Tubing *begins at the Y in Tahoe City; daily 9:30-3:30 June-Oct; $9/person; no children under 4.* What better way to spend a sunny summer Alpine day than floating down the peaceful Truckee River a la Huckleberry Finn? All you need is a swimsuit, waterproof shoes, some suntan lotion, and a raft. White-water enthusiasts stay away—this trip is so civilized that there are even portable toilets strategically placed along the riverbank. The three-hour trip ends at **River Ranch**, a restaurant featuring outdoor barbecue dining. Tahoe City concessionaires offer a package which includes raft, life jacket, paddles, and return ride. It is first-come, first-served, so get here before 11 a.m. to avoid crowds.

Sugar Pine Point State Park *on west shore, 916/525-7982 & 525-7232 (winter); daily 8-dusk; mansion: tours on the hour 11-4, July-Sept only; $3/car.* The Visitors Center is inside the three-story 1902 Queen Anne **Ehrman Mansion**; sixteen rooms are open for public viewing. Also on the property is the **General Phipps Cabin**, built of hand-split logs in 1870. Hiking trails are available, and campsites are open year-round. In winter, cross-country skiing and ranger-led snowshoe walks join the agenda.

Winter Activities. See pp.246 to 249.

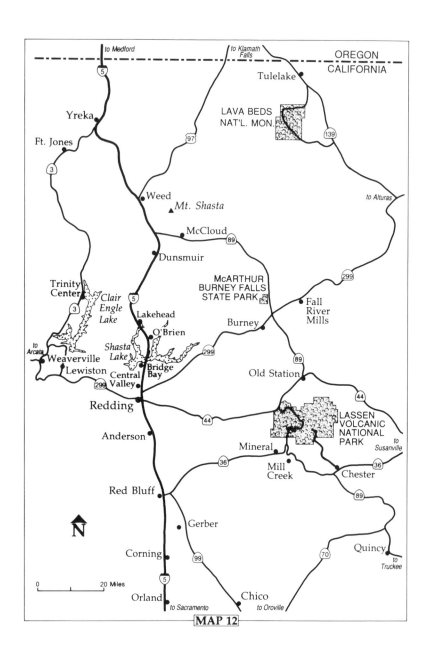

to Medford

to Klamath
Falls

OREGON
CALIFORNIA

5

Tulelake

LAVA BEDS
NAT'L. MON.

Yreka

139

Ft. Jones

3

97

to Alturas

Weed

Mt. Shasta

McCloud

89

McARTHUR
BURNEY FALLS
STATE PARK

299

Dunsmuir

Trinity
Center

3

5

Clair
Engle
Lake

Lakehead

O'Brien

Burney

Fall
River
Mills

to
Arcata

Shasta
Lake

299

89

Weaverville

Bridge
Bay

Lewiston

Central
Valley

Old Station

299

44

Redding

44

LASSEN
VOLCANIC
NATIONAL
PARK

to
Susanville

Anderson

Mineral

36

36

Mill
Creek

Chester

Red Bluff

89

N

Gerber

Quincy

70

to
Truckee

Corning

99

0   20 Miles

5

Orland

Chico

to Sacramento

to Oroville

MAP 12

MT. SHASTA AND VICINITY

■ *A LITTLE BACKGROUND*

Poet Joaquin Miller described Mount Shasta as "lonely as God and white as a winter moon."

■ *VISITOR INFORMATION*

Shasta-Cascade Wonderland Association *1250 Parkview Ave., Redding 96001, 916/243-2643.*

Shasta Dam Area Chamber of Commerce *P.O. Box 1368, (5232-C Shasta Dam Blvd.), Central Valley 96019, 800/367-2649, 916/275-8862.*

■ *ANNUAL EVENTS*

South Shasta Model Railroad *Sundays in April and May on even numbered years; 8620 Holmes Rd., Gerber, 12 miles south of Red Bluff, 916/385-1389.* This miniature 1/4-inch O-gauge reproduction of the Southern Pacific line from Gerber to Dunsmuir operates in a farmhouse basement. It includes 16 steam locomotives, 94 cars, and over 840 feet of track. Visitors may ride on a 2-foot gauge steam train. A **Threshing Bee** is held on odd numbered years.

■ *GETTING THERE*

Located approximately 235 miles north of San Francisco. Take Highway 80 north to Highway 5 north.

LAKE SHASTA

■ *WHERE TO STAY*

Houseboats. See pp.265 to 266.

Motels. Inexpensive motels are located at Bridge Bay and in the Lakehead area. Some inexpensive hotels are in McCloud.

■ *WHAT TO DO*

Lake Shasta Caverns *O'Brien, off Highway 5, 15 miles north of Redding, 911/238-2341; tours daily, call for schedule; adults $9, 4-12 $4.* Discovered in 1878, these caverns didn't open for tours until 1964. The 2 1/2-hour tour begins with a 15-minute catamaran cruise across the McCloud arm of Lake Shasta. Then visitors board a bus for a scenic, winding ride up the mountainside to where the caverns are located. In this case, getting there really is half the fun.

McCloud. Set in the shadow of Mt. Shasta, this scenic lumbermill town dates back to 1827. Try the **McCloud Cookhouse** *(424 Main)* for a lumberjack breakfast and Mexican-style dinners, or **Bellissimo Restaurant** *(204 Lake St.)* for homemade waffles and blintzes.

LASSEN VOLCANIC NATIONAL PARK

■ *A LITTLE BACKGROUND*

Imposing 10,457-foot Lassen Peak is a dormant volcano and is thought to be the largest plug dome volcano in the world. There are self-guided nature walks and, in the summer, guided hikes and campfire talks. Wooden catwalks guide visitors through popular **Bumpass Hell**, an area featuring geological oddities such as boiling springs and mud pots, pyrite pools, and noisy fumaroles. The trail covers three miles and takes about three hours round-trip. The park also offers over 150 miles of back country trails, including a 17-mile section of the **Pacific Crest Trail**. A free newsletter orients visitors and lists daily activities. The park has no lodging facilities, but seven campgrounds are available on a first-come, first-served basis. It is best to visit July through October, when the 30-mile road through the park is least likely to be closed by snow. For skiing information, see p.244. Park admission is $5/car.

■ *VISITOR INFORMATION*

Park Headquarters *P.O. Box 100, (38350 Highway 36E), Mineral 96063, 916/595-4444.*

NORTH

■ *WHERE TO STAY*

Hat Creek Resort *on Highway 89 just north of Highway 44, Old Station, 11 miles from Lassen Park, 916/335-7121; 2-4/$; 2-night minimum in cabins; 1 crib; some kitchens.* These motel units and old-time housekeeping cabins are located beside rushing Hat Creek. The cabins are available May through October only.

Little other lodging is available in this area, but many forest campsites are available on a first-come, first-served basis. Visitors must bear in mind that this area is remote and does not offer big-city facilities like supermarkets.

■ *WHERE TO EAT*

Uncle Runt's Place *Highway 44, Old Station, 916/335-7177; L/D Tu-Sun Apr-Nov, Th-Sun rest of year; highchairs, booster seats, children's portions; reservations suggested; $; no cards.* This cozy restaurant caters to locals and has a short-order menu of sandwiches, hamburgers, and dinner specials.

■ WHAT TO DO

McArthur-Burney Falls Memorial State Park *30 miles north of Old Station on Highway 44; $2/car.* A lovely one-mile nature trail winds past the soothing rush of the 129-foot falls and allows for closer inspection of the volcanic terrain for which this area is known. Paddle boats may be rented at man-made Lake Britton. Facilities include picnic tables, a sandy beach, and a wading area for children. Swimming is allowed only in designated areas as the lake has a steep drop-off. Campsites are also available. Five miles away, the town of Burney offers modern motels and supermarkets.

Spattercone Crest Trail *1/2 mile west of Old Station across the street from Hat Creek Campground; free.* This two-mile self-interpretive trail winds past a number of volcanic spattercones, lava tubes, domes, and blowholes. It take about two hours to walk and is best hiked in early morning or late afternoon.

Subway Cave *1 mile north of Old Station near junction of Highways 44*

& 89; free. Lava tubes were formed here about 2,000 years ago when the surface of a lava flow cooled and hardened while the liquid lava beneath the hard crust flowed away. This cave, actually a lava tube, winds 1,300 feet (about 1/4 mile). Always a cool 46 degrees, it makes a good place to visit on a hot afternoon. However, it is completely unlit inside, so you must bring along a powerful lantern. Even chickens can enjoy the cave—by making a furtive entry and then picnicking in the lovely surrounding woods.

SOUTH

■ *WHERE TO STAY*

Childs Meadows Resort o*n Highway 36, 9 miles from Lassen Park, Mill Creek, 916/595-4411; 2-4/$; weekends only in winter; cribs; some kitchens; restaurant; pool, tennis court.* Choose a motel unit or cabin. Lawn games, a recreation room, and horseback rentals round out the facilities.

Drakesbad Guest Ranch *end of Warner Valley Rd., 18 miles from Chester, 916/529-1512; $57-$79/person/day, includes 3 meals; closed Oct-May; 2-night minimum; cribs; some shared baths; natural hot springs pool.* In the mid-1800s, Drakesbad was a hot springs spa. It has been a guest ranch since the turn of the century. Most of the rustic cabins, bungalows, and lodge rooms have no electricity, so kerosene lanterns are used for light. Located in a secluded, scenic mountain valley in Lassen National Park, the ranch is close to some of Lassen's thermal sights: one mile from the steaming fumaroles at **Boiling Springs Lake** and two miles from the bubbling sulfurous mud pots at the **Devil's Kitchen.** Guests may rent horses from the ranch stables and take guided rides into these areas. Pack trips may also be arranged. Day visitors should call ahead for stables or dining reservations. All this and a good trout-fishing stream, too!

LAVA BEDS NATIONAL MONUMENT

■ *A LITTLE BACKGROUND*

It doesn't hurt to be warned ahead of time that Lava Beds is located in the middle of nowhere. Some people might even go so far as to call it a wasteland. Perhaps you've heard of the expression "out in the tules." This could be where it originated.

The monument has a campground, but the nearest motels and restaurants are far away in Tulelake. It's a good idea to pack-in picnic supplies as there is nowhere to buy food within many miles of the monument.

The area also buzzes with insects, is a haven for rattle-snakes, and, when I visited, had plague warnings posted. But it is still an unusual place and, in my opinion, worth the visit.

The Visitors Center at the southern entrance offers a good orientation. Historically this area is known as the site of the 1872 Modoc War—the only major Indian war to be fought in California. Geologically the area is of interest because of its concentration of caves—approximately 300. Park admission is $3 per car.

■ VISITOR INFORMATION

P.O. Box 867, Tulelake 96134, 916/667-2282.

■ GETTING THERE

Continue north from Lassen Park to Highway 299. Then head north on Highway 139 through sparsely populated forest and farmland.

■ STOPS ALONG THE WAY

Fort Crook Museum *Fall River Mills; daily 12-4 May-Nov only; free.* Six rooms of antique furniture, a blacksmith's shop, and the old Fall River jail are on display here. There is also a collection of early farm implements and Indian artifacts.

■ WHAT TO DO

Caves. Mushpot Cave, located in the Visitors Center parking lot, is the only lighted cave. It also has interpretive displays. A loop road provides access to most of the other nineteen caves which are open without passes. They have such descriptive names as Blue Grotto, Sunshine, and Natural Bridge; Catacombs must be crawled through. All are unlit; lanterns may be borrowed from the Visitors Center. Registering at the Visitors Center is required to explore some of the other caves… just in case.

Klamath Basin National Wildlife Refuge. The gravel road north out of the monument passes through this welcome sight. It is home to a variety of interesting birds which can be easily viewed from the car.

TRINITY ALPS

■ *A LITTLE BACKGROUND*

This is wonderful camping country. There really isn't much to do here except relax and perhaps fish, boat, or hike.

■ *WHERE TO STAY*

Cedar Stock Resort and Marina *on Highway 3, Lewiston, 15 miles east of Weaverville, 916/286-2225; 2-4/$; closed Dec-Feb; 1 week minimum in summer; kitchens; restaurant.* This quiet spot offers a cabin in the woods or a houseboat on Clair Engle Lake. Guests provide their own bedding and linens. The marina also rents boats and slips, and the bar and restaurant offer a terrific view of the lake.

Coffee Creek Guest Ranch *off Highway 3, Trinity Center, 40 miles north of Weaverville, 916/266-3343; $295-$345/person/week, includes 3 meals/day, special rates for children, under 2 free; 2-night minimum in spring & fall, 1-week minimum June-Aug; closed Nov-Apr; cribs; all bathtubs; some fireplaces; heated pool.* The private one- and two-bedroom cabins here are located in the woods. Planned activities include hayrides, movies, steak-frys, outdoor games, square dancing, archery, gun practice on a rifle range, gold-panning, and a kiddie korral with supervised activities for children 3 to 9. Horseback riding is available at additional charge. Inquire about cross-country skiing and ice skating in the winter.

Trinity Alps Resort *on Highway 3, Lewiston, 12 miles north of Weaverville, 916/286-2205; $330-$475/cabin/week, 1-week minimum June-Aug; spring & fall prices by the day; kitchens; restaurant; 1 tennis court.* Arranged especially to please families, this 90-acre resort offers 40 rustic 1920s brown-shingle cabins with sleeping verandas—all scattered along rushing Stuart Fork River. Guests provide their own linens. Simple pleasures include crossing the river via a suspension bridge, hanging out at the General Store, and gathering for theme meals in the dining room/patio over the river. Scheduled activities include square dancing and evening movies. Horseback riding is available at additional cost, and kids can ride their bikes endlessly.

■ *WHAT TO DO*

Joss House State Historic Park *Main/Oregon St., Weaverville, 916/ 623-5284; tours M-F on the hour 10-4, Sat & Sun on the half-hour; adults $1, 6-17 50¢.* Located in a shaded area beside a creek, this Chinese Taoist temple is still in use and provides a cool respite on a hot summer day. The fee includes same-day admission to the **Shasta Museum** located outside of Redding.

J.J. Jackson Memorial Museum *508 Main St., next door to Joss House, 916/623-5211; daily 10-5 Apr-Nov; by donation.* Trinity County's history is traced through mining equipment, old bottles, and photographs. A reconstructed blacksmith shop and miner's cabin are also on display. Outside a creekside picnic area beckons. A full-size stamp mill, located on the block just below the museum, is operated on holidays.

YREKA

■ *A LITTLE BACKGROUND*
This town is filled with beautifully maintained historic homes. The Chamber of Commerce provides a brochure pointing out the many homes built before 1900. A few are open to the public. If you have no brochure to guide you, head for the four blocks of Third Street located between Lennox and Miner.

■ *VISITOR INFORMATION*
Yreka Chamber of Commerce *1000 S. Main St., Yreka 96097, 916/ 842-1649.*

■ *WHAT TO DO*
Siskiyou County Museum *910 S. Main St., 916/842-3836, in summer daily M-Sat 9-5, Sun 1-5; closed Sun & M rest of year; free.* Local artifacts and history are emphasized. I was especially taken by the exhibit on the pioneer Terwilliger family. Of special interest is the **Outdoor Museum** located adjacent. Among its original and reconstructed historic buildings are a schoolhouse, a Catholic church, a blacksmith shop, and a miner's cabin. On the second Saturday of June each year, a **Historic Crafts Fair** demonstrates old-time crafts like horseshoeing and spinning. Call for details.

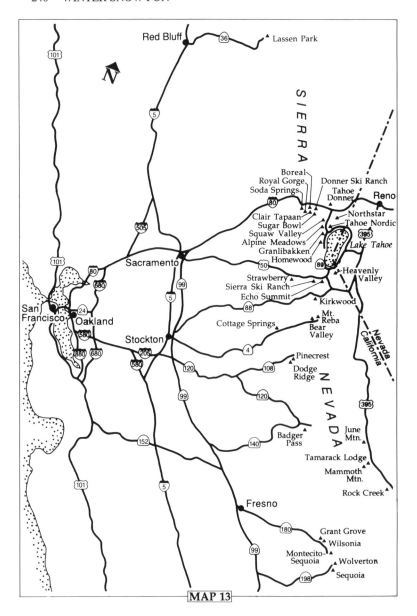

MAP 13

WINTER SNOW FUN

DOWNHILL SKIING

Ski areas are plentiful in Northern California. The season runs from the first snow, usually in late November, through the spring thaw in April. Several resorts are known for staying open longer.

Lifts usually operate daily from 9 to 4. Rates for an all-day lift ticket currently vary from a low of $11 to a high of $29; many resorts offer weekday discounts. To avoid parking problems and long lines for lift tickets and rentals, plan to arrive early. On-site equipment rentals run $10 to $16 per day, $6-$12 for children. Group downhill lessons range from $10 to $18 and average two hours. All-day childcare or children's ski schools range from $27 to $40. Many resorts offer lodging/lift, learn-to-ski, and bargain mid-week packages. Cross-country ski rentals range from $8 to $11, $5 to $7 for children.

The least crowded times at the resorts are the three weeks after Thanksgiving, the first two weeks in January, and late in the season. The two weeks around Christmas are ridiculous.

Those who know say it is worth your while to buy your own ski equipment if you ski more than fifteen days per season. Otherwise, it is in your favor financially to rent. Avoid buying children plastic skis; they break very easily.

CROSS-COUNTRY SKIING

Cross-country skiing is becoming more popular each year. One reason for this surging popularity is the advantages it has over downhill skiing. There are no lift tickets to purchase, and the equipment is less expensive. Also, the sport is considered safer, can be enjoyed in groups, and allows you to get away from crowds. But it also requires more stamina and is less exhilarating.

Specialized cross-country centers offer equipment rentals, lessons (average cost is $6 to $10 and reservations are usually required), maintained trails, and warming huts. Trail maps are usually available at the center headquarters. Some centers also offer lodging, guided tours, and the option of downhill facilities.

Children 4 and older are usually taught in classes with their parents, but some centers have special children's classes. If you have the strength, younger children can also be carried in a backpack.

It is a good idea for beginners to rent equipment and take a few lessons to learn safety guidelines and basic skiing techniques. Once the basics are learned, this sport can be practiced just about anywhere there is a foot of snow.

SNOW PLAY

Toboggans, saucers, inner tubes, and sleds are the equipment people bring for snow play. For safety's sake, take note that sleds are lots of fun to use but extremely dangerous. Truck inner tubes are also extremely dangerous because the rider is high off the ground with nothing to hold on to and no way to steer.

In fact, snow play can be generally dangerous, especially when people do not pay attention to safety rules. I once had the wind knocked out of me by an antsy bear of a man who didn't wait for me and my young child to come to a stop before he pushed down the same hill in his saucer. After the collision he said, "Sorry. But you shouldn't have been there." I'm sure worse stories are waiting to be told.

Many commercial snow play areas will let you use your own equipment, but some require that you rent their equipment.

Dress for cold, wet weather. Wear wool when possible, and pack a change of clothes. Protect feet with boots. If you don't have boots, a cheap improvisation is to wrap feet in newspapers and then in plastic bags, and then put shoes on. Also, a large plastic garbage bag can be used as a raincoat. Always wear gloves to protect hands from sharp, packed snow.

DRESSING KIDS FOR THE SNOW

Borrow clothing from friends or relatives until you know what you want or need.

I have found the following to be a comfortable, warm way to dress children for the snow. Most of the ideas carry over and work for adults as well. Many of the items you probably have on hand already. Others make excellent presents for Christmas or Hanukkah—which come just at the beginning of the season.

Dress children in thermal underwear which can afterwards be used for pajamas. Then put on a cotton turtleneck to keep out drafts. On top of that put a wool or wool-blend pullover sweater and insulated bib-front water-repellant pants or regular overalls treated with a water-repellant spray. Top it off with their regular winter jacket. For insulation use two layers of socks: a thin cotton liner and a thicker wool pair—unribbed to avoid blisters. If you have them, leg-warmers can add an extra layer of warmth worn over or under pants.

The best places to find good winter clothing for children include Sears, REI Co-op *(call 800/426-4840 for a free catalogue),* and Patagonia *(call 805/648-3386 for a free catalogue).*

To avoid loss of children's gloves or mittens, thread a length of elastic or thick yarn through their jacket sleeves and pin mittens to the ends. A wool hat that can be pulled down over their ears is essential (20 to 30% of body heat is lost through uncovered heads); some convert to face masks for windy days. Avoid long neck scarves as they have been known to become entangled in lift equipment, and we all know what happened to Isadora Duncan. For neck warmth try a square bandana instead; wool is best but cotton is better than nothing. Sunglasses with a safety strap or goggles are necessary to cut the glare. A warm pair of water-proof boots for after-skiing is useful; avoid rubber as it gets very cold. Good-looking, popular, and warm "moon boots" can be purchased inexpensively.

Zip into pockets: sun-block cream, chapstick, loose change for a snack, tissues, an identification slip (with name and address or location of parents), and perhaps a box of raisins or a candy bar snack.

Never let children ski alone. Lifts can be very dangerous without proper supervision. If you want time to ski without your children, consider signing them up for lessons in the morning and then spend the afternoon skiing together. Another alternative is the all-day childcare and ski schools available at many resorts.

Note: Adult prices are first/followed by children's prices. Difficulty of terrain is specified in percentages: %B (beginner), %I (intermediate), %A (advanced).

WAY UP NORTH

Coffee Creek. See p.237.

Lassen Park Ski Area *2150 N. Main #7, Red Bluff, 916/595-3376; 49* *miles east of Red Bluff; open F-Sun; downhill & cross-country; 1 triple chair, 1 surface; 40%B, 40%I, 20%A; lifts $16/$11; children's ski school (4-11); lodging nearby; packages available; snow play area.* California's "undiscovered National Park" is an excellent area for families and beginners. The scenery includes hot steam vents and mud pots, allowing for unusual and interesting cross-country ski touring. Snowshoe walks are sometimes scheduled. See also pp.233 to 235.

SOUTH LAKE TAHOE

Echo Summit Ski Area *South Lake Tahoe, 916/659-7154; on Highway 50, 8 miles west of the South Lake Tahoe "Y". Downhill: 2 double chairs, 1 surface; 40%B, 40%I, 20%A; lifts $15/$9; childcare, children's ski school (5-12). Cross-country: 916/659-7177; 15 trails (18 km), all groomed; 40%B, 40%I, 20%A; trail fee $4/$3. Lodging nearby 800/822-5922.* This family-oriented ski area is especially good for beginners and low intermediates.

Heavenly Valley *South Lake Tahoe, 916/541-1330; downhill only; tram, 6 triple chairs, 10 double, 9 surface; 25%B, 50%I, 25%A; lifts $29/$14; childcare (2-4), children's ski school (4-12); lodging nearby 800/822-5922, adjacent townhouses 800/822-5967, packages available.* This is one of the largest and most scenic ski areas in the country. Situated in two states, the runs on the California side offer breathtaking views of Lake Tahoe. Heavenly has been rated as having the best intermediate skiing in California. It also has exhilarating expert slopes and offers both night and helicopter skiing.

Kirkwood Ski Resort *Kirkwood, 209/258-6000; on Highway 88, 30 miles south of South Lake Tahoe; downhill only; 4 triple chairs, 6 double, 1 surface; 15%B, 50%I, 35%A; lifts $27/$10; childcare center (3-8), children's ski school (4-12); lodging on premises in condominiums 209/258-7247, nearby housekeeping cabins at **Kays Resort** 209/258-8598 & **Sorensen's** 916/694-2203.* This is a very large, uncrowded family area. It is said to be snowing here when it is raining at other Tahoe ski areas. The adjacent **Kirkwood Cross Country Ski Area** *(209/258-8864)* offers inexpensive Family Days as well as guided overnight trips including lodging and meals.

Sierra Ski Ranch *Twin Bridges, 916/659-7453; on Highway 50, 12 miles west of South Lake Tahoe; downhill only; 8 double chairs, 2 triple; 20%B, 60%I, 20%A; lifts $22/$12; children's ski school (3-5); lodging nearby 800/822-5922.* This family-run ski area is reputed to be particularly popular with college students and families with teenagers.

Strawberry Ski Touring Center *on Highway 50, Kyburz, 916/659-7200; 15 miles west of South Lake Tahoe; open Th-M; cross-country only; lodging nearby.* Snow camping and courses in survival are offered.

SNOW PLAY

Borges' Sleigh Rides *on Highway 50 across the street from Caesar's casino, 916/541-2953; daily 10-dusk, as snow conditions permit; adults $7, under 12 $4, reduced family rates.* Take a ride around a meadow in an old-fashioned "one-horse open sleigh."

Hansen's Resort *1360 Ski Run Blvd./Needle Peak Rd. near Heavenly Valley, South Lake Tahoe, 916/544-3361; daily 9-12 & 1-4; 3-hour toboggan rental $9 and up.* Facilities include a saucer hill and a packed toboggan run with banked turns. Equipment must be rented on the premises. Lodging facilities are available.

Snow Hikes. *Sierra State Parks, P.O. Drawer D, Tahoma 95733, 916/525-7232.* Request a schedule of free ranger-led snowshoe and cross-country hikes in Lake Tahoe area state parks by sending a stamped, self-addressed legal size envelope to the above address. Hikes are scheduled January through April.

Taylor Creek Ski Tour and Snow Play Area *at the end of Cathedral Rd., off Highway 89 west of Camp Richardson.* This informal, small area is good for younger children.

Winter Carnival *916/659-7519 & 659-7453.* Three days of theme sports and special snow activities are scheduled late in January. Call for details.

Winter Wonderland *3672 Verdon/Needle Peak Rd., South Lake Tahoe 916/544-7903; daily; free.* This snow play area is an open field located behind the Winter Wonderland ski rental shop. Saucers may be rented from the shop for $4 per day.

NORTH LAKE TAHOE

Alpine Meadows Ski Area *916/583-4232; off Highway 89, 4 miles north of Tahoe City; downhill only; 9 double chairs, 2 surface; 25%B, 40%I, 35%A; lifts $29/$12, under 7 $5; childcare snow school (3-6), children's ski school (6-12); lodging nearby 916/583-1045, packages available.* Alpine is usually open through Memorial Day and some years is open into July—giving it the longest ski season at Lake Tahoe. Ask about the five-day learn-to-ski program which begins each Monday. Reservations are necessary for the free one-hour guided tours offered on Saturdays and Sundays at 9:30 a.m. Tours show participants the main runs and how to avoid crowds. Alpine also hosts a free ski clinic for amputees and is known for having excellent ski instruction for the physically and mentally handicapped.

Granlibakken *800/543-3221, 916/583-4242; 1 mile south of Tahoe City; 2 surface; 50%B, 50%I; lifts $10/$6, free to lodging guests; snow play area.* This small ski area is protected from the wind and caters to beginners and families with small children. It is said to be the oldest ski resort at Tahoe and to have the least expensive lift ticket. See also p.223.

Homewood *916/525-7256; on Highway 89, 6 miles south of Tahoe City; downhill only; 1 quadruple chair, 2 triple, 2 double, 5 surface; 20%B, 50%I, 30%A; lifts $23/$8; children's ski school (4-6); lodging nearby 800/822-5959.* The slopes here are ideal for intermediates and provide great views of Lake Tahoe.

Northstar-at-Tahoe *916/562-1010; off Highway 267, 6 miles south of Truckee. Downhill: gondola, 3 triple chairs, 5 double, 2 surface; 25%B, 50%I, 25%A; lifts $27/$14; childcare center (2-6), children's ski schools (3-6 & 5-12). Cross-country: 14 trails (40km), all groomed; 20%B, 55%I, 25%A; trail fee $8/$4. Lodging in modern condos on premises 800/822-5987, packages available.* Lift ticket sales are limited to assure the slopes don't get overcrowded. This attractive area is said to be the least windy at Tahoe and is good for beginners and excellent for intermediates. It offers organized activities throughout the week and caters especially to families. Free two-hour introductory tours, in which participants are shown the best runs and given a history of the area, are available on Fridays and Sundays at 11 a.m. See also p.223.

Squaw Valley U.S.A. *Olympic Valley, 916/583-6985; off Highway 89, 5 miles north of Tahoe City; downhill only; aerial tramway, 6-passenger gondola, 2 quadruple chairs, 5 triple, 16 double, 2 surface; 25%B, 45%I, 30%A; lifts $30/$5; childcare (6 mo.-5), childcare snow school (3-5), children's ski school (6-12); lodging on premises 800/545-4350; packages available.* Squaw Valley made its name in 1960 when it was home to the VIII Winter Olympic Games.

Today it is a world-class ski area known internationally for its open slopes and predictably generous snowfall—which usually allows Squaw to stay open into May. Many avid skiers consider it to be the best ski resort in the state because it has the steepest, most challenging expert slopes. Indeed, there are good slopes for every ability level. Squaw Valley's Children's World, a special area for children under 12, is equipped with two platter pulls and a poma lift. Night skiing is available, and a free one- to two-hour introductory tour is scheduled each day at 1 p.m.

Tahoe Nordic Ski Center *925 Country Club Dr., 916/583-9858 & 583-0484; off Highway 28, 2 miles east of Tahoe City; weekends only; cross-country only; 12 trails (60 km), all groomed; 30%B, 40%I, 30%A; trail fee $8/$4, under 7 free; children's ski school (3-5), children's lessons (3-10); lodging nearby 800/824-6348.* Ask about the moonlight tours.

SNOW PLAY

Carnelian Woods Condominiums. See p. 223.

North Lake Tahoe Regional Park *off Highway 28 at the end of National Ave., Tahoe Vista, 916/546-7248; daily; free.* This 108-acre park has a snow play area for toboggans and saucers. Snowmobile rentals are available on weekends to use on a 1/4-mile oval racing track and 2 1/2 miles of trails. Cross-country trails and picnic tables round out the facilities.

Sugar Pine Point State Park. See p.229.

Snowfest *916/583-7625.* Held for a week each year in March, this is the largest winter carnival in the West. In the past activities have included a fireworks display over the slopes at Squaw Valley followed by the awe-inspiring sight of scores of torch-bearing skiers making a twisting descent down Exhibition Run. The popular **Great Ski Race**, a 30-kilometer nordic competition, is also part of the festivities. Call for details.

DONNER SUMMIT

Boreal *916/426-3666; Castle Peak exit off Highway 80, 10 miles west of Truckee; downhill only; 1 triple chair, 8 double; 30%B, 60%I, 10%A; lifts $20/$11; childcare center (2-12), children's lessons; lodging on premises 916/426-3668; packages available.* This area is known for being relatively inexpensive and convenient to the Bay Area. Facilities are especially good for beginners and low-intermediates, and night skiing is available.

Clair Tapaan Lodge *Norden, 916/426-3632; on Highway 40, 3 miles east of Norden/Soda Springs exit off I-80; cross-country only; 6 trails (7 km), all groomed; 30%B, 60%I, l0%A; trail fee: $4/$3.* This area is the snowiest in the continental U.S. The lodge and track system are owned and operated by the Sierra Club. The package rate of $29.50/$21.50 (less for members) includes bunk bed lodging, three hearty meals, and use of the trails. As in hostels, everyone is expected to do a chore. Overnight trips to wilderness areas can be arranged.

Donner Ski Ranch *Norden, 916/426-3635; on Highway 40, 3 miles from the Norden/Soda Springs exit off Highway 80; downhill only; 1 triple chair, 3 double; 25%B, 50%I, 25%A; lifts $20/$10; children's ski school (3-7); lodging on premises; packages available.* This area offers no frills and is best for beginners and intermediates.

Royal Gorge Cross Country Ski Resort *Soda Springs, 916/426-3871; at Soda Springs/Norden exit off Highway 80 near Donner Pass; cross-country only; 67 trails (280 km), all groomed; 45%B, 35%I, 20%A; trail fee $12/$6.50; childcare available, children's ski school (4-9); lodging on premises; packages available.* Modeled after Scandinavian ski resorts, the overnight **Wilderness Lodge** here is not easily accessible. Guests are brought in by snowcat-drawn sleigh (sorry, no reindeer or horses yet) and leave by skiing the two miles back

out. Accommodations are primitive. In the old 1920s hunting lodge, everyone shares the same toilet area. The bathing facilities are a choice of steaming in a sauna or soaking in an outdoor hot tub—both of which are reached by a short trek through the snow. Sleeping facilities are dormitory-style bunk beds and your own sleeping bag, making this a place to avoid for a romantic weekend. The food, however, is remarkably civilized. A chef works full-time in the kitchen preparing attractive, tasty, and bountiful French repasts. Oh, yes. The skiing. Guests may cross-country ski whenever they wish, and the capable staff gives lessons each morning and afternoon. A two-night weekend runs $180 per person (children under 14 $145) and includes everything except equipment, which may be rented on the premises. Lower rates are available midweek. Royal Gorge also operates a more accessible B&B nearby (**Rainbow Lodge** *916/426-3661*). The cross-country center is open to non-guests and features the largest cross-country track system in the U.S.

Soda Springs Ski Area *Soda Springs, 916/426-3666; at Soda Springs exit off Highway 80, 4 miles west of Donner Summit; open F-Sun; downhill only; 3 double chairs; 30%B, 50%I, 20%A; lifts $15/$8; children's ski school (4-12), children's lessons; lodging nearby.* This relatively new resort is built on the former site of one of the very first Sierra ski resorts and is very close to the Bay Area. If you have the bucks ($200 to $2,200), you can rent part—or all—of the resort on weekdays.

Sugar Bowl Ski Resort *Norden, 916/426-3651; on Highway 40, 3 miles from the Soda Springs exit off Highway 80; downhill only; 1 quadruple chair, 6 double; 20%B, 30%I, 50%A; lifts $26/$13; childcare (3-5); lodging on premises 800/435-4004; packages available.* Exuding a 1930s charm, this ski resort is one of the Sierra's oldest and is said to have had the first chairlift in the state. It is further known for having short lift lines, good runs at all ability levels, and a lack of hotdoggers. Skiers park their cars carefully (to avoid tickets) and then ride a gondola or chairlift up to the resort. Night skiing is available.

Tahoe Donner *Truckee, 916/587-9444; on Highway 40, 1/2 mile from the Truckee/Donner Lake exit off Highway 80. Downhill: 2 double chairs, 1 surface; 50%B, 50%I; lifts $16/$10; children's ski school (3-6). Cross-country: 916/587-9484; 27 trails (68 km), all groomed; 34%B, 31%I, 35%A; trail fee $10/$6, under 7 free; children's ski school on weekends (3-6). Lodging in modern condos and homes on premises 916/587-6586 & 587-5411.* This small resort is good for families. The number of lift tickets is limited, assuring that it never gets too crowded. The cross-country ski center offers lighted night skiing and schedules special tours: Ski With Santa, Morning Nature Tour, Sauna Tour, annual Donner Trail Tour.

SNOW PLAY

Ski Sport Museum *Boreal Ridge exit off I-80, 916/426-3313; Nov-May, Tu-F 12-4, Sat & Sun 11-5, call for rest of year; free.* See how cumbersome old-time ski equipment was. Ski films are shown upon request.

EAST

Bear Valley Nordic Ski Area *Bear Valley, 209/753-2834; on Highway 4, 49 miles east of Angels Camp; cross-country only; trail fee $9.50/ $6.50, under 8 free; 30 trails (90 km), all groomed; 40%B, 40%I, 20%A; children's ski program (4-7), childcare and lodging nearby.* This resort ranks second in Northern California in length of groomed trails. Overnight tours, complete with lodging and food, are available, as are snowbound cabins reachable only by snowcat.

Cottage Springs *209/795-1401; on Highway 4, 8 miles east of Arnold; downhill only; 1 double chair, 2 surface; 75%B, 25%I; lifts $15/ $10; lodging nearby; snow play area (fee).* This is a good area to learn to ski. Night skiing is available on Fridays and Saturdays.

Dodge Ridge *Pinecrest, 209/965-3474, 415/345-7763; 32 miles east of Sonora off Highway 108; downhill only; 2 triple chairs, 5 double, 3 surface; 20%B, 65%I, 15%A; lifts $21/$10; childcare center (2-8), children's ski school (3-12); lodging nearby 800/446-3333.* This low-key, family-oriented ski area is known for short lift lines. Classes are available in ballet skiing.

Mt. Reba/Bear Valley *Bear Valley, 209/753-2301; on Highway 4, 55 miles east of Angels Camp; downhill only; 2 triple chairs, 7 double; 20%B, 50%I, 30%A; lifts $25/$12, under 7 $8; childcare center (1-5), children's ski school (3-7); lodging in condos, homes, and lodge on premises 209/753-BEAR.* Intermediate or better ability skiers staying in this secluded resort village can ski the three-mile Home Run trail back to the resort area at the end of the day. A bus takes skiers to and from the village area lodgings and the slopes. Bear is one of the biggest ski areas in the state and generally has short lift lines. However, that Ski Bare campaign must have caught people's attention: Now there are lines where once there were none. It is popular with families and especially good for beginners and intermediates. More condos and lodge rooms are available *(800/247-9346);* inexpensive modern rooms with bathrooms down the hall are available at nearby **Red Dog Lodge** *(209/753-2344).*

Pinecrest Nordic Ski Area *on Dodge Ridge Rd. in Stanislaus National Forest, 35 miles east of Sonora, 209/965-3434; cross-country only; 10 trails (40 km), none groomed; 15%B, 75%I, 10%A; no trail fee; childcare and lodging nearby.* Ski through old-growth conifers in this area administered by the U.S. Forest Service.

SNOW PLAY

Bear River Lake Resort *on Bear River Reservoir, 209/295-4868; 20 miles east of Pioneer, 3 miles off Highway 88; daily 8am-8pm; free, parking $5/car.* Visitors may use their own equipment in this groomed snow play area. Snowcats, cross-country equipment, snowshoes, saucers, and tubes are available for rental, and back country cross-country trips may be arranged.

Calaveras Big Trees State Park *(see p.176).* Bring your own snowshoes or cross-country skis for the free ranger-led walks. Reservations must be made at least one week in advance *(209/795-2334).*

Leland Meadows *Pinecrest, 209/965-3745; 36 miles east of Sonora off Highway 108; daily 9-4:30, Dec-Apr only; admission $4, under 5 free, rentals $4-$8, visitors may bring own equipment but are charged $2/piece.* Tubes give the best ride on these supervised, groomed slopes, but toboggans and saucers may also be used. Bring a picnic, and plan to spend the day. Guests staying in the adjacent townhouses may use the facilities for half-price. Snowmobile tours and rentals and a cross-country ski area are also available.

Long Barn Lodge Ice Rink *Long Barn, 209/586-3533; 23 miles east of Sonora off Highway 108; call for schedule; adults $4.50, under 13 $3.50, skate rental $1.* This rink is located behind an old bar and restaurant built in 1925. The top is covered, but two sides are left open.

SOUTH

Badger Pass *Yosemite National Park (see pp.157-164.); off Highway 41 on Glacier Point Rd., 23 miles from the valley. Downhill: 209/ 372-1330; 1 triple chair, 3 double, 2 surface; 35%B, 50%I, 15%A; lifts $20.50/$10; childcare center (3 and older), children's ski school (3-6). Cross-country: 209/372-1244; 20%B, 60%I, 20%A; 13 trails (140km), 32km groomed; trail use free with park admission. Lodging nearby; packages available.* Badger Pass opened in 1935, making it California's first, and oldest, organized ski area. It is a prime spot for beginners and intermediates and is especially popular with families.

Its natural bowl has gentle slopes and provides shelter from wind. A free shuttle bus delivers valley guests to the slopes. Tickets must be picked up the day before at any lodging reservations desk. A snow play area is located several miles from the slopes; it is not always accessible and there are no equipment rentals. Cross-country skiing is arranged through the Mountaineering School—the oldest cross-country ski school on the West Coast. Survival courses, snow camping, and overnight tours including lodging and meals are also available. Ask about the bargain Midweek Ski Special.

Grant Grove Ski Touring Center *Kings Canyon National Park, 209/ 335-2314; in Grant Grove Village; children's lessons; lodging nearby.* Moonlight and guided overnight tours are available. Snow play areas are located at Azalea campground and Big Stump picnic area. See also pp.165 to 167.

June Mountain *June Lake, 619/648-7733; 4 miles south of Highway 395, 58 miles north of Bishop; downhill only; 1 aerial tram, 5 double chairs, 1 surface; 35%B, 45%I, 20%A; lifts $27/$14; childcare center (4-5), children's ski school (3-12); lodging nearby.* This compact, uncrowded area is excellent for beginners and popular with families. For lodging try the **June Lodge** *(714/648-7713).* A former hunting lodge, it was once a popular retreat for movie stars like Clark Gable and Humphrey Bogart.

The old days.

Mammoth Mountain *Mammoth Lakes, 619/934-2571; 50 miles north of Bishop; downhill only; 2 gondolas, 7 triple chairs, 16 double, 4 surface; 30%B, 40%I, 30%A; lifts $25/$13; infant care, childcare center (2-8), children's ski school (4-12); lodging on premises 619/ 934-2581.* One of the three largest ski areas in the country, Mammoth is located on a dormant volcano and has the highest elevation of any California ski area. It also is said to have some of the longest lift lines and one of the longest seasons, usually staying open through June and sometimes into July. A seven-hour drive from the Bay Area, it is actually more popular with Southern Californians.

Montecito-Sequoia Cross Country Ski Center *(see pp.166 & 262); on Highway 180 between Kings Canyon and Sequoia National Parks; cross-country only; 40%B, 40%I, 20%A; 26 trails (92km), 25km groomed; trail fee $8; childcare, children's lessons; lodging on premises; packages available; natural lake ice skating rink.* Skiers here enjoy breathtaking ski tours and snowshoe walks through groves of giant sequoias. Arrangements can be made for videotaping lessons. And lodge guests have plenty to do besides skiing. In the lodge they feast on "California fresh" cuisine. Plenty of movies are available for the VCR, and there are also board games and table tennis. Outside there are snow sculpture, igloo building, and snow football. But there is also the option of just resting in front of the massive stone fireplaces. Because of its high altitude location at 7,500 feet, the resort usually retains its snow and stays open for skiing through spring.

Rock Creek Winter Lodge *Mammoth Lakes, half-way between Mammoth Lakes and Bishop, 619/935-4464; cross-country only; 30%A, 45%I, 25%B; 14 trails (75km), 25km groomed; trail fee $3/$1.50; lodging on premises.* The $135 ski package includes snowcat transportation to the lodge, two nights in a cabin heated by a woodburning stove, breakfasts and dinners in the lodge, and a two-hour ski lesson. Children ages 5 to 9 are charged half-price; under 5 are free. Midweek rates are even lower.

Sequoia Ski Touring Center *Sequoia National Park, 209/565-3461; in Giant Forest Village (209/565-3461) & Grant Grove (209/335-2314); cross-country only; 25%B, 25%I, 50%A; 8 trails (40km), none groomed; trail use free with park admission; children's lessons; lodging nearby (see pp.166-167).* The big attraction here is the scenic national park ski trails through groves of cinnamon-colored giant sequoias. Free hot drinks are provided, and moonlight and overnight guided tours are available.

Tamarack Lodge Resort and Nordic Ski Center *Mammoth Lakes, 619/934-2442; on Twin Lakes, 2 1/2 miles from Mammoth Lakes Vil-*

lage; cross-country only; 50%B, 25%I, 25%A; 21 trails (55km), all groomed; trail fee $8, under 18 free; lodging on premises. For the hearty, expedition tours are scheduled in which participants spend the night in a snow cave or tent.

Wilsonia Ski Touring *Kings Canyon National Park, 209/335-2404; cross-country only; lodging on premises (see p.166).* Inexpensive overnight hut tours may be arranged.

Wolverton Ski Bowl *Sequoia National Park, 209/565-3381; off Highway 198, 52 miles east of Visalia; open weekends and holidays; 3 surface; 35%B, 65%I; lifts $13.50/$9.50; lodging nearby 209/561-3314.* This small, family-oriented area caters to beginners and has a snow play area. See also pp.165 to 167.

SNOW PLAY

Yosemite *(see pp.157-164).* Ice skate in the shadows of **Glacier Point** and **Half Dome** at the scenic outdoor rink in Curry Village. Skating pointers are free *(209/372-1442; call for schedule; adults $4.50,*

children $3.50, rentals $1.25). Open-air **snowcat rides** leave from Badger Pass *(209/372-1330; daily 10-3; reservations suggested; tickets $5).* Free ranger-led snowshoe walks are also available at Badger Pass *(209/372-4461).* A good place to snowshoe on your own is the **Sequoia Forest Trail** in Mariposa Grove.

FAMILY CAMPS

Remember the good old days when you were a kid and got to go away to summer camp? Bet you thought those days were gone for good. Well, they're not. Now you can go to family camp.

Family camps provide a reasonably-priced, organized vacation experience. They are sponsored by city recreation departments, university alumni organizations, and private enterprise. The city and private camps are open to anyone, but some university camps require a campus affiliation.

And you don't have to have children to attend. One year when I was at the Alumni Vacation Center in Santa Barbara, a couple was actually honeymooning! Elderly couples whose children have grown occasionally attend, and family reunions are sometimes held at a camp. Whole clubs have been known to book in at the same time.

Housing varies from primitive platform tents and cabins without electricity, plumbing, or bedding to comfortable campus dormitory apartments with daily maid service. Locations vary from the mountains to the sea. Predictably, costs also vary with the type of accommodations and facilities. Some camps allow stays of less than a week, but most require a week-long committment. Children are usually charged at a lower rate according to their age.

Most family camps operate during the summer months only and include meal preparation and clean-up, special programs for children, and recreation programs for everyone. Activities can include river or pool swimming, hikes, fishing, volleyball, table tennis, badminton, hayrides, tournaments, campfires, crafts programs, songfests, tennis, and horseback riding.

Each camp has its own special appeal, but all offer an informal atmosphere where guests can really unwind. Often over half the guests return. Repeat guests and their camp friends tend to choose the same week each year.

For detailed rate information, itemization of facilities, session dates, and route directions, contact the camp reservation offices directly and request a free brochure. Reserve early to avoid disappointment.

■ CITY/GROUP CAMPS

Camp Concord *Concord Department of Leisure Services, Concord, 415/671-3273; daily rates; located near Camp Richardson at South Lake Tahoe; cabins with electricity, provide own bedding, community bathrooms; cafeteria-style meals; special program for ages 3-6, and 7-16; horseback riding and river rafting available at extra charge.*

Camp Sacramento *Department of Parks and Community Services, Sacramento, 916/449-5195; daily rates; located in the El Dorado National Forest 17 miles south of Lake Tahoe; cabins with electricity, provide own bedding, community bathrooms; cafeteria-style meals; program for age 3 and older, babysitting available at extra charge.*

Camp Sierra *Associated Cooperatives Inc., Berkeley, 415/538-0454; weekly rates; located in a pine forest between Huntington and Shaver Lakes about 65 miles east of Fresno; some cabins with electricity, lodge rooms, or bring own tent; provide own bedding, community bathrooms; family-style meals; special activities for teens, playground and crafts program for younger children; special programs on consumer topics.*

Cazadero Family Music Camp *CAMPS Inc., Berkeley, 415/549-2396; weekly rates; located in the Russian River area; platform tents with* *electricity, dormitories; provide own bedding, community bathrooms; family-style meals; daycare for toddlers, program for ages 2-6.* The music classes are open to everyone regardless of ability or experience. Campers may learn anything from beginning musical theory to advanced steel drums. Private lessons are available on all instruments. Dance and art classes are also available.

Echo Lake Family Camp *CAMPS Inc., Berkeley, 415/549-2396; weekly rates; located on the western rim of the Lake Tahoe basin near the Desolation Wilderness Area; tent-cabins without electricity, provide own bedding, community bathrooms; family-style meals; infant care, program for toddlers and older children; swimming pool, seminars on nature exploration and survival techniques.*

Feather River Vacation Camp *Office of Parks and Recreation, Oakland, 415/273-3896; daily rates; located in the Plumas National Forest near Lake Tahoe; cabins and platform tents without electricity, provide own bedding, community bathrooms; family-style meals; play area and activities for ages 2-6, program for age 6 and older; theme weeks.*

Gualala Family Camp *Berkeley-Albany YMCA, Albany, 415/525-1130; 2-3 night weekend in July; located 7 miles inland from the coast near Gualala; shared cabins with electricity & lodge rooms, community bathrooms; meals provided; childcare for 1-6, programs for older children; fitness classes, canoeing, swimming, arts & crafts, hiking, campfire programs.*

Mather Family Camp *San Francisco Recreation and Park Department, San Francisco, 415/558-4870; daily rates; located on the rim of the Tuolumne River gorge near Yosemite National Park; cabins with electricity; provide own bedding, community bathrooms; cafeteria-style meals; playground area, program for age 6 and older; pool, horseback riding.*

San Jose Family Camp *San Jose Parks and Recreation Department, San Jose, 408/277-4666; daily rates; located in the Stanislaus National Forest 30 miles from Yosemite National Park; platform tents without electricity, provide own bedding, community bathrooms; buffet and family-style meals; play area, program for age 3 and older; pool.*

Silver Lake Resort *Department of Parks and Recreation, Stockton, 209/944-8206; daily rates; located 40 miles south of Lake Tahoe; platform tents without electricity, cabins with electricity; provide own bedding, community bathrooms; cafeteria-style meals; program for toddlers and older; swimming in lake, horseback riding.*

Tuolumne Family Camp *Berkeley Camps Office, Berkeley, 415/644-6520; daily rates; located on the south fork of the Tuolumne River near Yosemite National Park; platform tents without electricity, provide own bedding, community bathrooms; family-style meals; programs for toddlers-6, 6-12, teens; swimming instruction in river, cookout and breakfast hikes.*

■ PRIVATE ENTERPRISE CAMPS

Coffee Creek Guest Ranch. See p.237.

Emandal. See p.137.

Greenhorn Creek Guest Ranch *Spring Garden, 916/283-0930; weekly rates; located 70 miles north of Lake Tahoe in Feather River country; modern cabins and hotel units with maid service, private bathrooms; family-style meals; childcare for children 3-5 during horseback rides, babysitting available at additional charge; heated pool, swimming hole, horseback riding, hayrides, fishing, hiking; golf & tennis nearby.* All activities are included in the price. Most people seem to come here for the heavy schedule of horse-related activities. A special Thanksgiving Weekend is available, and in the spring and fall daily and weekend rates may be secured on a space-available basis. This is where you go to rough it in comfort.

Highland Ranch. See p.85.

Kennolyn's Family Camp *408/475-1430; no children under 3; 1 weeklong session in Aug; located 4 miles from Soquel in the Santa Cruz mountains; cabins with electricity, provide own bedding, some private bathrooms; family-style meals; programs for all ages; 3 tennis courts, pool, darkroom access for photographers; instruction in horseback riding, riflery, archery, gymnastics, crafts, sailing, windsurfing, skin diving, & soccer.*

Montecito-Sequoia High Sierra Vacation Camp *800/227-9900, 415/967-8612; weekly rates; located in Sequoia National Forest between Kings Canyon and Sequoia National Parks; lodge, bedding provided, private baths; also open cabins, provide own bedding, community bathrooms; buffet meals; programs for age 3 and older; 2 tennis courts, lake swimming, pool, sailing, canoeing, boating, archery, photography darkroom, fishing, riflery, water-skiing, horseback riding.* See also pp.166 and 255.

■ UNIVERSITY CAMPS

Alumni Vacation Center *sponsored by the University of California, Santa Barbara, 805/961-3123; weekly rates; located on U.C. cam-*

pus in Santa Barbara; dormitory suites with private bathrooms, refrigerators, and daily maid service; bedding provided; cafeteria-style meals; infant care, 8 hours of programs daily for all ages; 10 tennis courts, pool, swimming and tennis lessons, bicycle rentals.

Lair of the Bear *sponsored by the University of California, Berkeley, 415/642-0221; weekly rates; located in the Stanislaus National Forest near Pinecrest; tent cabins with electricity, provide own bedding, community bathrooms; family-style meals; supervised play for ages 2-6, program for 6 and older; 2 camps (***Camp Blue*** & ***Camp Gold***); pool, 3 tennis courts, swimming and tennis lessons.*

Floating campsite.

HOUSEBOATS

Living in a houseboat for a few days is an unusual way to get away from it all. You can dive off your boat for a refreshing swim, fish for dinner while you sunbathe, and dock in a sheltered, quiet cove for the night.

Houseboats are equipped with kitchens and flush toilets. Most rental agencies require that you provide your own bedding, linens, and groceries. Almost everything else is on your floating hotel—including life jackets.

Rates vary quite dramatically depending on the time of year (summer rentals are the highest) and how many people are in your party (a group of six to ten people gets the best rates). In-season weekly rates for six range from $750 to $1,050 and can go as high as $1,775— depending on the size and quality of the boat. Fuel is additional. Some rental facilities have enough boats to offer midweek specials and three-day weekends; some offer a Thanksgiving special which includes the turkey and pumpkin pie. During the off-season, some will even rent their boats for just a day. Contact rental facilities directly for their current stock and rates.

LAKE OROVILLE

Floating Campsites *800/444-7275, 619/452-1950; Apr-Oct; $50/night.*
Operated by the State Department of Parks and Recreation, these floating campsites have fully equipped kitchens and a sundeck on the roof.

Lime Saddle Marina *800/826-7517, 916/877-2414.*

For more information on this area contact:

Oroville Chamber of Commerce *1789 Montgomery, Oroville 95965, 916/533-2542.*

LAKE SHASTA

Bridge Bay Resort & Marina and **Digger Bay Marina** *800/752-9669, 702/294-1770.*

Holiday Flotels *916/221-5666.*

Holiday Harbor *800/258-BOAT, 916/238-2383.*

For more information on houseboating on Lake Shasta contact the Shasta-Cascade Wonderland Association or the Shasta Dam Area Chamber of Commerce (see p.231).

SACRAMENTO DELTA

Herman & Helen's Marina *209/951-4634.* Especially reasonable prices are available for four-person boats. Inquire about the special RV barge.

Paradise Point Marina *209/952-1000.*

For more information on houseboating on the Delta contact:

Rio Vista Chamber of Commerce *60 Main St., Rio Vista 94571, 707/ 374-2700.*

RIVER TRIPS

The adventure of rafting down a changing and unpredict-
able river offers a real escape for the harried, city-weary
participant. But don't expect it to be relaxing. Participants
are expected to help with setting up and breaking camp and
are sometimes mercilessly exposed to the elements. While
usually not dangerous when done with experienced guides,
an element of risk is involved. Still, most participants walk
away ecstatic and addicted to the experience.

The outfitter will provide shelter, food, and equipment
for the trip. You need only bring sleeping gear and personal

items. Costs range from $104 to $380 per person for an overnight run. Some day trips are available. Seasons and rivers vary with each company. The minimum age requirement for children ranges from 6 to 10. For details, contact the tour operators directly.

The American River Touring Association *Groveland, 800/323-ARTA, 209/962-7873.*

ECHO: The Wilderness Company *Oakland, 800/652-ECHO, 415/ 652-1600.*

Mariah Wilderness Expeditions *Point Richmond, 415/233-2303.* This is California's only woman-owned and operated whitewater raft and wilderness company. Special mother/daughter trips are scheduled, as well as father/son trips (with male guides). This outfit also schedules backpacking and cross-country ski trips.

Whitewater Voyages *El Sobrante, 415/222-5994.*

PACK TRIPS

Packing your equipment onto horses or mules allows for a much easier and luxurious trek into the wilderness than does backpacking. All necessary equipment, food, and paraphernalia can be packed onto these beasts of burden. You need simply to make the choice as to the type of pack trip you desire.

On a spot pack trip the packers will load the animals with your gear, take them to your prearranged campsite, unload your gear, and return to the pack station with the pack animals. They will return to repack your gear on the day you are to leave. You may either hike or ride on horses to your campsite. If you ride, you will usually have a choice of keeping the horses at your campsite or of having the packers take them back out. If you wish to keep them, you will need to arrange in advance for a corral and feed, and you should be experienced with horses. Do not bring along children who haven't had at least basic riding instruction.

A more rugged trip (where you move your campsite each day) or an easier trip (with all expenses and a guide included) can also usually be arranged with the packer.

This is not an inexpensive vacation. Prices will vary according to which of the above options you choose. Trips are usually available only in the summer. Often there are special rates for children, who must be at least five years old. For general information and a list of packers contact:

Eastern High Sierra Packers Association *690 N. Main St., Bishop 93514, 619/873-8405.*

Guided pack trips can also be taken with llamas. They're used to this chore, having been used for it for over 2,000 years in the Andes. And they are so gentle even a 4-year-old can lead one. For details, contact the following outfitters:

Mama's Llamas *P.O. Box 655, El Dorado 95623, 916/622-2566.* This was the first company in North America to make llamas available for pack trips.

Shasta Llamas *P.O. Box 1137, Mt. Shasta 96067, 916/926-3959.*

CAMPING

Because there are excellent resources available for information on campgrounds, I have mentioned only briefly ones which fit into the text. For your convenience I have also included them in the Index under "campsites." For more complete information, consult the following references:

The California-Nevada CampBook and its companion map list camping facilities and fees. They are available free to AAA members.

The Official Guide to California State Parks is an informative brochure with a map which pinpoints all state parks, reserves, recreation areas, historic parks, and campgrounds. It is available by mail for $2 from: Publications, Department of Parks and Recreation, P.O. Box 942896, Sacramento 94296.

■ *CAMPSITE RESERVATIONS*

Reservations are advisable at most state park campgrounds and can be made by phone for a small service fee. They may be made as early as eight weeks in advance. For general information on state park campgrounds and to make reservations call 800/444-7275 or 619/452-1950.

MISCELLANEOUS ADVENTURES

American Youth Hostels *San Francisco, 415/863-1444.* The idea behind hosteling is to save money, so accommodations are simple. Women bunk in one dormitory-style room and men in the other. Some hostels have separate rooms for couples and families. Guests provide their own bedding and linens (sleepsets can be rented), and bathrooms and kitchens are shared. All guests are expected to do a chore. Hostels are closed during the day, usually from 9:30 to 4:30, and lights go out at 11 p.m. Fees are low— ranging from $6.50 to $12 per person per night. Children under 18 with a parent are charged half-price. Hostel members receive a discount at most hostels as well as a newsletter and handbook of U.S. hostels. Package tours are available. Call for further information and a brochure listing all the hostels in Northern California.

Audubon Canyon Ranch *Stinson Beach, 415/868-9244.* Past weekend programs have included From Branches to Baskets (a weekend of weaving) and Small Animal Safari (especially for families). Lodging is in a bunkhouse featuring solar-heated water and toilets operated by wind power. Participants provide their own bedding and meals.

Backroads Bicycle Touring *San Leandro, 415/895-1783.* Bicycle tours include the Wine Country, Russian River, Point Reyes Seashore, Solvang, and Death Valley. Areas outside of California include the Oregon Coast, Grand Canyon, Colorado Rockies, and Yellowstone. Then there's Baja California, Hawaii, and New Zealand! The emphasis is not on endurance but on getting some exercise. Two tour guides accompany bikers, and a support vehicle transports equipment (and cyclists if they get tired). To allow for different ability levels, several routes are available on each trip. Accommodations are in either interesting hotels or comfortable campgrounds, and meals are included. Children are welcome, and fair discounts are given for them.

Bed & Breakfast International *Albany, 415/525-4569.* Lodging and full breakfast are provided in private homes throughout Northern California. Some of the 300 host homes located in 42 cities are appropriate for children. Most cannot accommodate more than two people in a room, but a 20% reduction is given for children staying in a second room. There is a two-night minimum.

California Academy of Sciences *San Francisco, 415/221-5100.* These nature study trips are headed by members of the academy staff. On some trips participants camp out and cook their own meals. On other less strenuous trips motel lodging and restaurant meals are included. Destinations include Lava Beds National Monument and Santa Cruz Island. The **Junior Academy** offers similar one-day and weekend trips for children ages 6 to 16.

California Adventures *University of California, Berkeley, 415/642-4000.* Adventure trips include rock climbing, backpacking, snow camping, cross-country skiing, river rafting, kayaking, sailing, and wind surfing. There is also a special program for children in grades 3 through 12.

Green Tortoise *San Francisco, 415/821-0803.* Travel on this laid-back alternative bus line is enjoyed at bargain rates, and children measuring under 4-feet 9-inches and accompanied by an adult are half-price. (Unfortunately a parent with more than one child is charged full fare for each additional child. The policy is one child per parent.) Clientelle tends to be the under-30s crowd, but all ages are welcome. Trips are available to almost anywhere on this continent. There are cross-country trips with stops at national parks, and there are river rafting trips to Baja. Usually the scenic route (not necessarily the most direct route) is followed. Overnight accommodations are often arranged in hostels, but sometimes riders must bring their own bedding. The jack-of-all-trades bus drivers often organize cookouts and get out and fix break-downs themselves. Passengers have also been known to get out and push when necessary. All in all, a trip on this bus line is really a trip.

Marin Discoveries *Corte Madera, 415/927-0410.* Overnight trips are varied and in the past have included a backpacking trip for parents with babies, a whale-watching trip to Monterey, and a ski tour of the Tahoe rim. There are day trips, weekend trips, and week-long trips. Many are centered in Marin County, but more ambitious trips are also arranged to Europe, Africa, and Asia.

Nature Explorations-Tuleyome *Palo Alto, 415/324-8737.* These teacher-led trips are mostly camping and backpacking—some specifically aimed at families and/or single-parent families. For example, in the winter there might be a snow camping trip and a cross-country ski weekend, in the spring a backpacking trip to the Sierras or a photography trip to Yosemite. The program also offers many day trips. The organization's objective is to foster in residents attachment to their environment.

Near Escapes *San Francisco, 415/921-1392.* Guided tours of unusual, closer-in destinations are the specialty of this business. Past escapes have included Shop Till You Drop (a shopping spree of clothing outlets) and Graveyard Shift: The Colma Cemeteries (a visit to the graves of Wyatt Earp, Levi Strauss, and Benny Bufano as well as a pet cemetery). Transportation, guide, and snack were included on both these trips. Children are welcome; minimum ages are always given.

Owner Builder Center *Berkeley, 415/848-6860.* One-, two-, and three-week camp programs giving participants experience in house building are held each summer in the Sierra foothills near Grass Valley. Students build in the morning and receive comprehensive classroom instruction in the afternoon. Step-by-step, they learn everything from foundations to finishing. But because it is vacation time, there are also rafting trips, barbecues, and softball games.

Point Reyes Field Seminars *Point Reyes National Seashore, 415/663-1200.* These interpretive programs are co-sponsored by the National Park Service and the Coastal Park Association. Instructors are experts in their fields, and courses include both day trips and overnight trips—some designed especially for families. Subjects include art, photography, horseback riding, cooking, whale and bird watching, and Indian culture.

San Damiano Retreat *Danville, 415/837-9141.* A person takes a retreat to experience solitude and meditate. Retreat weekends here are scheduled for groups of men, women, young adults, engaged couples, married couples, etc.

Sierra Club *San Francisco, 415/776-2211.* Service trips take participants to remote wilderness areas to maintain trails and clean up trash. Nature appreciation trips and special family trips are also scheduled. All trips are described in the January/February issue of *Sierra Magazine*—sent free to all members.

House building camp.

Slide Ranch *Muir Beach, 415/381-6155.* Perched dramatically on the ocean side of Highway 1 near Muir Beach, Slide Ranch offers the city-slicker a chance to get back to the land...a chance to learn about a self-sustaining rural lifestyle through exposure to frontier arts...a chance to slow the pace. During Family Days programs, children and adults learn together about things like cheesemaking, composting, and papermaking. Though the program varies according to the season and the ages of participants, a typical day begins with smiling staff members greeting visitors in a fragrant grove of eucalyptus. A visit to the sheep pen usually follows—giving children the chance to "pet a four-legged sweater." Then, turning the tables, children who really just want to be kids can don a sheepskin and wander disguised among the goats—who tend to stare quizzically and then run. A picnic lunch, nature walk, and visit inside the chicken pen round out this family experience. In addition to these day-long programs, the ranch offers Family Overnights. Participants spend the night in tents pitched under a lone cypress located about 1/4-mile from the ranch house. Communal meals are prepared in a geodesic dome built by high school students in a previous teen program.

University Extension. Contact your local state college or university about their travel/study extension program. **San Jose State University** offers a program of family vacations *(408/924-2625).* The **University of California** sponsors a program of research expeditions which are not appropriate for children under 16 *(415/642-6586).*

Volunteer Vacations. Get a job as a volunteer in a state park or forest. Host a campground, improve trails, collect data on wildlife, explain an area's history to visitors. Only a very few of these jobs reimburse travel and food costs or provide accommodations. For a sample issue of the periodical *Helping Out in the Outdoors* send $3 to: American Hiking Society, 1015 31st St. NW, Washington, D.C. 20007, 703/385-3252.

Wildlife Weekend *San Francisco Zoological Society, San Francisco, 415/661-2023.* This weekend trip for the whole family is usually scheduled for Labor Day weekend. It takes place on the Inverness Ridge near Point Reyes National Seashore and includes nature seminars and evening campfires. Participants provide their own transportation and camping equipment; some cabins are available. Meals are included in the nominal fee. This special program is for members of the Zoological Society only. A $35 family membership allows unlimited free admission to the zoo, a subscription to *Animal Kingdom Magazine,* invitations to other member-only events, discounts at the Zoo Shop, and free admission to 50 other U.S. zoos and aquariums.

INDEX

A

AAA, 3, 271
A&W Rootbeer Drive-In, 154
Abalonetti, 44
Accommodation Station, 217
A Child's Garden of Verses, 111
Adobe House Tour, 43
Adventures Aloft, 105
Aero Schellville, 99
The Ahwahnee, 158, 160, 161
airplanes, 32, 99, 115
Albion, 87
Alexander Valley, 135
Alexander's Restaurant, 225
Alger, Horatio, 176
Alice in Wonderland, 71
Alleghany, 198
Allen Knight Maritime Mus, 46
Alpine Meadows Ski Area, 246
Alta Sierra Resort Motel, 194
Alumni Vacation Ctr, 259, 262
Amador City, 187-188
Amador Cnty Fair Grounds, 181
Amador County Museum, 183
American Hiking Society, 277
American River Parkway, 206
The Amer River Tour Assoc 268
American River, 207
The American Victorian Museum
  Dining Room, 199
American Youth Hostels, 273
amputee ski clinic, 247
Amtrak, 69, 151, 204, 222
amusement parks, 27, 35, 130, 203,
  211, 219
Ancil Hoffman Park, 207
Anderson Vly Historical Mus 85
Anderson Valley Hostel, 85
Andril Fireplace Cottages, 51
Angels Bakery, 179
Angels Camp, 178-179
Angels Camp Museum, 179
Angora Lakes Trail, 219
Animal Tree, 20
Ano Nuevo State Reserve, 31
The Ansel Adams Gallery, 162
Antique Apple Tasting, 131
antique farm equipment, 228
Antique Rose Garden, 131
antique shops, 109, 142, 149, 183,
  188, 216
antique weapons, 141
Antonelli Bros Begonia Gdns, 41
Apple Fare, 199
Apple Hill, 189
aquariums, 37, 48, 74
The Arbor, 109
arboretums, 25, 39
Arcata, 138, 139
Armour, Philip, 189
Arneson, Robert, 216
Arnold, 176, 252
Asilomar Conference Center, 51
Asti, 135
Auberge Du Soleil, 109
Auburn, 169, 192, 222
Auburn Hotel, 192

Audubon Canyon Ranch, 273
autumn colors, 172, 197
The Ave of the Giants, 143-146
aviaries, 205, 210
Avila Beach, 75
Avila Hot Springs, 155
Awanichi Indians, 163

B

Babbling Brook B & B Inn, 33
Bach Festival, 54
Backroads Bicycle Touring, 273
Badger Pass, 253, 257
bakeries, 31, 58, 59, 88, 98, 106, 132,
  150, 179, 226
Bale Grist Mill S H P, 110
Bargetto Winery, 42, 47
Barrel Builders, 110
barrel tasting, 111
The Beach Boys, 32
Beachcomber Inn, 51
Beachcomber Motel, 91
Bear Mountain, 21
Bear River Lake Resort, 253
Bear Valley, 252
Bear Vly Nordic Ski Area, 252
Bear Wallow Resort, 85
Bearpaw, 166
Beaulieu Vineyard, 111
Bed & Breakfast Intl, 274
Bed & Breakfast San Juan, 150
Bedford Park, 190
beehive, 112
Beesley's Cottages, 224
Begonia Festival, 40
Bellissimo Restaurant, 232
Bellotti Inn, 184
Ben Lomond, 19, 20, 21, 22
Ben Lomond County Park, 22
Ben Lomond Hylton Motel, 19
Benbow Inn, 145
Beringer Vineyards, 111
Bernhard House, 192
Berry Creek Falls, 20
Bicentennial Museum, 200
bicycles, free use, 52, 86, 87, 143
bicycle paths, 47, 98, 120, 206, 219,
  227, 237
bicycle rentals, 30, 34, 47, 103, 145,
  162, 167, 219, 227, 263
bicycle tours, 273
Big Basin Redwoods S P, 20
Big River, 90
Big River Lodge, 87
Big Sur, 59, 64-67
Big Sur Inn, 66
Big Sur Lodge, 64
Big Sur River, 65
Big 3 Fountain, 97
Big Time Miwok Cele, 186
Bikini Beach, 167
Billy Jones Wildcat Railroad, 25
Bing Crosby Golf Tournament, 43, 62
bird sanctuaries, 25, 60, 72, 74, 237
Bishop Pine Lodge, 146
Black Bart, 176, 180
Black Bart Inn and Motel, 179

Black Bart Players, 176
blacksmiths, 174, 236, 238, 239
Bluegrass Festival, 193
Blue Heron Inn, 129
Blue Sail Inn, 72
boat tours, 31, 75, 120, 142, 204, 219,
  220
Bodega Bay, 79
Bodega Bay Lodge, 79
Boeger Winery, 190
Bogart, Humphrey, 254
Bohemian Grove, 127
Boiling Springs Lake, 235
Bonanza, 228
Bonny Doon, 37
Bonny Doon Vineyard, 37
bonsai, 125
Bookshop Santa Cruz, 38
Boontling dialect, 85
Boonville, 85
Bordeaux House, 102
Boreal, 249
Borges' Sleigh Rides, 246
Bothe-Napa Valley S P, 115
Boulder Creek, 20, 22
Boulder Creek Park, 22
Bourn Mansion, 19
Boyden Cavern, 167
Boyes Hot Springs, 97
Bracebridge Dinner, 158
Brambles Dinner House, 70
Brass Ass Saloon, 124
Brass Rubbing Centre, 60
Breakers Motel, 72
brewpubs, 35, 114, 136
Bridge Bay, 232
Bridge Bay Rsrt & Mar 266
Bridgeport Bridge, 195
Broadway Hotel, 181
Brockway Springs, 223
Brookside Lodge & Motel, 127
Brother Timothy's corkscrew
  collection, 111
Brussels Sprout Festival, 32
Buena Vista Winery & Vineyards,
  101
Bufano, Benny 80, 275
Buffalo Bob's Ice Cream Saloon, 206
Buffalo Chips Emporium, 187
Bumpass Hell, 233
Bunyan, Paul, 147
Burgundy House, 102
burro picnic, 164
Burton, Richard, 67
bus tours, 146, 162, 163, 274
Butterfly Grove Inn, 52, 53
Butterfly Town USA, 51
Butterfly Trees Lodge, 52, 53

C

C.T.M.'s Rule of the Road, 4
Caber Tossing Champs, 123
cable cars, 41, 208
Cabrillo Motel, 72
Cabrillo Music Festival, 32
cactus gardens, 99, 125
Caesars casino, 217; Cafe Roma, 218;

Cascade Showrm, 220
Cafe Amphora, 66
Cafe Beaujolais, 88
Cafe Delicias, 192
Cafe du Chai, 133
Cafe Les Stace, 200
Cal Poly, 155
Calaveras Big Trees S P, 176, 253
Calaveras County Fair, 179
Calaveras County Hist Mus, 180
California Academy of Sciences
  nature study trips, 274
California Adventures, 274
California Almond Growers Visitor
  Center, 207
Cal Caverns at Cave City, 180
California Heritage Guides, 46
California Market, 55
California Poly State U, 155
California Rail Museum, 204, 215,
  222
California Rodeo, 151
California's First Theater, 46
The California-Nevada CampBook,
  271
California State Auto Assoc, 3
California State Capitol Building, 202,
  207
California State Fair, 203
California State Indian Mus, 210
California State RR Mus, 208
California Western Railroad, 93
Calistoga, 112-118
Calistoga Inn, 114
Calistoga Soaring Center, 115
Calistoga Spa Hot Springs, 113
The Call of the Wild, 100
Cambria, 67-71
Cambria Pines Lodge, 70
camel rides, 211
Camino, 189
Campbell, 25
Campbell Hot Springs/Consciousness
  Village, 200
Camp Blue, 263
Camp Concord, 260
Camp Gold, 263
camping, campsites, 20, 23, 66, 67,
  79, 80, 111, 121, 128, 129, 136,
  145, 153, 159, 160, 166, 176, 177,
  186, 194, 198, 201, 217, 221, 227,
  229, 233, 234, 236, 265, 269, 271-
  272, 274, 275, 277
Camp Richardson, 221, 246, 260
Camp Richardson Corral, 221
Camp Sacramento, 260
Camp Sierra, 260
candle-light mission tour, 150
candy shops, 47, 59, 174
The Candy Store Gallery, 216
Cannery Row, 47, 53
Cannery Row, 47
cannons, 186, 210
canoe rentals, 130, 132, 262
Cantina Los Tres Hom 217, 226
Cap'n Flint's, 91
Cape Mendocino, 142
Capitola, 39-42
Capitola Inn, 40
Capitola Venetian Hotel, 40
car seat law, California, 6
Caravan to Nation's Christmas Tree,
  166
Carmel, 54-64
Carmel Bay, 64
Carmel Beach, 60
Carmel Mission, 54
Carmel River, 55, 56

Carmel River Inn, 55
Carmel River State Beach, 60
Carmel Valley, 57
Carmichael, 207
Carnelian Bay, 223, 225
Carnelian Woods, 223, 249
carousels, 27, 36, 47, 125
Carriage House Theater, 25
Carson Mansion, 141
Carter House, 139
Casa Blanca Motel, 33
Casa del Mar, 69
Casa Guttierez, 45
Casa Munras Garden Hotel, 43
Casa Soberanes, 49
casinos, 217, 218, 220, 225
Castro Adobe, 149
Castroville, 42
catamaran, 232
Catch A Canoe, 90
catch-your-own-trout, 128
Cavalier Inn, 70
caves, 167, 177, 180, 232, 234, 236
Cayucos, 75
Cazadero, 128
Cazadero Fmly Music Cmp, 260
Cazanoma Lodge, 128
Cedar Grove, 167
Cedar Stock Resrt & Mrna, 237
The Celebrated Jumping Frog of
  Calaveras County, 169
Cellar Bar, 89
The Cellar, 188
Centennial Stairway, 74
Central Pacific Passenger Station, 208
Central Valley, 231
Centrella Hotel, 52
Chamarita, 29
The Chart House, 23
Chateau Montelena Winery, 116
Chateau St. Jean Winery, 101 ·
cheese factories, 98, 159
chess board, giant, 74
Chester, 235
Chez Panisse Desserts, 132
Children's Forest, 145
children's programs, supervised, 85,
  114, 120, 163, 215, 223, 237, 241,
  246, 248, 249, 250, 251, 253, 255,
  260-263, 274, 245
Childs Meadows Resort, 235
Chinese junk, 116
Chinese Taoist temple, 238
Chinquapin, 223
The Chocolate Tree, 106
Cholame, 154
The Christian Bros, 111
Christmas B&B tour, 183
Christmas events, 150, 158, 166, 174,
  183, 189, 193, 197, 217
The Church of One Tree, 125
The Chutney Kitchen, 103, 106
Cinnabar Cafe, 114
City Hotel, 174, 175
Clair Engle Lake, 237
Clair Tapaan Lodge, 250
Clam Box Restaurant, 57
clam digging, 74
Clarke Memorial Museum, 141
Clear Lake, 118-121
Clearlake, 120, 121
Clemens, Samuel L., 170
Cleveland, President, 194
Clock Garden, 44
Clos Pegase Winery, 118
Cloverdale, 127
Coast North, 76-93
Coast Oyster Co., 141

Coast South, 28-75
Coast Starlight, 69
Coastways Ranch, 31
Cobblestone Theater, 187
Cocoanut Grove, 34
Coeur du Lac, 223
Coffee Creek Guest Ranch, 237, 244,
  262
Coloma, 190-191
Colonial Inn, 91
Colonial Terrace Inn, 55
Columbia Gem Motel, 175
Columbia State H P, 173
Come Fly a Kite, 60
Commons Beach, 227
Concours d'Elegance, 43
condominiums, 15, 34, 40, 217, 222-
  223, 225
Congress Springs Vineyards, 24
Constitution Day Parade, 197
Consuelo's, 44
Cooks' Corner Deli, 106
Cornish Christmas, 193
Cottage of Sweets, 57
Cottage Springs, 252
Country Squire Motel, 181
County Historical Museum, 155
Court House Theatre, 180
covered bridges, 21, 141, 160, 163,
  195
Crescent City, 146
Crocker Art Museum, 207
cross-country skiing, 223, 229, 237,
  241-257, 268, 274, 275
The Crow's Nest, 34
Crystal Cave, 167
Cunha Country Store, 30-31
Curry Village, 160, 161, 163, 256
Custom House, 49

D
Daffodil Hill, 185
Daily Planet, 126
Dale, Douglas, 227
dams, 227, 228
Dansk shops, 60, 111
Danville, 275
da Vinci, Leonardo, 39
Dean, James, 154
Degnan's Deli, 162
deLatour, Georges, 111
Del Monte Forest, 61
Delta region, 204, 266
DeMartin House, 147
demonstration forests, 85, 143
Dennis the Menace Playgrnd, 47
Depot Museum, 98
Desolation Wilderness Area, 261
Devil's Kitchen, 235
diaries, trip, 9, 11
Digger Bay Marina, 266
The Diner, 103
diving bell, 47
Dixieland Jazz Festival, 203
Dodge Ridge, 252
dolphins, 37
Domaine Chandon, 104, 106
Domaine M. Marion Winery, 24
Domike's Inn, 194
Donner Lake, 227
Donner Memorial S P, 227
Donner Party, 227
Donner Ski Ranch, 250
Donner Summit, 249-252
Donner Trail Tour, 252
Dom's Origl Breakers Cafe, 73
downhill skiing, 223, 241-257
Downieville, 169, 196, 199

Downtown Bakery, 132
Drakesbad Guest Ranch, 235
Dream Inn, 33
dressing kids for snow, 243-244
Drive-Thru Tree Park, 146
Dr. Wilkinson's Hot Sprngs, 113
Dry Creek Inn, 131
Dry Creek Vineyards, 133
Drytown, 188
Dunbar House, 1880, 175
Duncan, Isadora, 244
Duncans Mills, 129
Dunes Beach, 31
The Dunes Resort, 225
Dunlap, 167

E
Eagle House Theatre, 140
Eagle House Victorian Inn, 140
Earp, Wyatt, 275
Earthquake Trail, 79
East of Eden, 151
Easter egg hunts, 21, 174
Easter parade, 174
Eastwood, Clint, 58
Echo Lake Family Camp, 261
Echo Summit Ski Area, 245
ECHO:Wilderness Co, 268
ecological staircase, 92
Edgewater Packing Company, 47
Edmeades Vineyards, 85
Eel River, 137, 139, 143, 145, 146
Eel River Redwoods Hostel, 146
Effie Yeaw Nature Center, 207
Egghead Omelettes of Oz, 92
Ehrman Mansion, 229
El Bonita Motel, 107
El Capitan, 158
El Dorado, 188-18
El Dorado Cty Fairgrounds, 190
El Dorado Cty Hist Mus, 190
El Dorado Inn, 96
El Dorado National Forest, 260
elephant seals, 31
El Estero Park, 47
El Granada, 30
elk, 83
El Palomar, 34
El Pueblo Motel, 97
El Teatro Campesino, 150
Emandal Farm, 137, 262
Embassy Suites, 102, 154
Emerald Bay, 219, 220
Emerald Bay State Park, 221
Emigrant Trail Museum, 227
Em Le's, 57
Empire Mine S H P, 195
End of the Trail Indian Mus, 147
Esalen Institute, 65
Eureka, 137-147
The Eureka Inn, 140
Europa Coffee Shop, 172
Exploration Cruise Lines, 204

F
Fairfield, 204
Fairytale Town, 211
Falcon Crest, 112
Fallen Leaf Lake, 219
Fallon Hotel, 175
Fallon House Theatre, 175
Fall River Mills, 236
Family Adventure Packs, 146
family camps, 258-263
Fanny Ann's Saloon, 206
Fanny Bridge, 227
Fantasie Au Chocolat, 98
Farmers' Market, 154

farm map, 123
farms, 31, 41, 123, 125, 129, 133,
    137, 155, 189, 277
father/son trips, 268
Feather River country, 262
Feather River Vac Camp, 261
Felton, 20, 21
Fensalden Inn, 87
Fern Canyon, 146
Ferndale, 139, 142, 143
Fernwood Resort, 67
Ferris wheel, 27
Fiddletown, 169
fiesta, 61
Finn, Huckleberry, 229
Fiori's, 129
Firehouse Museum, 200
fire muster, 174
Fish Camp, 164
Fisherman's Wharf, 47, 49
fish hatchery, 134
fishing, 21, 47, 116, 128, 167, 189,
    197, 199, 211, 221, 228
Fitzgerald Marine Reserve, 30
floating campsites, 264, 265
Florence Lake, 166
Florentine Pasta Factory, 24
flume rides, 27, 36
folk opera, 150
Folsom, 215
Folsom Zoo, 215
Forbes Mill Museum, 25
Ford House, 90
Ford, President, 57
Forestville, 127, 129, 131
Fort Bragg, 91-93
The Fort Bragg Footlighters, 92
Fort Crook Museum, 236
Fort Humboldt S H P, 141
Fort Ross State Historic Park, 80
Four Seasons Restaurant, 161
4th of July Parade, 197
Freemark Abbey, 111
French Laundry, 104
Friar Tuck's, 200
Friendly Acres, 30

G
Gable, Clark, 254
gambling, 214
Garberville, 145
gardens, 25, 41, 80, 92, 125, 131, 142,
    185, 195, 196, 207
Garfield, President, 181, 194
Garrod Farms Stables, 24
The Gaslighter Theater, 25
Gatekeeper's Museum, 228
General Grant Grove, 167
General Phipps Cabin, 229
General Sherman Tree, 165, 167
General's Highway, 167
General Vallejo's home, 99
George Washington Park, 53
Georgia-Pacific Corp, 93, 141
Georgia-Pacific Tree Nurs, 92
Gerber, 231
Gerhards Sausage Kitchen, 106
geyser, 116
Geyser Peak Winery, 135
Geyserville, 134-135
ghost town, 201
Giant Artichoke Restaurant, 42
Giant Chess Board, 74
Giant Dipper, 36
Giant Forest, 165
The Gingerbread Mansion, 143
Glacier Point, 162, 163, 256
Glendeven, 87

Glen Ellen, 99
Glen Oaks Restaurant, 66
Gold Bluffs Beach, 146
Gold Bug Mine, 190
Gold Dust Days, 181
gold mines, 174, 190, 198, 201
gold panning, 171, 174, 181, 182, 198,
    237
Gold Prospecting Tours, 171
Gold Run Creek, 197
Gold Rush Country, 168-201
golf, 43, 56, 62, 72, 81, 88, 103, 108,
    120, 124, 145, 161, 194, 211, 223,
    224, 262
Gonzales, 152
The Good Earth, 23
goodie bags, 12-14
Grace Hudson Museum, 136
Grandmere's Inn, 197
Grand Prix, 43
Grani-Ann's Kayaking, 132
Granlibakken, 223, 247
Grant Grove, 167, 255
Grant Grove Ski Touring, 254
Grant, Pres U.S., 141, 176, 194
Grass Valley, 192-196, 197, 222, 275
Gravenstein Apple Fair, 127
Great America, 27
The Great Amer Fish Co, 73
The Great American Omelette
    Company, 226
great blue heron, 74
Great Pumpkin Parade, 29
The Great Santini, 4
Great Ski Race, 249
Greenhorn Crk Gst Ranch, 262
Greenhouse at the Farm, 41
The Green Lantern, 55
Green Tortoise, 274
Grey Fox Inn, 70
Grey Whale Bar, 86
The Grey Whale Inn, 91
Griffin's Fern Rvr Resort, 20
Groveland, 159
Groveland Motel, 159
Grover Hot Springs S P, 220
Gualala, 82, 261
Gualala Family Camp, 261
Guerneville, 126-131
Guest House Museum, 92
Gum Alley, 155
Gunn House, Motel, 172

H
Hacienda del Lago, 226
Hacienda Winery, 101
Hakone Japanese Gardens, 25
Half Dome, 256
Half Moon Bay, 29-31
Half Moon Bay Bakery, 31
handicapped skiing, 247
hang-gliding, 48
Hangtown Fry, 189
Hansen's Resort, 246
Harbor House, 83
Harbor Lights Motel, 41
Harrah's casino, 215, 217; Forest Buf-
    fet, 218; South Shore Room, 220
Harrison, President, 194
Harte, Bret, 170, 180
Hartsook Inn, 145
Harvest Inn, 107
Harvey's casino, 217; Carriage House,
    218
Hat Creek, 233
Hat Creek Resort, 233
haunted houses, 41, 49, 183, 191, 200
hayrides, 30, 228, 237, 262

Healdsburg, 131-133
Healdsburg Meml Beach, 132
Healdsburg Meml Pool, 132
Hearst Castle, 67-69
Hearst, William Randolph, 67
Heavenly Valley, 245
Hector De Smet Bakery, 58
The Heirloom, 182
helicopter skiing, 245
Helping Out in the Outdoors, 277
Henry Cowell Redwoods State Park, 20, 21
Heritage House, 87
Herman & Helen's Marina, 266
heron rookery, 72, 74
Herrington's Sierra Pines, 198
Hershey Chocolate Co, 160
Highland Ranch, 85, 262
Highlands County Park, 21
Highlands Inn, 55
High Noon, 174
High Sierra Camps, 160
High Sierra casino, 217; Theater, 220
Hiouchi, 146
Historic Automobile Races, 43
Historic Crafts Fair, 239
Hog's Breath Inn, 58
Holbrooke Hotel, 194
Holiday Flotels, 266
Holiday Harbor, 266
The Homestead, 55
Homewood ski area, 248
Hoover, President, 181
Hope-Bosworth House, 134
Hope-Merrill House, 134
Hop Kiln Winery, 132
Hopkins, Mark, 189
Hopland, 136
horseback riding, 24, 30, 56, 79, 81, 92, 100, 106, 129, 145, 146, 153, 163, 166, 167, 217, 221, 223, 235, 237, 260, 261, 262, 269, 275; English saddles, 61
hostels, 23, 30, 31, 33, 43, 78, 85, 146, 147, 161, 273
hot air balloon rides, 105-106
Hotel Carter, 139
Hotel La Rose, 125
Hotel Leger, 180
hot springs, 113, 118, 121, 136, 155, 166, 200, 220, 223, 235
houseboats, 232, 237, 264-266
The House of Happy Walls, 100
house rentals, 34, 80, 88, 128, 161, 217,
house tours, 27, 43, 49, 51, 64, 99, 136, 183, 192, 196, 197, 222
Howarth Memorial Park, 125
Humboldt Bay Cruise, 142
Humboldt Redwoods S P, 143
Humboldt State College, 138
Hungry Tiger, 73
Huntington Lake, 260
Hurd Beeswax Candles, 112
Hyatt Lake Tahoe Casino, 225
Hyatt Regency Monterey, 43

I

ice climbing, 163
ice cream parlors, 88, 106, 176, 182, 185, 187, 190, 191, 206, 218
ice skating, 237, 253, 255, 256
Incline Village, Nevada, 223, 225, 227, 228
India Joze, 34
Indian Creek City Park, 85
Indian Cultural Museum, 163
Indian Grinding Rock S H P, 186

Indian villages, 49, 79, 163, 186
The Inn at Morro Bay, 72
The Inn at Saratoga, 22
Inn By the Lake, 216
Inns of Point Reyes, 78
International Calamari Fest, 35
Intl Teddy Bear Convention, 196
Ione, 182
Italian Picnic, 181

J

Jack London Bookstore, 100
Jack London's Bar & Bistro, 58
Jack London S H P, 99
Jackson, 181-183
Jack Swan's Tavern, 47
Jacob Myers Park, 160
Jade Lake, 116
jails, 173, 180, 236
James Dean Memorial, 154
Jamestown, 169, 170-171
Jamestown Hotel, 170
Jardines de San Juan, 150
Jaye's Timberland Resort, 20
Jeffers, Robinson, 64
Jenner, 79-80
Jenny rail cars, 164
J.J. Jackson Meml Museum, 238
John Ash & Co., 124
John Gardiner's Tennis Rnch, 57
Johnson's Bch & Resrt, 127, 130
Jorgensen, Chris, 99
Joseph Long Marine Lab, 37
Joshua Grindle Inn, 85
Joss House S H P, 238
Judge Wlter Murray Adobe, 155
Jug and Rose Confectionery, 185
Jughandle State Reserve, 92
Jules Resort, 120
Julliard Park, 125
Jumping Frog Jubilee, 179
June Lake, 254
June Lodge, 254
June Mountain, 254
Junior Ranger Program, 163

K

Kalisa's, 47
Kanaka Creek, 198
Kaweah River, 167
kayaking, 48, 132, 146, 274
Kays Resort, 245
Keith Rosenthal Theatre, 106
Kelley House Museum, 90
Kelley, William H. 86, 90
kelp horn, 89
Kelseyville, 120, 121
Kendall-Jackson Winery, 121
Kennedy Gold Mine, 181
Kennedy, John F., 66
Kennedy Mine Tailng Whls, 183
Kennolyn's Family Camp, 262
Kenton Mine Lodge, 198
Kentucky Mine&Stmp Mill, 201
Kenwood, 96, 100, 101
Kenwood World Pillow Fighting Championships, 96
Ketchum, Hank, 47
Kinetic Sculpture Race, 139
King Richard's, 195
Kings Beach, 223, 225, 226
Kings Canyon National Park, 165-167, 254, 256, 262
Kings River Canyon, 167
Kingswood Village, 223
Kirkwood, 245
Kirkwood Cross Country, 245
Kirkwood Ski Resort, 245

Kitty Hawk Kites, 48
Klamath, 147
Klamath Basin National Wildlife Refuge, 237
Klamath River, 147
Knight's Ferry Cvrd Bridge, 160
koi, 25, 125
Kokanee salmon, 221
Konocti Harbor Inn, 120
Konocti Winery, 121
Korbel Champagne Cellars, 131
Kozlowski Farms, 129
Kruse Rhododendron St Res, 80
Kule Loklo, 79
Kyburz, 246
Kyoto Koi & Garden Cntr, 125

L

La Boheme Restaurant, 58
Laguna Seca Races, 43
La Hacienda Inn, 22
Lair of the Bear, 263
Lake Berryessa, 111
Lake Britton, 234
Lakehead, 232
Lake House Pizza, 226
Lakeland Village, 217
Lake Oroville, 265-266
Lakeport, 120, 121
Lake Ralphine, 125
Lake Shasta, 232, 266
Lake Shasta Caverns, 232
Lakeshore, 166
Lakeside Chalets, 225
Lake Sonoma, 134
Lake Tahoe, 212-229, 261
Lake Tahoe Accom, 217
Lake Tahoe Cruises, 219
Lake Tahoe Hist Soc Mus, 221
Lake Tahoe Visitor Center, 221
Lamp Lighters Inn, 55
La Pastorela, 150
La Playa Hotel, 55
Larkin House, 49
Lassen Volcanic National Park, 233-235; Ski Area, 244
The Last Supper, 39
Lava Beds Ntl Mt, 235-237, 274
Lazio's Seafood Restaurant, 140
Leggett, 146
Leland Meadows, 253
Lewiston, 237
Lighthouse Point, 37
lighthouses, 30, 31, 37, 53, 67, 79, 82
Lime Saddle Marina, 266
Lime Spur, 171
Lincoln Green Inn, 56
Little House on the Prairie, 174
Little River, 87
Little River Inn, 88
llamas, 87, 190, 270
Locke, 204
The Lodge at Pebble Bch, 56, 63
Lodgepole, 167
log cabins, 228, 229
logging museum, 143
London, Jack, 100
Lone Cypress, 62
Long Barn, 253
Long Barn Lodge Ice Rink, 253
Los Gatos, 22-27
Los Gatos Garden Inn, 23
Los Gatos Lodge, 23
Los Gatos Museum, 25
Los Padres, 206
Los Posadas, 150
Lover's Point Marina, 53
The Luck of Roaring Camp, 170

Luther Burbank Meml Gdn, 125

M
MacCallum, Daisy, 86, 90
MacCallum House Inn, 86
Madonna Inn, 154
Magic Carpet Golf, 218
Magnolia Hotel, 102
Maidu Indians, 192
Malakoff Diggins S H P, 201
Mama Nina's, 104
Mama's Llamas, 190, 270
Mammoth Lakes, 255
Mammoth Mountain, 255
Manteca, 159
Mariah Wilderness Expeds, 268
Marin County, 275
Marin Discoveries, 274
Mariposa, 169
Mariposa Grove of Big Trees, 161,
  163, 257
Mark Abbott Meml Lghthse, 37
Markleeville, 220
Mark Thomas' Outrigger, 45
Mark West Vineyards, 131
Marquee Theatre, 126
Marshall Gold Disc S H P, 191
Marshall, James, 190
Marshall's Pasties, 195
Martin Eden, 100
Mar Vista Cottages, 82
Masonite Corp Demo Forest, 85
Mather Air Force Base, 210
Mather Family Camp, 261
Mayacamas Mountains, 134
maze, 47
McArthur-Burney Falls Memorial
  State Park, 234
McCloud, 232
McCloud Cookhouse, 232
Meadowood Resort, 107
Mediterranean Market, 58
melodrama, 26, 47, 126, 174, 188
Mendocino, 83-90
Mendocino Art Center, 90
Mendocino Bakery, 24
Mendocino Brewing Co Hopland
  Brewery Tavern, 136
Mendocino Coast Bot Grdns, 92
Mendocino Cst Holiday Reser, 88
Mendocino Headlands S P, 90
Mendocino Hotel, 84, 86, 88
Mendocino Ice Cream Co., 88
Mendocino Village Inn, 86
Mercer Caverns, 177
Merrybrook Lodge, 20
merry-go-rounds: see carousels
Midpines, 161
Midsummer Mozart Fest, 101
mid-week special rates, 160, 225, 241,
  251, 254, 265
Mike's Seafood, 45
Mill Creek, 235
Miller, Joaquin, 231
Miller Park, 208
Mimi's, 23
Mimi's Ice Cream Cart, 41
Mine House Inn, 187
Mineral, 233
Mineral King, 167
Miners Christmas, 174
Miners Foundry, 199
miniature golf, 36, 120, 130, 218
Miramonte Restaurant, 109
Miranda, 145
Miranda Gardens Resort, 145
Mission San Carlos Borromeo del Rio
  Carmelo, 61

Mission San Francisco Solano, 99
Mission San Juan Bautista, 149
Mission San Luis Obispo de Tolosa,
  155
Mission San Miguel Arcangel, 153
Mission Santa Cruz, 37
Miwok Indians, 79, 186
Miwok Village, 186
Moaning Cavern, 177
Modoc War, 236
Mokelumne Hill, 180
Mokelumne River, 182
Monarch butterflies, 37, 50, 52, 53,
  71, 74
monorail, 203
Montara, 30
Montara Lighthouse Hostel, 30
Montecito-Sequoia Cross Country Ski
  Center, 166, 255; High Sierra Vac
  Camp, 262
Monterey, 42-49
Monterey Bay Aquarium, 47, 48
Monterey Bay Kayaks, 48
Monterey Beach Hotel, 43
Monterey Jazz Festival, 43
Monterey Peninsula, 42-64
Monterey Peninsula Hostel, 43
Monterey Pen Mus of Art, 49
Monterey Sheraton, 43
Monterey State Historic Park, 49
The Monterey Vineyard, 152
Monte Rio bridge, 130
Montez, Lola, 192
Morgan Horse Ranch, 79
Morgan, J.P., 176
Morro Bay, 69, 72-75
Morro Bay Aquarium, 74
Morro Bay State Park, 72, 74
Morro Rock, 72
Morton's Warm Springs, 100
Motel Inn, 154
Motel rows, 33, 44, 52, 140, 217, 225
mother/daughter trips, 268
Mother Lode area, 169, 173
Mother Lode vein, 169
Mountain Charley's, 24
Mountain Home Ranch, 113
Mountain Room Bar, 162
Mountain Room Broiler, 162
Mount Konocti, 118
Mount St. Helena, 113
Mount Tamalpais State Park, 78
Mount View Hotel, 114
Mourelatos' Lakeshore Rsrt, 225
Mrs. Dubblebee's Pasties, 194
Mrs. M's Fudge, 59
M.S. Dixie, 220
Mt. Reba/Bear Valley, 252
Mt. Shasta and Vicinity, 230-239
Mt. Whitney, 165
M/V Madaket, 142
mud bath, 113
Muir Beach, 78, 277
Muir, John, 157, 176, 180
Muir Trail Ranch, 166
mule rides, 163
Murphys, 175-178
Murphys Hotel, 176
Murphy's Jenner Inn, 79
Murrietta, Joaquin, 153
Museum of Natural History, 74
Mushpot Cave, 236
Music Circus, 207
Mustards, 104
Myers Flat, 145
Mystery Spot, 37

N
Napa, 103, 106
Napa Valley Balloons, 106
Napa Valley Lodge, 103
Napa Vly Olive Oil Co., 110
Napa Valley Railway Inn, 103
Napa Valley Show, 106
Napa Valley Wine Library, 111
National Hotel, 181, 197
national parks, 146, 147, 156-167,
  233, 253, 254, 255, 256, 274
Nation's Christmas Tree, 166
Natural Bridges State Beach, 37
Nature Explorations-Tul, 275
Navarro, 85
Navarro Vineyards, 85
Near Escapes, 275
Negri's, 129
Nepenthe, 66
Nevada City, 169, 196-201, 222
Nevada City Hist Trolly Tour of Vic-
  torian Homes, 197
Nevada City Winery, 200
Nevada Theatre, 200
Nick's, 30
Nixon, President, 57
Norden, 250, 251
Normandy Inn, 56
North Bloomfield, 201
Northcoast Daylight, 139
Northern Queen Motel, 197
North Lake Tahoe, 222-229, 246-249
North Lake Tahoe Reg Prk, 249
Northstar-Tahoe, 223, 224, 248
North Star Mine stamp mill, 183
North Star Mining Museum and Pel-
  ton Wheel Exhibit, 196
North West Pacific RR Statn, 98
Noyo Harbor, 92
nude beaches, 126
The Nut Tree, 205, 215, 222

O
Oakdale, 159, 160
Oak Meadow Park, 25
Oakville, 110
Oakville Grocery, 110
Oakwood Lake Resort, 159
O'Brien, 232
Occidental, 129
Ocean Echo Motel, 33
Oceanic Society, 31
Octagon County Histl Mus, 37
*The Official Guide to California State
  Parks*, 271
Old Abe Cannon, 186
Old Bath House, 53
Old Del Monte Golf Course, 43
Old Eagle Theatre, 208
Old Faithful Geyser, 116
The Old General Store, 47
Old Governor's Mansion, 207
The Old Milano Hotel, 82
Old Sacramento, 206, 208
Old Station, 233, 234
Old Theatre Cafe, 35
Old Timers Museum, 175
Old Town, Eureka, 142
Old Town, Los Gatos, 23, 25
Olympic Valley, 225, 248
Oregon Creek Swim Hole, 201
Orick, 146
Oroville, 266
Orr Hot Springs, 136
Owner Builder Center, 275, 276
oyster processing plant tour, 141

P

Pacifica, 30
Pacific Crest Trail, 233
Pacific Garden Mall, 38
Pacific Grove, 50-54
Pacific Grove Mus Nat Hist, 53
Pacific Lumber Company, 143
Packer Lake, 198
Packer Lake Lodge, 198
pack trips, 269-270
pagodas, 116
Pajaro Dunes, 34
parades, 29, 40, 181, 197; floating, 40
Paradise Point Marina, 266
Paso Robles, 153-154
Pat Paulsen Vineyards, 135
Patagonia, 244
Patisserie Boissiere, 59
Peanuts, 126
Pebble Beach, 43, 56, 61, 62
Pebble Beach Equestrian Ctr, 61
Pebble Beach Golf Course, 62
Pedro's, 24
Pee Wee Glf/J's Amusmnts, 130
The Pelican Inn, 78
The Peppermint Stick, 176
Pepperwood, 143
Pescadero, 31
Petrified Forest, 116
petroglyphs, 186
Petticoat Junction, 183
petting zoos, 142, 203, 228
Pewter Plough Playhouse, 71
Pfeiffer Beach, 67
Pfeiffer-Big Sur S P, 65, 67
Phillipsville, 143
Philo, 85
Phoenix gift shop, 66
Pickford House, 70
Pickle Barrel Deli, 179
pick-your-own, 31
Picnique in the Pines, 70
Piercy, 145, 146
Piety Hill Inn, 197
Pigeon Point Lighthouse Hstl, 31
Pine Beach Inn, 91
Pinecrest, 252, 253, 263
Pinecrest Nordic Ski Area, 253
Pine Grove, 182, 186
Pine Inn, 56
Pine Ridge Winery, 107
Pinnacles Natl Monmnt, 153
Pioneer History Center, 163
Piper Playhouse, 188
Piper Sonoma Cellars, 133
Pismo clams, 74
Placer County Historic Mus, 192
Placerville, 189-190, 216
planetarium, 27
Plaza Hotel, 150
Pleasant Valley, 195
Plumas National Forest, 261
Plymouth, 181, 183
Point Arena, 82-83
Point Arena Lighthouse, 82
Point Lobos State Reserve, 62
Point Motel, 72
Point Pinos Lighthouse, 53
Point Reyes, 78-79
Point Reyes Field Seminars, 275
Point Reyes Hostel, 78
Point Reyes Lighthouse, 79
Point Reyes National Seashore, 78, 273, 275, 277
Point Sur Light Station, 67
Polka Dots, 124
Polk, Willis, 195
Pollock Pines, 189

Pomo Indns, 118, 136, 137, 210
Ponderosa Ranch, 228
Pony Express reenactment, 189
pony rides, 24, 125, 134, 152, 164, 189, 203, 211
Poor Man's 17-Mile Drive, 54
Poor Red's, 188, 216
Pope-Baldwin Recrn Area, 219
portable crib, 5
post cards, 11
Prairie Creek Redwds S P, 146
Presidio of Monterey Mus 49
Princeton-By-The-Sea, 31
Pumpkin Festival, 29
puppet shows, 205, 210
Pygmy Forest, 90, 92

R

Railroad Square, 125
Railtown 1897 S H P, 171
Rainbow Lake, 137
Rainbow Lodge, 251
The Ranch, 153
Rancho Cordova, 210
rappel tour, 177, 178
Reagan, President, 57
Red Bluff, 244
Red Caboose Saloon, 21
Red Castle Inn, 197
Redding, 231, 238
Red Dog Lodge, 252
The Red Pony, 152
Redwood Empire Ice Arena, 126
Redwood Hostel, 147
Redwood Natl Park, 146, 147
redwoods, 137-147
The Redwoods, 161
Redwood Trail, 20
REI Co-op, 244
Requa Inn, 147
Rescue, 169
reservations services, 54, 88, 215, 217, 225, 274
Restless Sea, 62
Rhine House, 111
Richardson Grove S P, 145
Ricochet Ridge Ranch, 92
Ridenhour Ranch Inn, 128
rifle range, 237
Right on Main, 182
Rio Vista, 204, 266
Ripley, Robert, 125
Ripplewood Resort, 65
Riverbank, 159
Riverbank Cheese Co, 159
Riverlane Resort, 128
River Ranch, 229
river trips, 146, 163, 207, 229, 267-268, 274
Roaring Camp & Big Trees Narrow-Gauge Railroad, 21
Roaring Camp Mining Co., 182
Robert L. Ripley Mem Mus, 125
rock climbing lessons, 163, 274
rock collecting, 121, 182
Rock Creek Winter Lodge, 255
Rockefeller Forest, 145
rocking horse rides, 205
Rocky Point, 59
rodeo, 151
Rodney Strong Vineyards, 133
roller coasters, 27, 36
roller skating rink, 159
Romano Gabriel Wooden Sculpture Garden, 142
romantic spots, 20, 30, 33, 41, 45, 52, 53, 55, 56, 57, 58, 66, 70, 80, 82, 83, 85, 86, 87, 91, 97, 102, 104,

108, 109, 128, 134, 139, 175, 182, 183, 191, 194, 197, 227,
Roosevelt elk, 146, 147
Rose's Landing, 73
Rosicrucian Egyptian Mus, 27
roundhouse tour, 171
Royal Gorge Cross Country Ski Resort, 250
Royal Vahalla, 216
Russian Gulch Park, 93
Russian River, 79, 126-131, 132, 260, 273
Russian River Jazz Festival, 127
Russian River Wine Road, 127
Rutherford, 107, 109, 111, 112
Rutherford Hill Winry, 107, 112

S

Sacramento, 202-211, 215, 222
Sacramento Civic Theater, 207
Sacramento Delta, 266
Sacramento History Center, 209
Sacramento Sci Ctr Jr Mus, 210
Sacramento Zoo, 211
Sail In Motel, 216
The Salame Tree Deli, 132
Salinas, 151-152
Salmon Lake Lodge, 199
Salt Point Lodge, 79
Salt Point State Park, 80
Same Time Next Year, 88
Samoa Cookhouse, 141
Sam's Town, 188, 216
San Antonio House, 56
San Benito House, 30
Sanborn Park Hostel, 23
Sanborn-Skyline Cnty Park, 23
Sancho Panza, 45
sand castle contests, 40, 60
San Damiano Retreat, 275
Sand Harbor Beach, 227
The Sandpiper, 67
Sanger, 166
San Jose, 27
San Jose Creek, 60
San Jose Family Camp, 261
San Jose State University, 277
San Juan Bakery, 150
San Juan Bautista, 149-150
San Juan Bautista S H P, 149
San Lorenzo River, 21
San Lorenzo Valley, 19-22
San Luis Obispo, 69, 154-155
San Miguel, 153
San Simeon, 67-71
Santa Barbara, 259, 262
Santa Clara, 27
Santa Cruz, 31-39, 41
Santa Cruz Art Center, 35
Santa Cruz Art League galry, 39
Santa Cruz Bch & Boardwlk, 35
Santa Cruz Boardwalk, 32
Santa Cruz Brewing Co, 35
Santa Cruz City Museum, 38
Santa Cruz Hostel, 33
Santa Cruz Mountns, 18-27, 262
Santa Cruz Municipal Wharf, 37
Santa Cruz Surfing Museum, 37
Santa Cruz Yacht Harbor, 34
Santa Maria-style barbecue, 150
Santa Rosa, 123-126
Saratoga, 22-27
Saratoga Creek, 22
The Sardine Factory, 45
Sausalito, 204
Scandia, 59
schoolhouses, 210, 239
Schulz, Charles, 126

Scopazzi's Restaurant, 20
Scotia, 143
Scotia Inn, 143
Scottish Games, 43, 123
scuba divers, 60, 80
Sea Breeze Motel, 30
Seabright Beach, 39
Sea Gull Inn, 84, 86
Sea Gull of Mendocino, 89, 90
Sea Horse Ranch, 30
Seal and Bird Rock, 62
Seal Rock, 37
seals, 31, 34, 37, 47, 62, 74
sea otters, 48, 53, 62
Sea Ranch, 80-82
Sea Rock B & B Inn, 87
Sears, 244
Sears House Inn, 87
Sears Point Intl Raceway, 101
Sea View Inn, 56
Sebastiani Vineyards, 101
Sebastian's General Store, 70
seismograph, 79
Senate Group and House Group of
  Sequoias, 167
Sequoia Natl Forest, 167, 262
Sequoia National Park, 165-167, 255,
  256, 262
Sequoia Park & Zoo, 142
Sequoia Ski Touring Center, 255
sequoias, 163, 165, 167, 176, 255
Serenisea, 82
Serra, Father Junipero 49, 61
Seven Brides for Seven Bros, 176
Seven Gables Inn, 52
17-Mile Drive, 56, 62; Poor Man's, 54
Shadowbrook, 41
Sharpsteen Museum and Sam Brannan
  Cottage, 116
Shasta Llamas, 270
Shasta Museum, 238
Shaver Lake, 260
Sheraton Round Barn Inn, 124
Shingle Springs, 188
The Shining, 198
Shirley Lake, 225
shooting gallery, 218
Shrine Drive-Thru Tree, 145
Sierra City, 198, 199, 201
Sierra Club, 250, 275
Sierra Cnty Histor Pk Mus, 201
Sierra Magazine, 275
Sierra Nevada House III, 190
Sierra Nevadas, 198, 213, 275
Sierra Shangri-La, 199
Sierra Ski Ranch, 245
Sierraville, 200
Sierra Vista Winery, 190
Silverado Resort, 103
Silverado Museum, 111
Silverado Restaurant, 114
The Silverado Squatters, 112
The Silverado Trail, 107, 112
Silver Lake Resort, 261
Silver Wings Aviation Mus, 210
Simi Winery, 133
Sing Kee's Store, 187
Siskiyou County Museum, 239
Sivananda Ashram Vrindavan Yoga
  Farm, 194
Ski Run Marina, 220
Ski With Santa, 252
Skippy's Hacienda Inn, 129
Skunk Train, 93
Skylark Motel, 121
sleigh rides, 217, 221, 246, 250
Slide Ranch, 78, 277
Slug Fest, 127

Smith River, 146
Smith's Mount St. Helena Trout
  Farm, 116
The Smoke Cafe, 171
Smothers Brothers Wines, 101
Smurf Woods, 27
Snoopy Gift Shop, 126
snow camping, 246, 254, 274, 275
snowcat ride, 257
snow caves, 256
Snowfest, 249
snow hikes, 246
Snowline Lodge, 167
snow play areas, 223, 242-243, 246,
  247, 249, 252, 253, 256-257
snowshoe walks, 229, 243
Soda Springs, 250, 251
Soda Springs Ski Area, 251
sod roofs, 178, 182, 222
The Soldier Factory, 71
Sonoma, 96-102
Sonoma Antque Appl Nrsy, 131
Sonoma Cattle Company, 100
Sonoma Cheese Factory, 98
Sonoma Cty Farm Trails, 123
Sonoma County Museum, 126
Sonoma French Bakery, 98
Sonoma Gaslght &Wstrn RR, 99
Sonoma Hotel, 97
Sonoma Mission Inn & Spa, 97
Sonoma Sausage Company, 98
Sonoma State Historic Park, 98
Sonoma Town Square Park, 99
Sonora, 172-173
Soquel, 41, 262
Soquel Creek, 39, 40, 42
Sorensen's, 245
Sourdough Jack, 185
South Lake Tahoe, 213-222, 245-246,
  260
South Shasta Model RR, 231
South Shore Marina, 220
Southside Resort, 128
Souverain Winery, 134
spelunking tour, 180
Spirit of Monterey Wax Mus, 47
Spring Garden, 262
Spring in the Sierra House and Garden
  Tour, 196
Spring Mountain Vineyards, 112
Squaw Creek, 225
Squaw Valley U.S.A., 219, 248
Stage-A-Picnic, 134
stagecoach rides, 134, 163, 173
stamp mills, 183, 198, 201, 238
Stanislaus Cnty Cheese Co, 159
Stanislaus National Forest, 253, 261,
  263
Stanislaus River, 160
Star Harbor, 223
state historic parks, 49, 80, 98, 110,
  141, 149, 171, 173, 186, 191, 195,
  201, 210, 238, 271
Stateline, 221
Stateline Stables, 221
state parks, 20, 21, 65, 74, 78, 80, 90,
  115, 143, 145, 146, 176, 220, 221,
  227, 229, 234, 271
steam donkeys, 92, 141, 142
Steamer's Lane, 37
Steelhead Special, 21
Steep Ravine Cabins, 78
Steinbeck Festival, 151
The Steinbeck House, 151
Steinbeck Library, 152
Steinbeck, John, 47, 53, 151, 152
Steinbeck, Mary, 152
Sterling Vineyards, 117, 118

Stevenot Winery, 177
Stevenson House, 49
Stevenson, Robert Louis, 62, 111, 112
St. George Hotel, 185
St. Helena, 107-112
Stinson Beach, 78, 273
Stockton, 204
Stonehouse Inn, 57
St. Orres, 82
Strauss, Levi, 275
Strawberry Ski Touring, 245
streetcars, 204
Stuart Fork River, 237
Studebaker, John, 189, 190
Stump Cove, 80
Subway Cave, 234
Sugar Bowl Ski Resort, 251
Sugar Pine Point S P, 229, 249
sugarplums, 59
The Sundae Times, 190
Sun House, 136
Sunnyside Restaurant, 226
surfing, 37, 262
suspension bridges, 47, 237
Sutter Creek, 181, 182, 183-184
Sutter Creek Inn, 183
Sutter Creek Palace, 184
Sutter Home Inn, 108
Sutter Home Winery, 108
Sutter, John A., 210
Sutter sawmill, 191
Sutter's Fort S H P, 210
swans, 102
Swedish Restaurant, 59
Sycamore Mineral Springs, 155

T
Tahoe Amusement Park, 219
Tahoe Beach and Ski Club, 216
Tahoe City, 223, 225, 226, 227, 228,
  229, 246, 247, 248, 249
Tahoe City Bakery, 226
Tahoe Donner, 251
The Tahoe Escape, 225
Tahoe Keys, 220
Tahoe Marina Inn, 216
Tahoe National Forest, 201
Tahoe Nordic Ski Center, 249
Tahoe Park, 226
Tahoe Pines, 227
Tahoe Queen, 219
Tahoe Trout Farm, 221
Tahoe Vista, 224, 225, 249
Tallic Historic Site Estates, 221
Tall Trees Grove Shuttle, 146
Tamarack Ldge & Nord Ski, 255
Tampico Kitchen, 35
Taylor Crk Snow Play Area, 246
Taylor Creek Stream Profile
  Chamber, 221
Taylor, Elizabeth, 67
teens, 14-15, 245, 262, 277
Tender Loving Care, 215
Ten Mile Beach, 93
tennis clinics, 57
tepees, 159, 186
Terwilliger family, 239
Thanksgiving wkends, 262, 265
Thinker Toys, 63
thoroughbred racing, 151, 203
Three Rivers, 165
Threshing Bee, 231
The Thunderbird, 59
tidepools, 30, 37, 48, 83
Tiger's Folly II, 75
Timber Cove Inn, 80
Timber Cove Lodge, 216
Timber Cove Marina, 220

Timber Crest Farms, 133
Timberhill Ranch, 128
Tinnery, 53
Tioga Pass, 161
Tofanelli's, 195
Toll House Inn, 85
Top Gun, 116
Top of the Tram, 218
topiary garden, 24
Topolos Russ Rvr Vnyrds, 129
Tor House, 64
Toscano Hotel, 99
Towe Ford Museum, 210
train excursions, 21, 25, 93, 99, 125,
139, 146, 151, 164, 171, 189, 204,
205, 208, 222, 231
Train Town, 99
tram rides, 218, 225, 245, 248
travel/study programs, 277
Treasure Island, 62, 111
Tree House Hostel, 161
Trees of Mystery, 147
trees, unusual 20, 21, 62, 125, 145,
147, 165, 166, 167
Trentadue Winery, 135
Trinidad, 146
Trinity Alps, 237-238
Trinity Alps Resort, 237
Trinity Center, 237
Troupers of the Gold Coast, 47
Truckee, 222, 223, 227, 248, 249, 251
Truckee River, 227, 229
Truckee River Bridge, 227
Tuck Box Tea Room, 60
Tulelake, 236
Tuolumne Cty Mus Hst Ctr, 173
Tuolumne Family Camp, 262
Tuolumne Meadows, 163
Tuolumne Meadows Lodge, 161
Tuolumne River, 262
Twain, Mark, 170, 176, 180, 203, 213
Twin Bridges, 245
Twin Lakes, 255
Tyrolean Inn, 20

U
Ukiah, 136-137
Uncle Runt's Place, 233
Union Hotel, 129
University of California, 277
University of California, Santa Cruz
campus, 32, 39
University of Pacific repertory theatre
company, 175
Upper Sunrise Recrea Area, 207
Utica Park, 179

V
Vacaville, 205
Vagabond's House Inn, 57
Vallecito, 177
Vallejo, General, 97, 98
Valley of the Moon, 100
Valley Stables, 163
Vasona Lake County Park, 25
Vasquez House, 99
vegetarian meals, 129, 194, 201
Ventana Inn, 66
Vertigo, 149
Victorian Christmas, 197
Victorian homes, 126, 138, 142, 152,
196, 239
Victorian Home Tour, 51
video arcades, 215, 218
Vikingsholm Castle, 221
The Village Green, 115
Villa Montalvo, 25
Villa Vista Resort, 225

Vines, 109
The Vineyard House, 191
Vins Le Salon, 106
Vintage 1870, 103, 106
Vintners Inn, 124
Vintners Village, 109
Volcano, 184-187
volcanoes, 233
Volcano Pioneers Community Theatre
Group, 187
Volunteer Fire Department, 83
volunteer vacations, 277
V. Sattui Winery, 112

W
The Warehouse Restaurant, 45
waterbeds, 52, 132, 197
waterfalls, 20, 158, 162, 219, 225, 234
water-skiing, 121, 220, 262
waterslides, 133, 159, 203
Water Wheel, 226
Watsonville, 32
Watsonville Fly-In, 32
Wawona, 161
Wawona Hotel, 161
The Way Station, 75
Wayne, John, 181
W.C."Bob" Trowbridge Canoe Trips,
132
Weaverville, 238
Wells Fargo Restaurant, 182
Weott, 143, 145
Whale Center, 31
whale skeleton, 37
whale-watching, 31, 79, 83, 90, 275
Whale Watch Inn, 82
Wharfside Restaurant, 46
What Cheer Saloon, 175
Whispering Pines Motel, 145
Whitegate Inn, 87
Whitewater Voyages, 268
White Wolf Lodge, 161
Whole Earth Restaurant, 39
Wilbur Hot Springs, 121
Wild Horse Valley Ranch, 106
Wilderness Lodge, 250
wildflowers, 53, 153
Wildlife Weekend, 277
Wildwood Park, 22
William B. Layton Park, 228
William G. Stone Lock, 210
Wm Hearst State Beach, 71
William Kent Beach, 227
William Land Park, 211
Williams, 121
Williams Grove, 145
Willie Bird's Restaurant, 124
Willits, 93, 137, 139
Will-o-Point Resort, 121
Wilsonia Lodge, 166
Wilsonia Ski Touring, 256
Winchester Mystery House, 27
Winchester, Sarah, 27
Wind & Weather, 90
Windsor, 132, 133
Windsor Vineyards, 133
Windsor Waterworks, 133
wind surfing, 220, 274
Wine & Cheese Zephyr, 171
Wine Country, 94-121, 273
The Wine Country Inn, 109
wineries, 24, 37, 42, 47, 85, 101-102,
106-107, 108, 111-112, 116-118,
121, 129, 131, 132, 133, 134, 135,
152, 154, 177, 183, 190, 200
The Winery at Asti, 135
winery maps, 127, 154, 183
Wine School, 108

Winter Carnival, 246
Winter Snow Fun, 240-257
Winter Wonderland, 246
Wishart's Bakery, 59
Wolf Creek, 196
Wolfdale's, 227
Wolf House, 100
Wolverton, 167
Wolverton Ski Bowl, 256
Woodpecker Nature Trail, 79
Woodwind, 220
World's Largst Salmon BBQ, 91
Wright, Frank Lloyd, 66

X
Xcelsior Brewery, 125

Y
Yeager, Chuck, 210
Yosemite Falls, 158, 162
Yosemite Guide, 163
Yosemite Lodge, 160, 162
Yosemite Lodge Cafeteria, 161
Yosemite Mt Sugr Pine RR, 164
Yosemite Mountaineering School,
163, 254
Yosemite National Park, 156-164,
165, 253, 261, 162, 256, 275
Yountville, 102-107
Yountville Pastry Shop, 106
Youth Science Institute, 23, 25
Yreka, 239
Yuba River, 195, 198, 199, 201

Z
Zen garden, 25
Zephyr Cove Resort, 217
Zephyr Cove, Nevada, 217, 220
zoos, 142, 211, 215

CREDITS

Typesetting and layout: Doug Burnet, The Cooperative Type

Cover illustration and design: Ron Chan

Maps: John Parsons and Mark Williams, Eureka Cartography

Printing: McNaughton & Gunn, Inc.

Computer Wizardry: Gene Meyers

Photos:

page 21: Roaring Camp & Big Trees Narrow-Gauge Railroad

page 26: Great America

page 27: Winchester Mystery House

pages 32, 36: Santa Cruz Beach & Boardwalk

pages 38, 40, 46, 61, 62, 63, 65, 68, 78, 100, 115, 139, 142, 144, 173, 193, 195, 202, 209, 243, 264: California Department of Parks and Recreation

page 48: Monterey Bay Aquarium

page 49: Jerry Lebeck, Monterey Peninsula Visitors & Convention Bureau

page 50: Pete Amos, California Department of Parks and Recreation

page 71: Theodore Osmundson, California Department of Parks and Recreation

page 73: John Kaestner, California Department of Parks and Recreation

pages 81, 89, 93, 117, 119, 130, 271: Redwood Empire Association

pages 84, 147: Ansel Adams, Redwood Empire Association

page 105: Balloon Aviation of Napa Valley, Redwood Empire Association

page 108: Meadowood Napa Valley

page 135: Pat Paulsen Vineyards

page 140: Eureka Inn

page 152: Valley Guild, courtesy of the Steinbeck Library

pages 157, 162, 254, 256: Yosemite Park and Curry Company

page 159: John Michael Flint, Oakwood Lake

pages 164, 258: John M. Giosso, San Francisco Recreation and Park Department

page 170: Patt Gilman Public Relations

pages 177, 186, 191, 211: Larry Paynter, California Dept of Parks and Recreation

page 178: Moaning Cavern

page 179: 39th District Agricultural Association

page 205: Harre W. Demoro,

page 214: Greater Reno Chamber of Commerce

page 219: Travel Systems Ltd.

page 224, 248: Northstar-at-Tahoe

page 228: Tahoe North Visitors and Convention Bureau

pages 232, 234, 238: John F. Reginato, Shasta-Cascade Wonderland Association

page 247: Bob Everson, Alpine Meadows

page 250: Royal Gorge Nordic Ski Resort

page 266: Shasta-Cascade Wonderland Association

page 267: Dick Linford, ECHO

page 268: Wilderness Adventures

page 270: Shasta Llamas

page 276: Owner Builder Center

page 287: Mike Maloney, San Francisco Chronicle

ABOUT THE AUTHOR

Carole Terwilliger Meyers, a native San Franciscan, holds a
B.A. degree in anthropology from San Francisco State Uni-
versity and an elementary teaching credential from Fresno
State College. Currently she is a columnist and contributing
editor for *Parents' Press,* a columnist for *San Francisco
Focus,* and a weekly guest authority on "family fun" on C.J.
Bronson's KNBR radio show in San Francisco. In the past she
has been a columnist for *California* magazine, the *San Jose
Mercury News,* and *California Travel Report.* She has also
been an editor for *Goodlife* magazine and the *San Francisco
Bay Area ASPO* (Lamaze natural childbirth) *Newsletter.* Her
articles have been published in *Image* and *San Francisco* magazines as well as numerous other magazines and newspapers.
Ms. Meyers resides in Berkeley with her husband and two
children.

BOOKS..

EATING OUT WITH THE KIDS IN SAN FRANCISCO AND THE BAY AREA *by Carole Terwilliger Meyers. $7.95. 194pp; b&w photos and illus.* Written by a native, San Francisco's only family restaurant guide tips visitors to over 200 restaurants appropriate for dining *en famille*. Destinations for family fun are tied in with the restaurants and include museums, amusement parks, tours, and live entertainment.

MAKE YOUR OWN CRAZY ANIMALS *$4.95.* **MAKE YOUR OWN CRAZY MONSTERS** *$4.95. Both created by Bruce Lansky.* Children can punch out the full-color cardboard animal or monster body pieces and accessories in these books and then rearrange them to make 927,360 different "crazy animals" or 302,526 different "crazy monsters." The punched out spaces then become stencils. When you add felt tip pens, a pad of paper, and a glue stick, the car fun becomes almost limitless.

HOW TO ORGANIZE A BABYSITTING COOPERATIVE AND GET SOME FREE TIME AWAY FROM THE KIDS *by Carole Terwilliger Meyers. $3.95; hardcover/$8.95. 82pp; b&w illus.* A babysitting cooperative is simply a group of parents who exchange babysitting services with one another, usually in their own homes. No money is involved. This valuable resource is the only book available on the subject and is essential for anyone who is having trouble finding, or paying for, babysitters.

WHAT TO DO BETWEEN HERE & THERE: ACTIVITIES FOR FAMILIES ON THE GO *by Susan Kirsch. $4.95. 128pp; b&w illus.* Perfect for the glove compartment, this book promises to "turn humdrum traveling time into fun-filled hours of discovery." Filled with topics that stimulate discussion, the book is designed to improve communication. Among the 260 numbered activities designed to test, tax, and toy with your imagination: sing a song about yourself; describe your mother; plan the movie about your life. All you have to do is select a number and start talking. *(See Order Form for information on how to get this book for **FREE**!)*

WEEKEND ADVENTURES FOR CITY-WEARY PEOPLE: OVERNIGHT TRIPS IN NORTHERN CALIFORNIA *by Carole Terwilliger Meyers. $11.95. 294pp; b&w photos, maps.*

A FAMILY TRAVEL GUIDES catalogue describing over 100 family-oriented travel books and games is included free with each order. Otherwise, send $1 (refundable with future order) to: FAMILY TRAVEL GUIDES, P.O. Box 6061-wa, Albany, CA 94706.

FAMILY TRAVEL TIMES. *$35/year within the U.S., $39 to Canada, $48 overseas.* Each month this newsletter publishes world-wide travel news of interest to families. It also often includes detailed reports on specific destination cities. The focus tends toward upscale travel—luxury hotels and resorts, cruises, Europe—but more reasonably-priced accommodations are also covered. Detailed reports are given on children's programs, with age range, price, and babysitting availability included.

TRAVEL PAPERS

Travel Papers are short, information-packed articles about a particular destination. Unless otherwise noted, all are written by California-based travel writer Carole Terwilliger Meyers—a family travel authority. Most of the **Travel Papers** offered here supplement general guidebooks by including useful, detailed information of value to families. Articles range from 3 to 7 pages. They are single-spaced and printed on one side of letter-size paper.

CALIFORNIA
- **Budget Family Vacations in Northern California** ($3) Five ideas for an inexpensive family vacation.
- **Cross-country Skiing Hideaway** ($3) Take your family to an isolated Sierra ski lodge where you can really get away from it all. Guests are brought in to the snowbound lodge by sleigh; when their visit is over, they ski out. A 4-hour drive from San Francisco.
- **Disneyland** ($4) Details about the park which are of interest to families. The best place to stay, plus several alternate lodging suggestions.
- **Good Eats at Disneyland** *by Lee Kucera* ($3) Suggestions on where to find wholesome, good-tasting food in this fantasyland of fast food.
- **Going Hollywood...In Search of the Stars** ($3) Good restaurants and hotels for families, plus information on Universal Studios and how to see movies being filmed.
- **Knott's Berry Farm, plus A Trip Back in Time** ($3) Details about the park and its famous restaurant, plus information on Medieval Times—a new attraction located across the street.
- **The Missions** ($4) The scoop on the 21 Franciscan Missions that stretch from San Diego to Sonoma.

- **The Queen Mary & Spruce Goose: Sites to Sea** ($3) Detailed descriptions of this famous floating hotel and unusual airplane attraction.
- **San Diego** ($4) The best hotels and attractions, plus several sidetrips.
- **San Francisco Family Sleepers** ($4) The best family lodgings in everyone's favorite city.
- **San Francisco's Floating Museums** ($4) Details on visiting the largest collection of historic ships in the world, plus several dine/sail excursions on the bay.
- **Santa Barbara** ($4) Beachfront lodgings, plus where to eat and what to see.
- **Solvang** ($3) Where to stay and eat and what to see and do in this replica Danish town located just north of Santa Barbara.

CANADA
- **The English Side of Victoria, British Columbia** ($3) Experience a bit of England in this lovely seaside town. Where to stay, eat, and sightsee.
- **Polar Bear Express** *by Norma Watts* ($3) Enjoy an interesting train ride to this remote area of Ontario.

THE CARIBBEAN
- **Sail the Caribbean in Style** *by Marilynn Mansfield* ($3) Charter a yacht and sail the British Virgin Islands.

FLORIDA
- **Swim with a Dolphin** *by Christie Costanzo* ($3) Two facilities in the Florida Keys where you can actually get in the water with these creatures, plus information on other activities and nearby camping.

HAWAII

- **Kauai, or "Pooped Parents Visit Poipu Beach"** ($4) Detailed description of a great family resort, plus restaurants and 1 1/2-day sightseeing itinerary.
- **On Top of the Volcano** ($3) Have a mountain experience on the Big Island. Where to stay and what to do at Hawaii Volcanoes National Park.

MEXICO

- **A Weekend in Ensenada** ($3) Where families should stay and eat and what they should do in this close-to-the-border town. An easy driving sidetrip from San Diego.

NEVADA

- **Reno** ($2) Where to stay and eat and what to see and do in "the biggest little city in the world."
- **Virginia City** ($2) What to see and do in the "the liveliest ghost town in the west." It is an interesting and easy side trip from Lake Tahoe.

NEW YORK

- **Fun in New York City...with the Kids!** ($4) Where to stay and eat and six days worth of sightseeing.
- **Tracking Down Tickets to CATS** ($3) Don't be disappointed when you try to get tickets to this block-buster musical.

OREGON

- **Ashland Shakespeare Festival** ($4) Information on this famous festival as well as family-oriented lodgings (including many B&Bs), restaurants, and activities. Information on sidetrips to Jacksonville and Oregon Caves National Monument, plus Jet Boating on the Rogue River.
- **Camping Favorites** ($3) Three special spots—one offers the option of renting a tepee complete with an open firepit for cooking.
- **Eugene** ($3) Family-oriented lodgings, restaurants, and attractions in this pleasant college town.

- **Highway Attractions** ($4) Detailed descriptions of attractions along Coast Route 101 and Highway 5.
- **Portland** ($4) Where to stay, where to eat, and what to do in this scenic city.

TAHITI

- **Paradise on a Budget: A Family Vacation in Tahiti** by Joyce Gregory Wyels ($3) Details on a great family resort, plus some helpful hints on planning your trip.

WASHINGTON D.C.

- **Washington D.C.** ($4) Lodgings and restaurants amenable to families as well as don't-miss sights and sidetrip suggestions.

WASHINGTON STATE

- **Seattle** ($4) The best attractions to enjoy with kids, plus details on two worthwhile sidetrips in southern Washington: Mount St. Helens and Northwest Trek Wildlife Park.

MISCELLANEOUS

- **Helpful Hints for Traveling with Children** ($4) Hints for planning trips, car comfort and entertainment, even ideas for when things degenerate. More hints on souvenirs and, horrors, traveling with teens.
- **Miscellaneous Guides and Coloring/Activity Books** ($3) Useful items which for an assortment of reasons could not be included in this catalogue. A short review and ordering instructions are included for each. Guides cover the cities of Chicago, Milwaukee, Minneapolis/St. Paul, Philadelphia, and Santa Cruz CA, plus the states of Maine and Texas. One also details a lengthy family canoe trip, with young children, through New England and Canada. Coloring/activity books cover Baton Rouge, Los Angeles, Dallas, California, Hawaii, Oregon, Washington, and San Francisco.
- **No More Motion Sickness** by Larrie Todd ($3) Ways to cope in the car and on planes, with special hints for children.

ORDER FORM

SPECIAL FREE OFFER: With an order of $30 or more, you receive a *free* copy of **WHAT TO DO BETWEEN HERE AND THERE.** OFFER GOOD WHILE SUPPLIES LAST.

Please Print: Date_____

Name_____

Street Address _____

City/State/Zip _____

Title	Quantity	Price
_____	_____	_____
_____	_____	_____
_____	_____	_____
_____	_____	_____
_____	_____	_____
_____	_____	_____
_____	_____	_____
_____	_____	_____

Subtotal _____

☐ bonus copy of WHAT TO DO (if subtotal is $30 or more) _____ free _____

California residents add 7% sales tax _____

Shipping Charges (circle choice)			
continental U.S. (UPS ground)	Alaska/Hawaii (UPS air)	(postal grnd)	Canada (postal grnd)
Under $25 $2.50	$8.00	$3.50	$5.00
$25-$50 $3.50	$11.00	$4.50	$6.50
over $50 $4.50	$14.00	$6.50	$8.50
All shipments are insured.			

shipping and handling _____

TOTAL _____

Gift certificates are available in any amount over $10. Send us the recipient's name and address, and we'll send a certificate along with our latest catalogue.

Method of Payment: ☐ **MasterCard**   ☐ **VISA**   ☐ **Check**

Card Number: Expiration date:

☐☐☐☐☐☐☐☐☐☐☐☐☐☐☐☐   ☐☐   ☐☐

Minimum order on charges—$20.00   mo.   yr.

Signature _____

Enclose check or money order payable to:

All payments must be in U.S. dollars.

☐ Please send fund-raising information.

Carousel Press
FAMILY TRAVEL GUIDES
Order Dept. WA
P.O. Box 6061
Albany, CA 94706
415/527-5849

Feedback

I am annoyed when I find out a place doesn't have a feature I've been led to expect. Please let me know if this happens to you at any of the listings in this book. I'll look into it, complain on your behalf, and fix the misinformation in the Fifth Edition of WEEKEND ADVENTURES FOR CITY-WEARY PEOPLE.

Also, let me hear from you about any new places you discover which you feel belong in this book.

Sincerely,
Carole Terwilliger Meyers
c/o Carousel Press, P.O. Box 6061, Albany, CA 94706

Your Name _____

Address _____

City, State, Zip _____

Telephone (_____)_____

Listing Name _____

Address _____

City, State, Zip _____

Telephone (_____)_____

Describe your annoyance or discovery:

_____

_____

_____ __

_____

_____